MW00910308

LOVE AND MONEY

When people speak about love and money, they are usually referring to a conflict: love distorted by the desire for money. Such statements imply that love has a distinct form before economics interferes, but this book aims to show that such a view simplifies what is going on, because people have always been deeply shaped by everything in the social order, including economics. So when people say that money is distorting love, what they are really saying is that the current relationship of love and economics is different from an earlier relationship. This book seeks then to demonstrate the intertwining of the discourses of love and money over a long history by focusing on moments when parallel conceptions appear in economic theories and love stories. The two discourses intersect because both seek to define qualities and behaviors of human beings that are most valuable and hence most desirable. Similar descriptions of valuable behaviors appear at roughly the same time in economic theories of how to acquire wealth and literary stories of how to find ideal lovers.

By tracking mutual expressions of desire, value, and acquisition in economics and love stories, this book argues for the ubiquity of the intertwining of these discourses while exploring shifts in conceptions of value. It focuses on four eras when economic and romantic conceptions of what is most desirable were actively changing in English discourses: the early modern 17th century, the Victorian 19th, the modernist 20th, and the postmodern present.

Michael Tratner received a Ph.D. in English from the University of California, Berkeley, and is currently the Mary E. Garrett Alumnae Professor of English at Bryn Mawr College. He has published three books: *Modernism and Mass Politics: Joyce, Woolf, Eliot, Yeats*; *Deficits, Desires: Economics and Sexuality in Twentieth-Century Literature*; and *Crowd Scenes: Movies and Mass Politics*.

LOVE AND MONEY

A Literary History of Desires

Michael Tratner

Routledge
Taylor & Francis Group
NEW YORK AND LONDON

First published 2021
by Routledge
52 Vanderbilt Avenue, New York, NY 10017

and by Routledge
2 Park Square, Milton Park, Abingdon, Oxon OX14 4RN

Routledge is an imprint of the Taylor & Francis Group, an informa business

© 2021 Taylor & Francis

The right of Michael Tratner to be identified as author of this work has been asserted by them in accordance with sections 77 and 78 of the Copyright, Designs and Patents Act 1988.

All rights reserved. No part of this book may be reprinted or reproduced or utilised in any form or by any electronic, mechanical, or other means, now known or hereafter invented, including photocopying and recording, or in any information storage or retrieval system, without permission in writing from the publishers.

Trademark notice: Product or corporate names may be trademarks or registered trademarks, and are used only for identification and explanation without intent to infringe.

Library of Congress Cataloging-in-Publication Data
A catalog record for this title has been requested

ISBN: 978-0-367-50494-6 (hbk)
ISBN: 978-0-367-50490-8 (pbk)
ISBN: 978-1-003-05009-4 (ebk)

Typeset in Bembo
by Taylor & Francis Books

CONTENTS

ACKNOWLEDGEMENTS

This book would never have been completed without the advice of Howard Horwitz and Jamie Taylor; they commented on early versions of some parts of the book, suggesting readings I had not encountered, helping me expand my ideas. Howard also read full drafts of multiple chapters and has provided superb suggestions for revising. This project has also benefitted from ideas first put forth by students in my classes at Bryn Mawr College, where I have taught a course entitled "Love and Money" several times. Roy Scott has turned the project into a single image for the cover that beautifully captures the essence of the whole. I also wish to thank Michelle Salyga, my editor, and her assistant, Bryony Reece, who have provided guidance that has made the publishing process smooth and productive. My family has supported me by being a mostly willing audience so I could rehearse various versions of broad ideas. In particular, Leda Sportolari has suggested numerous perspectives on topics I was writing about and has supported the process of working on something for much too long.

PERMISSIONS

"To Elsie" and "A Foot-Note" by William Carlos Williams (*Collected Poems Volume I 1909–1939*, 2018) are reprinted here by kind permission of Carcanet Press Ltd, Manchester, UK.

All Louis Zukofsky materials copyright © Musical Observations, Inc. Used by permission.

"Spring and All" by William Carlos Williams, from *The Collected Poems: Volume I, 1909–1939*, copyright ©1938 by New Directions Publishing Corp. Reprinted by permission of New Directions Publishing Corp.

Paterson by William Carlos Williams, copyright ©1946, 1948, 1949, 1951, 1958 by William Carlos Williams. Reprinted by permission of New Directions Publishing Corp.

The Cantos of Ezra Pound by Ezra Pound, from *The Cantos of Ezra Pound*, copyright ©1934, 1937, 1940, 1948, 1950, 1956, 1959, 1962, 1963, 1965, 1966, 1968, 1970, and 1971 by Ezra Pound. Reprinted by permission of New Directions Publishing Corp.

The Waste Land by T.S. Eliot reprinted by permission of Faber & Faber.

INTRODUCTION

When people speak about love and money, they are usually referring to a conflict: love distorted by the desire for money. Such statements imply that love has a distinct form before economics interferes, but this book aims to show that such a view simplifies what is going on, because people have always been deeply shaped from the beginnings of their lives by everything in the social order, including economics. So when people say that money is distorting love, what they are really pointing out is that the current relationship of love and economics is different from an earlier relationship. This book seeks then to demonstrate the intertwining of the discourses of love and money over a long history by focusing on moments when parallel conceptions appear in economic theories and love stories. Such parallels may seem surprising, but there is a fairly simple explanation of why they occur: the two discourses repeatedly intersect because both involve describing or prescribing qualities and behaviors of human beings which are most valuable and hence most desirable. One economist who highlighted this intersection as central to economics—Dennis Holme Robertson—wrote in 1956,

> What does the economist economize? Tis love ... if we economists mind our own business, and do that business well, we can, I believe, contribute mightily to the economizing, that is to the full but thrifty utilization, of that scarce resource, Love—which *we* know, just as well as anybody else, to be the most precious thing in the world.
>
> (154)

Robertson's statement may seem rather unusual for an economist, but he bases it on a plausible notion of what all economic theories aim at: to identify and help people maximize what they deem most precious. Of course, most economists do not so dramatically identify love as the most precious quantity. However, the relation of love to what other economic theories seek to maximize can be seen throughout history when similar descriptions of valuable behaviors appear at roughly the same time in economic theories of how to acquire wealth and literary stories of how to find the ideal lover. By tracking mutual expressions of desire, value, and acquisition in economics and love stories, this book argues for the ubiquity of the intertwining of these discourses while exploring shifts in conceptions of value over a long history.

Some critics have examined the intertwining of economics and romance, generally focusing on a single era. For example, Carmen Nocentelli argues that in the early modern era there is an "intimate connection between the emergence of mercantile imperialism and the rise of new socio-sexual ideas" (136). Jen Cadwallader shows that in the Victorian era, the new economics which values labor over visible wealth transforms what is romantically attractive in *Jane Eyre* (234–46). And I wrote a book in 2001 about the 20th century, tracing intersections between macroeconomics and the Freudian vision of sexuality. This book builds on such critical analyses in order to bring out what is difficult to see when examining an era alone, namely that in every era there are tensions between long past and emergent conceptions. In economic treatises and literary works, stories and metaphors in effect stage debates about what is most valuable, debates within the texts about whether prospective changes in economics and in romantic notions are welcome or destructive.

Now one caveat: I am not claiming that all love stories and all economic theories in each age share the same vision of desire. There are always conflicting theories present. What I am tracing in each era are parallels between a fairly central set of economic theories that appear in that era and a fairly central body of contemporary English literary texts about love. These parallels suggest that economic theories are tied to arenas of human action not usually thought of as "economic," and also that romance is not just a personal interaction, but one influenced by seemingly unrelated aspects of society.

I am not suggesting that the connections between economics and love stories are causal in either direction; I do not support the Marxist idea that economics is behind every other cultural phenomenon, nor the psychoanalytic project of finding libido as the underlying force in all human behavior. Rather, I consider that changes emerge haphazardly in various realms, but then, since individuals and groups and institutions act in multiple realms, the disparate changes intertwine. The discourses, metaphors, images, and behaviors developed in one realm find support or are hindered by the discourses, metaphors, images, and behaviors developed in other realms. As Roland Greene describes this process, there emerge "reciprocal protocol[s] of representation": the terms in one discourse turn out to be useful to represent elements in another (9). Love has been repeatedly described as a form of wealth, and wealth as an attractive object like a lover. But there are more than merely metaphoric connections between these discourses. Economic

systems have emotional consequences in people's lives, and th
are often visible in romantic tales. And treatises about love crea
desires are and how they function, visions that sometimes er
economic theories.

Economic theories and love stories thus present conceptions of the sour
value, of what to do and where to go to gain access to valuable things or people,
and such presentations are most dramatic when a writer is proposing a change. So
I am going to focus on four eras when economic and romantic conceptions of
what is most valuable or desirable were actively changing in English discourses:
the early modern 17th century, the Victorian 19th, the modernist 20th, and the
postmodern present. I can summarize my overall argument with a chart giving a
rough sense of the parallels between economics and love stories in the four eras I
am exploring:

Century	Emerging Source of Economic Value	Parallel Source of Romantic Attraction
17th	Foreign Treasure	Foreign beauty
19th	Capital	Character
20th	Demand	Desire
21st	Information	Virtual self

In tracing a long historical process, I will clearly be painting in broad strokes,
ignoring elements which experts in each era and each discourse would regard as
crucial. But I believe that something is gained by trying to see across eras that
tend to be studied in isolation from each other, in particular the ways that writers
are struggling with unsettled, shifting conceptions.

The first chapter of my account, entitled "Digesting Foreign Treasure: Early
Modern Mercantilist Lovers," examines the early modern era, an era often considered the beginning of economics as a discipline. A beginning is a reaction to
something else, so I wish to set the early modern conception of value against the
medieval conception, which was in some ways not economic at all. As D. Vance
Smith notes, "Medieval texts do not describe lack or scarcity as constitutive of
either self or society; they describe the political economy as beginning with an
initial grant, the constitutive surplus of life" (xvi). People did not have to seek
what is desirable; it was granted to them as part of their "household," and granted
in surplus. So the economic question was not how to acquire what one desired,
but rather how those who controlled the wealth granted—the nobles—could
distribute that surplus of desirable things to create "Magnificence" and provide
"Benevolence" to those in lesser positions. Supporting this household economics
was the biological theory of humoralism, which says that ethers and fluids in the
environment maintain one's body and personality. In medieval theory, everything
needed for wealth and health is found in the household, surrounding and supporting the individual, all of it granted by God.

But something happens around the 16th century that challenges these medieval conceptions: great wealth began being brought into European nations from foreign cultures. Goods from the New World and the success of the East India Company threaten to overwhelm the initial grants that had previously seemed to comprise the wealth of England. Relying on an initial grant starts to seem insufficient and texts begin to appear calling for "increase." But to get that increase from other, foreign, realms could seem to violate the divine distribution of goods. It could seem an act of theft. Furthermore, the means of acquisition was often violent conquest, so it became crucial to develop ways to justify the transfer of wealth. And one of the central ways of justifying it was by claiming that once in contact with Europeans, those others in the Eastern and Western continents became enamored of Europe and just naturally wished to transfer their wealth.

While increasing wealth, foreign trade also produces a problem: the goods themselves are foreign, so bringing them into the country threatens the balance of humors. New biological theories emerge prescribing how to make the foreign contribute to health. Thus, in one of the most important treatises on the newly emerging economic system, Thomas Mun's essay entitled *Englands Treasure by Forraign Trade. or The Ballance of our Forraign Trade is The Rule of our Treasure*, the economic and the biological unite when Mun says that the Prince needs to tax away all the profits merchants gain from foreign trade and then distribute benefits to those merchants, thereby becoming what Mun calls the "stomach" of the nation that digests foreign wealth and converts it to domestic nutrition (chap. 18, para. 3). The royal household gains a new function, not merely making use of the initial grant but also processing incoming foreign wealth. And this new function serves to convert the new source of wealth into what appears to be the old: after digestion, foreign wealth seems to derive from the "body" of the nation, from the royal household, as it should in the medieval economic system. The conversion of the people of foreign lands is followed by the conversion of their goods: everything is then in a sense as the divine grant intended, purely English.

During the early modern era, the glittering attraction of the foreign becomes a dominant metaphor to describe nearly anything that seems desirable, in particular lovers. When Romeo first sees Juliet, he describes her as "a rich jewel in an Ethiop's ear" (1.5.53) and later says he would "adventure far for such merchandise" (2.2.89). Romeo is describing his love as a mercantile adventure, but he has clearly not traveled to any foreign land: Juliet's seeming foreignness derives from a division inside Romeo's homeland, which has led to endless violence between noble families. The overall play, then, is about eliminating the sense of foreignness between the Capulets and Montagues. That is brought about at the end, when each family erects a gold statue of the other family's child, and they dedicate these statues to Verona. They are in effect paying the taxes Mun recommends so the prince can "digest" the seeming foreignness that their competition had created and installed within their children. The romance in the play transforms the regime; the two families convert to being parts of one united realm. Romance rather more directly functions to convert foreign lands into European colonies and thereby end and cover up violence in a popular English play based on the Pocahontas story, *The Island Princess* by John Fletcher. Mercantilist language is also at the core of the *Merchant of Venice* and permeates Shakespeare's sonnets. In a coda to this chapter, I trace how mercantilist ideas reappear in later eras in the many versions of the fictionalized love story of Pocahontas.

The second chapter of this book, entitled "Disconnecting Bloodlines: Moving to Capitalist Romance" traces changes emerging at the end of the 18th century. The rise of industry as an even greater source of wealth than foreign trade leads to a new source of economic value and a new goal in love stories: both discourses turn to the value of hidden, internal potential rather than glittering visible attractiveness. A crucial narrative becomes central to both discourses: the search for the object of desire, which is distinctly not visible. To acquire value is to resist what seems valuable. Capital—wealth that must be invested, not spent or enjoyed—replaces treasure as the key economic value, and character replaces external beauty as the key romantic value. Hence "plain Jane" Eyre is much less attractive than Blanche Ingram—but while Blanche just sits around being beautiful, Jane labors as a governess, and that incites a new kind of desire in Rochester. Rochester himself is "more remarkable for character than beauty" (124). Romeo would never have noticed Jane, and Juliet would have been horrified at being approached by Rochester.

These new values do not just emerge full-blown: there is a long period of transition, and it is not easy. When one has a great source of wealth, via inheritance or foreign trade, it seems to fill up one with all that one needs. But Adam Smith describes this as a false sense of being full and satisfied—indeed, a kind of disease. Speaking of how England is gorging on wealth from the Americas, he says the country is like a person with a swollen blood vessel connected to another body (801). He calls for the blood vessel to be disconnected and the blood pumped into some currently undeveloped part of the domestic body.

The image of cutting off and reattaching a blood vessel is disturbing, but fits what we see in many Victorian love stories: characters from wealthy families are cut off from sources of foreign wealth or from inheritance and then undergo what is often a fairly violent process of learning to acquire wealth through their own labor. And it is only when they are disconnected that these characters can find love, because only then can they see beyond the visible wealth that in effect defined what was most desirable in earlier eras. The process of transforming a disinherited aristocrat into a capitalist devoted to the value of labor is quite physical and even violent. To cut Rochester off from the wealth supporting his profligate lifestyle requires burning his house, killing his Jamaican wife, and maiming him. Similarly, *Goblin Market* traces a violent shift in women's desires, transforming them so that they no longer succumb to irresistibly attractive foreign objects from goblin men but rather attach to the domestic household, producing another form of "domestic labor"—children, seemingly without involvement of any men at all.

While *Goblin Market* is clearly rejecting the foreign fruits of the goblin men, those fruits are extremely attractive and dangerously seductive. One could almost see the turn to the domestic in that poem as a loss of what is exciting, and that is very much what structures *Wuthering Heights*. Heathcliff is, as many critics have described him, a foreign or alien insertion into a peaceful feudal order of estates. But even though he is represented as using illicit or immoral means of rising into wealth (gambling and lying), Heathcliff remains the most attractive character in the novel. The novel ultimately expels him and replaces him with the same kind of figure I have been tracing in other novels—a disinherited aristocrat who takes on the role of laborer for most of the book. But that character, Hareton Earnshaw, remains a lesser figure than the dynamic Heathcliff. The book is thus torn by the loss of the exciting mercantilist possibilities in the move to a stable capitalism.

Our Mutual Friend is structured around a remarkable image of wealth being cut off from its ties to an estate. The wealth of what was once a rich estate is buried inside huge piles of dust and will only be fully possessed again through a process of labor. And as happened in *Jane Eyre*, the process of recovering that wealth requires someone to be disinherited, cut off from bloodlines: John Harmon, the son directly in line to inherit all the wealth, is accidentally declared dead, and he finds that that frees him to go to work: he becomes the business manager or "Secretary" for his father's servants who temporarily inherit the wealth, and his industrious behavior transforms a woman who would have been in effect purchased for him in his father's will so that she no longer would do anything for money but rather marries him as a secretary for love. Virtuous labor undoes the greed that had turned humans themselves into little more than piles of dust.

The third chapter of my history, entitled "Usury in the Bedroom: Financing Desire," begins at the end of the 19th century. In an earlier book—*Deficits and Desires: Economics and Sexuality in Twentieth Century Literature*—I explored the way early 20th-century writers advocated that young people indulge both sexual and economic desires. Those who are not sexual before marriage and those who will not borrow to buy things before earning enough to pay for them are described in the 20th century as repressed and destined to be unhappy. There is a general sense of a need to escape what is described as a debilitating state of inhibition. In that book I discussed this as a general sense of gaining a new kind of freedom and did not examine what in history had led up to this new vision. Placing that book in a longer history has led me to revise my view of that era. It is not simply a new sense of freedom that allows credit cards and premarital sex but nearly the opposite, a sense that both economic and sexual desires have been distorted by historical forces in ways that cannot be easily undone. At the end of the 19th century there emerge both economic and psychological theories that claim that desires are not entirely inside people—rather they are partly responding to external forces and past events. Darwin and Freud highlight the impact of historical biological processes on desires; Marx highlights the impact of historical economic structures. The dominant mainstream capitalist economist of the early 20th century—John Maynard Keynes—develops what could be called a mixture of these theories: he proposes that the government can "stimulate demand"—increase people's desires—by increasing government spending. This notion that internal states of people can be altered by the actions of completely external agencies such as government spending transforms the very conception of what desires are.

The new literature that emerges in the early 20th century—modernism—is full of visions of people's desires distorted by social and historical forces, and a surprising number of modernists directly call for economic change to alter the way romantic desires operate. Perhaps the most dramatic such statement comes from Ezra Pound, who says that a bad system of credit has "brought palsey to bed. Lyeth / between the young bride and her bridegroom" (Pound, *The Cantos*, 230). William Carlos Williams joins Pound in calling for an end to what he calls the war of "Love versus Usury" (Williams, *Selected Essays*: 168). Gertrude Stein suggests that government intervention in the monetary system has ruined romance (194). Louis Zukofsky advocates love and bodily pleasure as forms of resistance to the alienation of labor under capitalism. And Virginia Woolf writes a treatise, *Three Guineas*, arguing that economics has distorted the relations of the sexes so completely that all desires lead to war.

My fourth chapter, entitled "Leaving the Body to Become Information," brings this book up to the present. The present is of course difficult to summarize, so the best I can say I am doing is tracing a certain category of economic theorizing and a certain body of love stories. What unites the works I am examining in this last chapter is that they all propose that what people really desire can be disconnected from the body and so escape the distortions that modernists and Keynesians describe. In this chapter, I follow the economic historians Philip Mirowski and John B. Davis who argue that late 20th-century economic theories present individuals as essentially information-processing units. A new genre of literary works known as cyberfiction traces the possibility of humans becoming virtual versions of themselves, and many such works include accounts of a new dematerialized economic system. But a striking feature of such works is that the process of achieving an immaterial consciousness involves separating the "self" from the body, but the body does not simply disappear: rather it becomes a residue left behind, a mass of flesh, non-human. And what had been significant physical interactions, such as sexuality, become disturbingly separated from consciousness. So the literary works suggest that we are not quite able to fully imagine the transformation into virtuality: the new value of information has not become fully established. To trace this half-step into the world of information, I turn first to several recent novels that focus on finance: *Cryptonomicon* by Neal Stephenson, *The Corrections* by Jonathan Franzen, and *American Psycho* by Brett Easton Ellis.

The move away from the body into the information economy is allegorically represented in an unusual way in a series of sword-and-sorcery novels by Samuel

Delany called Nevèrÿon. The plot of the books is a move beyond slavery to what is called a "New Market," which one might expect to be an image of early capitalism, but instead wealth in the new economy derives from, as one wealthy woman puts it, "manipulations of the real" (*Tales*, 92). The series parallels this seemingly distant historical transformation to the current move into a financial, immaterial world, suggesting that the transformation to non-physical forms of social control has the potential to release people from various physical and sexual oppressions. However, the series suggests that this transformation has so far only created "synthetic" images of people that make it very hard for anyone to know the self (*Return*, 93). Delany writes in a footnote to the last of the series that "the job is to find a better metaphor," one that would change our understanding of all of human history in order to build a culture that would free people from various forms of enslavement, including the enslavement to heterosexual relationships (*Flight*, 187).

A number of recent movies have turned to ways people can find love by becoming in a sense images of their original selves, and this process is connected to financial economics. *Moulin Rouge* is a movie in which the body as performed on stage becomes the locus of true love, but to create that body requires financing by a rich sponsor who keeps interfering with the performance. The body off stage, when people are not playing a role, becomes incapable of even continuing to exist after love is finally enacted on stage; the off-stage body of the lover who is pursued throughout the film succumbs to "consumption" at the moment of perfect on-stage love. The physical world is "consumed" when the characters fully transform into performances (or we might say virtual copies) of themselves.

The most popular movie of all time, *Avatar*, provides a vision of a new, electronic body replacing human physicality. It focuses on a man whose human body is failing—his legs are paralyzed—but he gains through an electronic process a temporary new, perfect body on an alien planet as part of the effort of Earthlings to colonize that planet. Eventually the man falls in love with a female alien and leads a revolt that drives the Earthlings out. The love story at the center of the movie thus breaks with a crucial feature of the entire previous history of love stories: this is a love that has no relation to one's own human body, a love based entirely on what is in one's mind, which can be transferred to a new body.

The new world of the lovers looks like a pre-modern utterly natural world, but it is actually an image of postmodern cyborg existence, not pre-modern naturalism, because it turns out that everything in this world is connected electronically to everything else: the new bodies have plugs that allow them to plug in to animals, trees, and each other. And this cyborg world is also an image of pure financial economics: everything anyone has is explicitly described as "lent" to them by the planet, including their personalities, and they return it all when they die. The planet is in effect a giant bank, with all of life—including love—turned into a process of withdrawals and deposits from a global reserve bank. The climactic love scene shows the two lovers holding each other while they are each plugged into what seem electrical cords draped from a cosmic tree. Human bodies and their physical act of love disappear, replaced by this new way of being connected electronically. At the end, the main character's human body is left as a corpse on the grass as he walks away in his constructed alien body.

As each new conception of value emerges, older economic and romantic theories do not disappear. In this present 21st-century era, 19th-century plots of learning to value hard work and inner character continue to appear in popular movies. And the newest sources of value—the economics of information and the attraction of virtual selves—often seem unfamiliar and even disturbing. It may be that the present as a world valuing information is only be a step toward something else. Or perhaps by recognizing that so much of what we value now is a residue of the beliefs of past eras, we can learn to see the present—and indeed every era—as a shifting spot in the history of discourses.

References

Brantlinger, Patrick. *Fictions of State: Culture and Credit in Britain, 1694–1994*. Ithaca: Cornell University Press, 1996.

Bronte, Charlotte. *Jane Eyre*. New York: Tom Doherty, 1994.

Bronte, Emily. *Wuthering Heights*. New York: Barnes & Noble, 2004.

Cadwallader, Jen. "Formed for Labour, Not for Love: Plain Jane and the Limits of Female Beauty." *Bronte Studies*, vol. 34, no. 3, 2009, pp. 234–246.

Davis, John. *Captain Smith and Princess Pocahontas, an Indian Tale*. First published 1805. Early American Imprints, 2nd series, no. 8301.

Davis, John B. *The Theory of the Individual in Economics: Identity and Value*. New York: Routledge, 2003.

Delany, Paul. *Literature, Money and the Market: From Trollope to Amis*. Basingstoke, UK: Palgrave, 2002.

Delany, Samuel. *Flight From Nevèrÿon* (Book 3 in the Nevèrÿon series). New York: Open Road Media, 2014.

Delany, Samuel. *Neveryóna, Or the Tale of Signs and Cities* (Book 2 in the Nevèrÿon series). New York: Open Road Media, 2014.

Delany, Samuel. *Return to Nevèrÿon* (Book 4 in the Nevèrÿon series). New York: Open Road Media, 2014.

Delany, Samuel. *Tales of Nevèrÿon* (Book 1 in the Nevèrÿon series). New York: Open Road Media, 2014.

Dickens, Charles. *Our Mutual Friend*. Ed. Adrian Poole. London: Penguin Books, 1865/1997.

Ellis, Brett Easton. *American Psycho*. New York: Vintage Books, 1991.

Fletcher, John. *The Island Princess*. In Francis Beaumont and John Fletcher, *Comedies and Tragedies*. London: Printed for Humphrey Robinson, at the three Pidgeons, 1647. Online from the Folger Shakespeare Library at https://emed.folger.edu/ip.

Franzen, Jonathan. *The Corrections*. New York: Picador, 2001.

Greene, Roland *Unrequited Conquests: Love and Empire in the Colonial Americas*Chicago: University of Chicago Press, 1999.

Goux, Jean-Joseph. *Symbolic Economies: After Marx and Freud*. Tr. Jennifer Curtiss Gage. Ithaca: Cornell University Press, 1990.

Mirowski, Philip. *Machine Dreams: Economics Becomes a Cyborg Science*. Cambridge: Cambridge University Press, 2002.

Mun, Thomas. *Englands Treasure by Forraign Trade. or The Ballance of our Forraign Trade is The Rule of our Treasure*. Published for the common good by his son John Mun of Bearsted in the County of Kent, Esquire. London, Printed by J.G. for Thomas Clark, 1664. Online at http://socserv2.socsci.mcmaster.ca/~econ/ugcm/3ll3/mun/treasure.txt.

Nocentelli, Carmen. "The Erotics of Mercantile Imperialism: Cross-Cultural Requitedness in the Early Modern Period." *Journal for Early Modern Cultural Studies*, vol. 8, no. 1, 2008, pp. 134–152.

Osteen, Mark and Martha Woodmansee, eds. *The New Economic Criticism: Studies at the Interface of Literature and Economics*. New York: Routledge, 1999.

Poovey, Mary. *Genres of the Credit Economy: Mediating Value in Eighteenth- and Nineteenth-Century Britain*. Chicago: University of Chicago Press, 2008.

Pound, Ezra. *The Cantos of Ezra Pound*. New York: New Directions, 1986.

Robertson, Sir DennisHolme. "What Does the Economist Economize?" *Economic Commentaries*. London: Staples Press, 1956.

Rossetti, Christina. *Goblin Market and Other Poems*. Cambridge: Macmillan, 1862. Online at http://rpo.library.utoronto.ca/poems/goblin-market.

Seybold, Matt and Michelle Chihara. *The Routledge Companion to Literature and Economics*. New York: Routledge, 2019.

Shakespeare, William. *Shakespeare's Sonnets*. Ed. Stephen Booth. New Haven, CT: Yale University Press, 1977.

Shakespeare, William. *The Merchant of Venice: Texts and Context*. Ed. Lindsay Kaplan. Boston: Bedford/St. Martin's, 2002.

Shakespeare, William. *Romeo and Juliet*. Folger Library digital texts. Online at https://shakespeare.folger.edu/shakespeares-works/romeo-and-juliet/download-romeo-and-juliet/.

Shakespeare, William. *The Tragedy of Othello, The Moor of Venice*. Folger Library digital texts. Online at https://shakespeare.folger.edu/shakespeares-works/othello/download-othello/.

Shell, Marc. *Money, Language and Thought: Literary and Philosophic Economies from the Medieval to the Modern Era*. Baltimore, MD: Johns Hopkins University Press, 1993.

Smith, Adam. *An Inquiry into the Nature and Causes of the Wealth of Nations*. First published 1776. London: Electric Book Company, 2001. Online at https://ebookcentral.proquest.com/lib/brynmawr/detail.action?docID=3008435.

Smith, D. Vance. *Arts of Possession: The Middle English Household Imaginary*. Minneapolis, MI: University of Minnesota Press, 2003.

Stein, Gertrude. *The Geographical History of America or the Relation of Human Nature to the Human Mind*. New York: Random House, 1936.

Stephenson, Neal. *Cryptonomicon*. New York: Avon Books, 1999.

Tratner, Michael. *Deficits and Desires: Economics and Sexuality in Twentieth-Century Literature*. Stanford: Stanford University Press, 2001.

Williams, William Carlos. *Selected Essays of William Carlos Williams*. New York: Random House, 1954.

Williams, William Carlos. *Paterson*. New York: New Directions, 1963.

Williams, William Carlos. *The Collected Poems of William Carlos Williams, Volume I: 1909–1939*. New York: New Directions, 1986.

Woolf, Virginia. *Three Guineas*. New York: Harcourt Brace Jovanovich, 1966

Zukofsky, Louis. *"A"*. New York: New Directions, 2011.

1

DIGESTING FOREIGN TREASURE

Early Modern Mercantilist Lovers

We misinterpret the past rather instinctively, precisely because so much seems easily understandable. When Romeo and Juliet fall in love, we fall into their emotions with about as much thought as they have, and we then presume that we are sharing their excitement and then their horror as events go awry. The play works because it seems to tap into something universal, something constant in human life. And it is probably true that sexual excitement was as confusingly pleasurable in Shakespeare's day as it is today. But if we look closely at what the lovers say, it is not so easy to simply imagine ourselves saying those lines. The very first thing Romeo says to himself upon seeing Juliet is that she looks like "a rich jewel in an Ethiop's ear" (1.5.53). If we notice the phrase at all, we have to ask ourselves, what would cause such an image to appear in Romeo's mind as he gazes at the woman he will fall instantly in love with? And this image is entirely Shakespeare's addition to the text he borrowed the story from. In the *Tragical Romance of Romeus and Juliet* by Arthur Brooke, on which Shakespeare based his play, when Romeus sees Juliet, the text says she is "a maid, right fair, of perfect shape, Which Theseus or Paris would have chosen" (197–8)—in other words, Juliet is comparable to Helen of Troy, the classical image of perfect beauty. Shakespeare decides to move from Greece to Ethiopia for his image of beauty, and to compare Juliet to jewelry, not to an ideal woman. If we turn to examining where the language of jewels from countries like Ethiopia appear in Shakespeare's day, we would find that Romeo is borrowing from a particular economic practice that was rather rapidly transforming England and Europe: mercantilism, seeking wealth from voyages to other continents. In Act 2, Romeo even more directly turns to the language of mercantilism, saying, "I am no pilot, yet wert thou as far / As that vast shore washed with the farthest sea, / I should adventure for such merchandise" (2.2.87–9).

The phrases that seem so odd in Romeo's first reaction to Juliet are actually quite common in Elizabethan romances. One even finds such language in guides to a good marriage, as Carmen Nocentelli notes:

> marriage manuals and conduct books routinely troped courtship and marriage as mercantile adventures ... "[W]ho so ever marries a wife may well be called a *Merchant venture*"—commented Barnabe Rich in *The Excellency of Good Women (1613)*—"for he makes a great adventure that adventures his credit, his reputation, his estate, his quiet, his libertye."
>
> *(141)*

And it was of course not merely marriage that was a merchant adventure: sexual pursuits of all kinds were described similarly. Edmund Spenser writes in Sonnet XV of his *Amoretti* that a lover can provide all that "ye tradeful merchants" seek when "both the Indias of their treasure spoil" (1–3); he concludes that "my love doth in her selfe contain / all this world's riches that may farre be found" (5–6). John Donne similarly says of his mistress in "The Sunne Rising" that "both the India's of spice and Myne ... lie here with mee" (17–18). The extensive use of such imagery leads Nocentelli to conclude that during that era there is "an intimate connection between the emergence of mercantile imperialism and the rise of new socio-sexual ideals" (136).

The relationship between love stories and mercantile adventures also shaped descriptions of actual voyages to gain wealth from foreign lands. Roland Greene says that during the early modern era, "a reciprocal protocol of representation took hold, charging the two areas of experience, romantic love and cross-cultural conquest, with each other's import and force" (9). Greene analyzes such texts as Columbus's journals, showing that they are full of the language of love poems. Greene proposes a term for the common form of such treatises: he says they are forms of "anaculturalism" or the "virtual crossing of cultures"—imagining oneself in another culture. He notes that "Probably the most prevalent of the ideologemes of anaculturalism is the trope of the frustrated lover as sailing ship which is launched in early modern lyric by Petrarch's *Canzoniere 189*" (14).

But there is much more to the relationship of mercantilism and romance in the early modern era than these brief quotes reveal, and to get at the deep way that the rise of mercantilism around the 1500s transformed romance and sexuality, we need to examine carefully what the emergence of mercantilist economics did to fundamental conceptions of what humans are. The economic system of early modern England is very difficult to describe, partly because people did not conceive of economics as forming a distinct system. Those who wrote about trade and commerce were either giving advice about some specific transaction or considering trade as part of broad religious, philosophical or even biological questions. Economic historians in general do not treat the 1500s-1700s as a distinct era, but rather as a period of transition between feudalism and capitalism, between a society imagined as having a stable, divinely ordered hierarchy based on inheritance and a society in which individuals can change their status based on economic activity: a transition from divinity to the marketplace as the "invisible hand" shaping events.

Literary critics, drawing on this sense of economic transition, end up aligning Shakespeare with nearly every possible attitude about the change: he could be rejecting capitalism for its crass market mentality (Grav, *Shakespeare*); he could be promoting capitalism as bringing freedom from inherited inequalities and authoritarianism (Cohen); or he could simply be seeing the instability of all values and so developing a pragmatic way of proceeding without relying on any set norms (Engle). It is probably impossible to pin down Shakespeare's views on the new economics emerging, and one reason for that is that there was no way for Shakespeare to see clearly what was coming, to recognize capitalism in the forms it would later take. The shift from feudalism to capitalism spanned hundreds of years—say, from 1200–1800—so it is hard to imagine that anyone in 1600 could have recognized what the future would bring.

But if it is implausible to imagine anyone in the early modern era having an opinion about the new economics of capitalism, we can look at what kinds of changes in understanding the role of wealth were written about during that era. What were people advocating as new ways of thinking of wealth? Once we can understand what the debates of the day were about, we can with some greater plausibility see how Shakespeare and other literary figures were negotiating those debates.

During the early modern era, treatises of economics were written that are often considered the early beginnings of that field. But a beginning is always a break with something else, and several historians and literary critics have examined earlier views of wealth and concluded that in a sense they are not "economics" since they do not deal with that fundamental question of economics, how to acquire wealth. The reason this question was not addressed was that there was a sense that there was no need to acquire wealth. As D. Vance Smith puts it,

> Medieval texts do not describe lack or scarcity as constitutive of either self or society; they describe the political economy as beginning with an initial grant, the constitutive surplus of life and the teeming, abundant world that writers from Aristotle on describe. The fundamental problem that the presence of surplus poses is to discover how to live ethically in a world in which one is confronted with more than is strictly necessary to sustain life.
>
> *(xvi)*

Note that Smith's description merges notions of economics and notions of the self, the body: the initial grant provided more than was needed for wealth and more than what was needed for health. And that grant was mediated through the "household," a term used to describe every nobleman's resources—even the king's. Thus, the household became "the basic constituent of the national economy" (1). The medieval era followed the Aristotelian ideal which specified that the proper use of that initial grant was "Magnificence," which involved both a glorious display and also a form of outflow to those higher in the hierarchy (via taxes) and to those lower (as beneficence). Aristotle states rather directly the anti-economic nature of that ideal, saying that the magnificent person is one who "prefers his possessions to be beautiful and useless rather than that they should be profitable and meant for use, because this goes to show that he is sufficient to himself" (125).

Such ideals began slipping during the years 1300–1500, when there was a shift in the way the household economies were understood. For one thing, the feudal system of support up and down the hierarchy was slipping into a competitive system which David Starkey describes as "bastard feudalism" (285). Nobles hired their own armies and competed not only with each other but with the king. This development created the sense that the relationships among nobles and kings was not simply inherited and set by nature: noble houses could fall, and depended as much on their ability to compete with others as on what had seemed their "initial grant" of wealth.

But of course what most radically changed the medieval notion of the initial grant was the discovery of the New World, which seemed a vast reservoir of wealth never before known—allowing countries such as Spain to rise far above their "initial grant" and making it seem that maintaining one's nation and one's self required increasing what was in the household, not merely using it magnificently.

There then emerged that basic economic question: how to increase what one had? And the answer most often provided emerged directly from the events of the 1500s: as the most influential theorist, Thomas Mun, states quite bluntly, "the ordinary means ... to encrease our wealth and treasure is by Forraign Trade" (chap. 2, para.1). He titles his treatise to focus on this single goal: "England's Treasure by Forraign Trade or The Ballance of our Forraign Trade is The Rule of our Treasure." Mun is proposing a vision of the circulation of wealth that works in a very different way from the ethics of the distribution of surpluses. And it is this economic philosophy of the value of the foreign that has become labeled "mercantilism." Actually, the term "mercantilism" was not coined till long after Shakespeare's death, but theories of the centrality of merchants to the wealth of the state were extensively debated during the early modern era and codified in treatises written in the 1600s, a time when Shakespeare was writing his plays.

Mercantilism made much of the distinction between domestic and foreign territories, far more than the distinctiveness of each noble estate. So the economic historians Robert B. Ekelund, Jr., and Robert D. Tollison have argued that "the driving force of mercantilism was the creation of states and the strivings of statesmen after power and authority" (11). It is an economics that involves drawing people's allegiances away from their separate families—particularly the noble families that structured feudalism. The importance of foreign trade led to a sense that internal competition among noble households was a waste of energy. As one treatise on trade puts it: "whatsoever is gained by one Native from another in one part of this Kingdome must necessarily by lost in another part, and so the public Stock nothing thereby Augmented" ("Certain considerations relating to the Royal African Company of England," qtd. in Appleby, 161). And as a corollary of that belief, the treatise adds that "Increase and Wealth of All States is ever more made upon the Forreigner." Mercantilism is not merely a supplement to household economics, as jewels from foreign lands might seem decorations on top of the basic substance created as part of the household: because merchant trade becomes a necessary source of the substance that nobles have, it changes the nature of how one conceives what one is. Instead of just being a product of the locale, the estate, the household, or even a product of the state, a noble is in part a product of something from outside that estate—or in part the product of a human process rather than entirely the product of a divine gift. And there is a change in the personal qualities that are valuable: added to magnificence as a key virtue with which to approach the issue of how to use wealth is the willingness to "hazard," to "venture." Of course, those with estates do not venture themselves on mercantile journeys, but they finance them and so use their money in ways rather different from just displaying magnificence. There is still a belief that the ultimate goal of economics is the glory of the domestic realm, but that goal requires letting part of the realm leave for a foreign land and return in materials that cannot just be considered divine growth from within the estate.

Mercantilism required the merchants to have an ethical system rather different from that of nobles: merchants need to take advantage of differences of value. To gain in foreign trade, there must be an inequality in the transaction. This could be accomplished by deception or violence, and both were of course extensively involved in the gaining of wealth from foreign lands, but economic theories sought to justify the extraction of wealth from other countries as something other than theft by violence. But to justify keeping foreign wealth, people developed ways of conceiving what could seem unfair and forced trades as voluntary exchanges. This was accomplished by considering foreigners as simply acting according to values different from those in one's own country. Or even that objects have different values in different cultures. As one cultural historian of the era, Valerie Forman, puts it, "wares had power precisely because they were differently valued in Europe than in the Indies and thus could be sold at a profit" (615). Taking an object across a border transforms its value: value is not stolen from the foreign land, it emerges in the new land, and not via just one transformation—merchants traded wool from England for Sugar from the West Indies and then traded the sugar for wine from France. Mun summarizes the process, saying that those who have money "turn that into wares, whereby they multiply their Mony, and so by a continual and orderly change of one into the other grow rich" (chap. 4, sec. 3, para. 3).

This process of continual change of one thing into another leads to an unusual way of understanding what a commodity is. As Wolfram Schmidgen puts it, "The uneven spaces of mercantile capitalism do not only volatilize value, they also produce a porous commodity whose identity is shaped by the markedly different zones it inhabits" (32). Commodities were not the only things that were porous and found their identity shaped by the zones they inhabited: merchants were threatened by the same possibility. Mercantilist exchange is always risky, even to the merchant himself. Forman points out that "what becomes visible in … East India Company tracts and documents is that wares and money not only have the ability to transform into each other, but like clothing they have transformative powers" (617). When in contact with foreign commodities, instead of the commodity being converted into a domestic product, a person might find himself converted into part of a foreign culture. And this was not merely a cultural result, but a real physical transformation. To understand how that seemed possible, we need to examine a biological theory connected deeply to early modern economics, and that is humoralism.

Humoralism is a theory that everything is made up of four elements. In the cosmos these are earth, fire, air, water; in the human body, they take the form of the four humors, four fluids which shape everything humans are: phlegm, black bile, yellow bile, and blood. To get a sense of this biological system, imagine that you are not solid, but rather fluid, and not simply one fluid, but a swirling mixture of different fluids which pour into and out of the space that is your body. And imagine that the world around you does not consist of solid objects either, but of flows of liquids which, nonetheless, create the appearance of solid objects when the flows remain steady (as a waterfall can appear a solid tube if viewed from a distance). Everything about you is a result of the particular mix of fluids coursing through you, including your thoughts and perceptions, which shift and flow themselves as you move through this fluid universe.

Gail Kern Paster, Katherine Rowe, and Mary Floyd-Wilson thus conclude that the early modern body was understood to be a "porous, labile arena of contesting fluids" (15). The mind itself was considered "a leaky organ, forever escaping its 'natural' confines and mingling shamelessly with body and with world" (Clark, 53). Of course, individuals looked as solid and separated as they do now, but this appearance was considered an illusion which would dissolve if only someone could see with better eyes—such as God's eyes. Furthermore, the substances inside people were considered in some sense alive, referred to as "animal spirits" that responded to what surrounded those people and thus "linked the human body to the cosmos in natural philosophy and medicine as well as in theological contexts" (Sutton, 34)—and, as we will see, in economic contexts too. As we will see in Chapter 3, John Maynard Keynes revived the term "animal spirits" very much to return to this notion of the individual mind as deeply tied to the surroundings and to the body, after 18th- and 19th-century scientists and economists argued for a self-contained and self-moving individual.

This vision of the permeable human body became the dominant model upon which to understand all other bodies, such as the state, the church, and even God himself. In the early modern era, invisible flows are everywhere; objects have only a thin surface constantly penetrated by winds, vapors, ethers, and spirits. One did not have to breach the skins of these bodies to identify the flows within: it was believed possible to read signs on the surface. Experts of all types—priests, doctors, philosophers, alchemists, princes, playwrights, and even economists—were called to interpret those signs, thereby translating solid stable "things" into myriad flows that could be manipulated for various goals—to cure disease, to increase the nation's wealth, to win love.

What made each person distinctive in this world of constantly interacting flows was a distinctive "complexion" created by a distinctive balance or "ecrasia" of the four humors. To remain constantly the same requires then a constant balance of flows in and out, which is what the household economy was supposed to provide. The humoral theory of the body also applied to the "body" of the state. As Jonathan Gil Harris puts it, the norm before the 1500s was a "discourse of commonwealth, in which the health of the body politic is synonymous with its internally generated wealth. Economic as much as corporeal health is similarly understood ... as an endogenous phenomemon, deriving from internal balance" (22). But in the 1500s, Harris notes, there was emerging a "new economic phenomenon ... the alienability of money and identity across national borders" (53). The alienability of identity, in humoral theory, is a transformation of the body: crossing natural borders changed the balance of humors and so changed the temperament and identity of people.

But risking that alienability became crucial as mercantilism grew. The view that the state needed the increase in wealth from foreign trade required people to risk losing their identity by crossing into new lands (as Othello does). And there is another problem: if there is a continuous inflow of foreign elements, then according to humoral theory the state should gradually transform into something at least partly foreign to what it once was. To maintain order in this process of continual transformation, another element is thus needed to transform the foreign materials brought by merchants into domestic "nutrition" that can feed the original balance of humors. Thomas Mun is quite explicit about this need, and he calls for the ruler, the "Prince," to perform this deed, using what may seem a surprising technique: taxation. Mun says, "the gain of [the merchants'] Forraign Trade must be the rule of laying up [the Prince's] treasure" (chap. 18, para. 3); in other words, the Prince should tax away *all* the gain that merchants make. The Prince then gives back some of that wealth in services, bequests, and loans. Mun explains the logic of this policy: "a Prince ... is like the stomach in the body, which if it cease to digest and distribute to the other members, it doth no sooner corrupt them, but it destroyes it self" (chap. 18, para. 3). Letting the merchants keep their profits would be like allowing the hands or the mouth to keep food to themselves rather than first passing it through the stomach. Merchants who do that destroy themselves: their profits remain foreign influences, corrupting their usual British identities. To maintain one's self or one's wealth—to even be a person—one has to be inserted somewhere in a royal system, and one has to pass one's wealth through the body of the Prince before making use of it in order to avoid being corrupted. Taxes are not something the state takes away from private individuals, but rather they are a means by which the state creates individuals, or more precisely, keeps those individuals healthy. Instead of just inheriting and growing value from where one lives, one now has a process of conversion of external matter into value that maintains what one has inherited and grown from one's land. The "grounds" of one's value function in a new way: in the medieval household economy, the "grounds" where one lived simply bestowed value on those who lived there (and enough value to provide surplus); now the grounds are not simply one's household, but the entire state, and those grounds have to have implanted in them "foreign" elements which are then converted into domestic value.

The comparison of the flow of money to the biological flow through the body of the state is not simply a rhetorical gesture of Mun's: it is part of the way money is understood in this era. We can see a similar and even more extreme version of this logic in another economic treatise, by Edward Misselden, about the East India Company. Misselden says that this company is causing the "decay" of trade and fears this will "draw our Currency out"; then he turns biological:

> And thus the *Hepatitis* of this *great Body* of our being opened, & such profu-sion of the *life blood* let out; and the *liver* or fountaine *obstructed*, and wea-kened, which should succour the same; needes must this *great Body languish*, and at length fall into a *Marasmum* [a miasma].
>
> *(Chap. 1, para. 12)*

Misselden's diagnosis is couched in language that must seem very strange to us; we might imagine an economist saying the lifeblood was draining out of the economy, but not that the "liver" of the economy is "obstructed." What Misselden is thinking is that there is a source within the state for the "life blood" which sustains trade, and that source is in effect an "organ" in the "body" of the state. According to early modern biology, the liver creates blood and so there must be a liver in the state, which is the "fountaine" from which trade gushes. Misselden goes on to describe how to restore this fountain, and again the language is strange to our modern ears:

> The *Remedy* whereof, is in the *Princely Power and Gratious Favour* of His *Majestie* to apply at His pleasure to this *Languishing* body. And if HIs *Sacred Majestie* will vouchsafe to apply His Gratious *Mouth*, to *this Mount*: His waking *Eye*, to *this Eye*: His powerfull *Hand* to *this Hand*: then surely this fainted *Body* will receive *Breath* and *Life*, from the powerfull influence of so *Great* a *Majestie*, and revive also the many other *fainting* Trades, that are *fallen* in it.
>
> *(Chap. 7, para. 8)*

Misselden describes a very physical interaction between royalty and the "fainted Body" of trade: somehow the mouth and eye and hand of the Prince touching the mouth and eye and hand of the body of trade would give it "Breath and Life." We might see this as suggesting that the Prince should make decrees with his mouth and write them with his hand and keep track of what is happening with his eye. But there is much more implied here: the notion of breath flowing from the Prince into trade is part of the way things like trade were understood: as flows of liquids and vapors which determined whether the regime was healthy or suffered from diseases like hepatitis. The flow of money and wares becomes a "vital spirit" moving through the state and the Prince, a spirit that produces health only if carefully controlled by the Prince.

The notion that the Prince should control the flows through the state went very far: to not only taxing away the excess of foreign trade but also regulating each industry within the nation. As historians Jacob Oser and Stanley L. Brue observe, "mercantilists placed little trust in their own judgement and honesty, believing that the common interest of merchants required the government to prohibit poor workmanship and shoddy materials. The result was a bewildering maze of regulations concerning the production of goods" (17). When Oser and Brue call the regulations a "bewildering maze," they are imposing a much later perspective, which would criticize government regulations as hindrances to entrepreneurs. Instead, we have to view the regulations from within the overall vision of mercantilism: I would suggest that the appearance of bewilderment is part of the system, is what makes the mind of the Prince seem different from the mind of the merchants: the merchants subject themselves without requiring that they understand the system to which they subject themselves. The Prince is of course getting some of the qualities of God in this structure.

The structure I have been outlining—of persons traveling to foreign realms and striving to bring back foreign elements that then need to be converted into domestic substance by the ruling prince—becomes a distinct plot structure in several Shakespeare plays. *Romeo and Juliet* is a play about young people whose love draws them away from their households. In their rejection of their households, they foreshadow the new source of value arising with mercantilism: Romeo's attraction to Juliet is couched repeatedly in terms that make her the prize in a foreign adventure. But Romeo is misapplying what is "foreign" precisely because he is applying the earlier conception of households as independent entities and not recognizing that the newly congealing state should unite the two households as one domestic realm. That coalescing of households is the end of the play, couched in decidedly economic terms.

The play is often interpreted as a play about individual passions, about freedom of the individual against any kind of social interference. The work thus seems to point toward the much later emergence of democratic ideals. But if we look at how the story is set up by the prologue and the opening scenes, we can see that Shakespeare is not really presenting the story as a tale of individuals and families, but rather as a tale about a diseased public body that contains everyone in the tale. And that disease is internal competition, which produces violence very much akin to imperial violence, as each family considers the other dangerously "foreign." The play is set precisely at the moment when the household economy is no longer working; it has become in this play a form of bastard feudalism, in which each household has its own army and competes with others and with the royal center. The resolution at the end of the play is the transformation from separate households to a unified Verona, the crucial step in creating a mercantilist state. Romeo's mercantilist language treating Juliet as a foreign jewel foreshadows that ending, but it is also the source of the disaster that ensues because he is misapplying mercantilism: the Capulets are not Ethiopians, but Italians like him, and it is the uniting of the households, brought about by the prince that transforms this feudal enclave into a mercantilist state.

The Prologue of the play uses biological terms to describe the state as suffering from self-inflicted wounds: "fair Verona" is drenched with "civil blood" that makes "civil hands unclean" (Prologue 2–4). The body politic, the body of the state, is not holding itself together: civil blood is pouring out, visibly staining the hands, the members of the state. The continual bleeding in this town derives from "rage": as the prince says a few lines into the first act, the two families are attempting to "quench the fire of your pernicious rage / With purple fountains issuing from your veins" (1.1.86–7). Note that his language suggests they are cutting themselves, not "others"—he is attempting to make the competing families feel as one "body." And of course the shed blood does not put out the fire because what enters into the "civil bodies" of the two families to replace their lost blood, from the air, is just more "civil brawls bred of an airy word" (1.1.91) As a result, the elders of the town take up partisans (cudgels) which are "Cankered with peace to part your cankered hate" (1.1.97). In other words, the town is suffering from a form of cancer that has made even peace cancerous. The elders can no more end the cancerous hate than the flow of blood can. The prince tells the battling families to "Throw your mistempered weapons to the ground" (1.1.89), identifying what is needed to cure the imbalanced tempers of everyone in town: ground, or the humor "earth," which is distinctly lacking in the early part of the play, the humor which could calm and cool the fire, blood, and airy words causing brawls. The violence that keeps erupting in the play is an image of imperial violence mistakenly projected onto the two families because they do not see themselves as having "common ground" and do not imagine a way to convert either family to the other, so they seek only to eliminate violently the otherness they see.

But it is not merely ground that is missing: the prince does not have the power to unify the city and so is not functioning as the "stomach." The two families are in effect keeping what they value as their own, so their separate stocks of wealth remain "foreign" and hence poisonous to each other. The body of the state is cleaved in two, and there is no flow across the two families to unite them and no "common ground" that can stand outside their private quarrel. The result is a town full of "airy", ungrounded words and fiery rage.

The prologue promises that the death of the two lovers will cure this diseased state. But what is even more important is that their passion is in fact produced by the diseased state. From the "fatal loins" of these two families come the "star-crossed lovers": they are products of the air and fire of the town and are therefore hot-headed, too quick acting; as "star-crossed" and "misadventured," the lovers are being compared to a voyage, a venture that has gone the wrong way (Prologue, 6–7). Or more to the point, a voyage with no way to get home because they are not "grounded" when they set forth on their love affair. Love should be what unites houses; but in this play, it is what removes the two young people from their houses. Note that when Romeo describes what love is to him, he mentions three of the four humors, notably leaving out ground, earth, the humor that could bring the lover home after being carried away with love. He says, "Love is a smoke made with the fume of sighs … a fire sparkling in lovers' eyes; … a sea nourished with loving tears. What is it else? A madness" (1.1.197–200).

And after Romeo describes Juliet as a foreign jewel, he identifies the central problem of their love, saying she is "for Earth too dear" (1.5.54): their love has no grounds, no way to come to earth; it remains from beginning to end a mercantile voyage with no destination. And the two lovers cannot imagine any way to transform the difference between them into a unified domestic substance. Juliet says at the end of Act II, "my true love is grown to such excess / I cannot sum up sum of half my wealth" (2.6.32–3). That excess, which is her increased value due to love, is what threatens both households: mercantilism says that excess wealth such as Juliet sees in herself has to be taxed away by the prince and converted to state treasure; we will see something like that does occur in the play.

Romeo's wooing of Juliet seems then to have accomplished what mercantilism requires: he has transformed the value of the "jewel" he has found. However, he cannot finish his "venture" because he has no domestic space to bring the rich jewel to. I would suggest that this is what lies behind the problem of names that generates the famous lines, "What's in a name? That which we call a rose / By any other word would smell as sweet" (2.2.46–7). These lines, extracted from the play, seems to indicate that the play is about the conflict between natural essence and culture—culture gives the word, but nature gives the smell. Hence, it seems to suggest that Romeo and Juliet, if they did not have their family names, would be free to be what they naturally are—sweet young lovers. But I think it a mistake to see the desire of Romeo and Juliet to "doff" their names as a desire to be natural individuals completely outside the social order. What Juliet is talking about is giving another word to roses, not having roses remain outside language or culture. Similarly, what Romeo and Juliet need is not the absence of names but a name other than Capulet or Montague—a name that they could share, a name that would identify them as part of a social body that was not internally divided. The only word they can find is the word "this," the word Romeo uses when he says he wants Juliet to forget "any other home but this" (2.3.189). The word "this" seems to point to something but he is pointing to empty space. What

Romeo and Juliet need is a name other than Capulet or Montague that defines a group of people to which they can both belong, and that name is clear: it is "Verona." But so long as civil strife divides the principality, "Verona" is in effect not a name at all. Verona cannot be "this," the home, the domestic space the two can share because it is undermined by its division into Capulet and Montague, which destroys its ability to function as a unified, mercantilist, monopoly nation-state.

Verona should function as the base, the "ground" upon which their love could grow as a marriage of their two houses. But as the play indicates throughout, this town lacks "ground," lacks the humor that would balance all the fire and air that is driving the quarrels. The metaphoric sea-voyage that is their love finally comes to ground, or rather becomes the ground upon which the city-state of Verona can be built. Shakespeare emphasizes this function of their deaths in the repeated use of the word "ground" in the watchman's description of their bodies in the last act:

> The ground is bloody ...
> We see the ground whereon these woes do lie
> But the true ground of all these piteous woes
> We cannot without circumstance descry.
>   *(5.3.176–86)*

What seems a shift from physical to metaphoric "ground" in these lines is more a shift from the physical to the humoral sense of the word: what is missing in this town is the "true ground" of all actions, the humor that would balance all the heat and air flying around. And that true ground can only be provided by the prince—if every family in Verona is willing to consider itself a "member" of the "body politic" rather than a separate "body" of its own. The prince takes charge of the task the watchman sets—to "descry the circumstances" that produced the confusing sight of these dead lovers. And what is needed to "clear these ambiguities," he says, is to "know their spring, their head, their true descent, / And then I will be general of your woes" (5.3.225–228). A spring provides water from the ground: it comprises exactly the two humors (earth and cool water) needed to counter the fiery, airy disease of the town. The town has actually been missing a "head": the prince is in a sense the cause of the trouble because he has not been strong enough to unite these feuding households. The end of the play installs the prince as the one deciding everyone's fate and, by transcending the families, providing the "ground" on which a state can grow.

For the prince to ground the state, the two families have to agree to share the one proper name, Verona. That name is finally granted to the two lovers and their families in the perfect mercantilist end of the play, when the dead lovers are essentially converted into treasure that is given to the state. `Montague says of Juliet, "I will ray her statue in pure gold, / That whiles Verona by that name is known, / There shall be no figure at such rate be set / As that of true and faithful

Juliet" (5.3.310–13). Note the strange position of the word "name" in this dedication. The phrasing implies that the meaning of the statue and of the name "Verona" are intertwined. And after Montague, Capulet similarly donates a statue of Romeo. Two gold statues, each given by one of the previously warring families in honor of the other, establish that the two families accept the prince's overruling of their own desires and judgments; they accept that they are parts of the principality, not autonomous units, and they mark this acceptance by transferring part of their private wealth into public wealth, into something that adorns and marks the power and glory of the prince. The two statues are models of how to contribute to the magnificence of the state: they are beautiful and useless; the prince will not sell these gold statues to finance something else. But there is a hint of some other usage of the statues that partly undermines their magnificence: Montague says that Juliet will become a "figure" who will be set "at such a rate" that no other figure will equal her. This seems to be the language of interest rates, of lending and borrowing. Perhaps what is being said by this transfer of gold from Montague to Verona is that Juliet is going to become a source of interest for Verona, for the prince. The statue will identify Verona as a place where internal competition can have a resolution without war, making it a haven for bringing mercantile goods home.

The prince goes on to present himself as the arbiter of disagreements, particularly ones that might become violent. In effect he promises to put an end to the woeful result of excess competition. He says, "Some shall be pardoned, and some punished. / For never was a story of more woe / Than this of Juliet and her Romeo" (5.3.319–21). The prince will decide what punishments are deserved for causing the woe of these lovers. But the play ends before he says who will be punished and who pardoned. We do not get to hear this final interpretation: we have to guess, or maybe it would be better to say we have to accept the prince's judgements without worrying about understanding them.

And who are the persons most at risk from his judgments? There are three main ones: Montague, Capulet, and the Friar. Note how neatly these three define the old feudal order, representing the noble feudal lords and the Catholic Church, which particularly in Italy could be an alternative governing body dividing the state. In this last scene we watch all three clearly indicate that they will accept the judgment of the prince: the Friar indicates this by giving his confession to the prince and being willing to accept whatever the prince allots as penance: he is giving the distinctive power of the priesthood over to the prince. Montague and Capulet indicate their acceptance of the royal center by giving a significant sum of gold over to the public glory of the state. So the net effect of this love story is to establish the prince as having the authority to judge and overrule the actions of the Catholic Church and the feudal families within his nation. Verona is thus cured of its divisive cancer and converted into a proper mercantilist state.

Love in this play is part of a vast heavenly plan, not something that emerges in private relationships. Love is a crucial part of the structure of flows that maintains each individual and the state: love of the king keeps people English, and saves them from the dangers of mercantile encounters with foreigners.

While mercantilist imagery begins the story of Romeo and Juliet, similar imagery ends the story of Othello. Killing Desdemona is not merely a private act: Othello's final words identify it as a disruption of the entire state. It deprives the whole "tribe"—all of Venice. And Othello describes that loss in terms that parallel what Romeo first says about Juliet: that she is a jewel possessed by a foreign figure who doesn't recognize its value. Othello likens himself to "the base Judean," who "threw a pearl away / Richer than all his tribe" (V.2.406). And he goes further, identifying himself as not merely a foolish foreign figure but the most immediate foreign threat to the state:

> ... Set you down this
> And say besides, that in Aleppo once
> Where a malignant and a turbaned Turk
> Beat a Venetian and traduced the state,
> I took by the throat th'circumcised dog
> And smote him thus. *(He stabs himself.)*
> *(5.2.412–16)*

Othello at that moment is both the Turk who "traduced the state" and the Venetian who restores domestic unity. Othello does not see what has happened as his having been deceived by one wicked man (Iago), but rather as his accepting that he is an alien, not a Venetian—as Iago argued from the beginning. As Imtiaz Habib has described, "This is the colonized black who will have become the inevitable perpetuator of the colonizer's dominion over the world, the subaltern deployed efficiently in his own irrecoverable silencing" (25–6).

The ending can be read as expressing what Ania Loomba calls "the absolute 'otherness' of black-skinned characters who cannot be washed white, cannot be assimilated into the Christian family" (86). His suicide ends the cultural division within himself by an act of imperial violence, eliminating the alien presence within Italy—just as the two families joining together to erect gold statues for Verona unifies the city-state in *Romeo and Juliet*. These plays present variations on a mercantilist theme: that to maintain the wealth and health of the state, all foreign elements which have been brought in must be "digested" into domestic unity or destroyed.

In Romeo and Juliet, it is the two families who in effect convert to being part of one unified realm, but in most plays that mix mercantilist themes and love stories it is far more often the conversion of a non-European woman. As Loomba notes, this trope was common in early modern texts and deeply tied to the mercantilist venture: "In English writings, the desire of the non-European for

Europeans becomes a way of suggesting the supposed reciprocity, mutuality, and equality of international and colonial trade, and, in many instances, a way of disguising its violence and asymmetry" (72). This use of love to justify mercantilist conquest is embodied in *The Island Princess*, a play by John Fletcher, one of the most popular early modern English playwrights. In that play, a princess from an Indonesian island converts to Christianity in an act that is part of what saves a Portuguese man from being killed by her family—a plot that parallels and could have been based on the Pocahontas story. But there is another transformation of identity that is crucial to saving the European hero: the unmasking of a fake religious prophet who had demanded the European man be killed. In a sense, this unmasking is also a conversion, suggesting as does the princess's conversion, that what justifies what could seem just conquest is a discovery by those "conquered" of a flaw in their own culture, so that the Europeans seem to be bringing in a better religion, a better moral code, a better way of life.

The play is set in two Indonesian Islands, Ternate and Tidore, islands that are competing with each other before the play begins, and the actions of the play are set off by the efforts of the governor of Ternate to become the sole ruler of both islands. His first act is to capture and imprison the king of Tidore, and this act of island-island violence is overcome by a kind of European invasion: the Portuguese hero, Armusia, leads troops to rescue the King (the Governor and King are identified only by these terms, so I capitalize them as the play does). The rescue of the King, early in the play, is the first suggestion of how the Europeans are reforming the islanders: they are overcoming an evil within the island community, so seemingly represent a universal morality.

The act of rescuing the king is also troped as part of a love affair, because what leads to the rescue is that the King's sister, Quisara, says she will marry whoever saves him. She insists that the rescue be by force, not persuasion—in other words, not by conversion; she wants the Governor punished, not turned into a good man. The person she expects to carry out that rescue operation is Ruy Dias, a Portuguese man who is her paramour at that point. But Ruy Dias hesitates, and Armusia appears out of nowhere with his soldiers to accomplish the military rescue and then claim Quisara's hand. This is thus quite directly a European invasion as an act of romantic pursuit.

However, the way Armusia manages the rescue seems to suggest something less than ideal about European contact with the islanders. He disguises his troops as merchants, which allows them to get close to the prison where the King is being held. When they are sufficiently close, they cast off their merchant disguises and blow up the prison, rescuing the brother. This is the first unmasking in the play, the first moment of people being revealed as something other than what they seemed. But this "conversion" in some sense undermines the conversions that end the play. The ones at the end all imply that the Europeans win out because they are recognized as being nobler, more moral. This early unmasking, however, suggests that the appearance of the Europeans being there just for friendly trade is merely a way of disguising what is really violent conquest. Just before Armusia's action he overtly states that he uses the appearance of being a merchant to disguise his military goals: "Powder is ready ... No man but suspecting what I am but a merchant" (l. 0790). He also suggests that his romantic passion, his desire for Quisara, which he calls "the fire" that drew him to the Islands, is equally just a cover for violence: "The fire I brought here with me shall do something / Shall burst into material flames, and bright ones" (l. 0786–7). Michael Neill sees Armusia's speech as rather ironically undermining the whole ethos of universal goodness that the play claims at the end:

> in the marvelously telling metamorphosis of love's fire into the 'material flames' of Ternata, Fletcher's language discloses the links among sexual desire, mercantile greed, and imperial violence which the play's official ideology struggles in vain to suppress.
>
> *(125)*

After Armusia's successful rescue of the King by disguising his soldiers as merchants, another disguise plays a large part in the plot. This time it involves the Governor, whom Armusia had defeated. In order to get revenge and keep alive the possibility of ruling both islands by wedding Quisara, the Governor disguises himself "like a Moor Priest" (l. 1935) and demands that the King require Armusia to convert to the island religion to marry Quisara. The island's religion is not really identified, but seems a mix of Muslim, Hindu and possibly American Indian elements.

The Governor's argument is that Armusia's marrying the princess will result in his destroying their culture because he is a Christian. The Governor asks if the islanders will be forced "To change our worships now, and our Religion? / To be traitor to our God?" (l. 2014–5). He convinces the King, but Armusia refuses to convert and vehemently condemns the island religion, so the King, at the Governor's insistence, threatens to kill him. But then there are two more "conversions" that resolve the standoff without violence: first, Armusia's noble stance wins over Quisara, who says she is convinced Christianity is the better religion and that her brother would be a heathen if he killed Armusia. And then the disguised Governor is "converted" from a Moorish priest by having his false beard and hair forcibly removed by Portuguese soldiers of Armusisa's camp. In a sense, the religion the Governor has been promoting is exposed as a fraud by the Portuguese, and this leads the King to release Armusia. As with Armusia's earlier rescue of the King from the treacherous Governor, this act seems to show the Portuguese restoring the internal goodness of the islands. The King then says he will "seize" the lands of the Governor because "His father and himself have both usurped it" (l. 3069). In other words, the King is curing an internal moral flaw in the government of the islands, but it is the Portuguese who have brought this flaw to light. The wicked Governor's town and castle are then given to Pyniero, the Portuguese man who unmasked him. In effect, a Portuguese colony is set up not by trade or conquest but by exposing fraud and wickedness within the colonized land. Colonization is thus represented not as conquest but rather as the cure for immorality within the world of the colonized.

But though the two "conversions" at the end of the play—of Quisara and the Governor—seem to resolve the conflicts by revealing true goodness (of Armusia and the European religion) and exposing wicked fraud (of the Governor), the play nonetheless surrounds these acts with a very definite threat of colonizing violence. While the transformations of the Governor and Quisara are occurring, the Portuguese are arrayed in military force outside the royal court, ready to save Armusia. They are clearly identified as strong enough to conquer the islands. But this threat is never acted upon. Thus, even though the play presents the triumph of morality over fraud as the reason for the Portuguese success in acquiring land and the love of the princess, the play still raises the specter of European military power standing behind such seemingly moral actions.

The play ends with a dismissal of all the various forms of threatened violence: the last lines are the King's, when he declares:

> No more guns now, nor hates but joys and triumphs,
> An universal gladness fly about us:
> And know however subtle men dare cast,
> And promise wrack, the gods give peace at last.
>
> *(l. 3082–5)*

The "gods" referred to in that last line bringing "universal gladness" to everyone seem to be both the Christian and the island deities; the King even tells Arumusia, "You have half persuaded me to be a Christian ... Why what dream have we dwelt in?" (l. 3053–5). The play thus ends by justifying mercantile conquest as the bringing of a universal religion that exposes the illusions or dreams of non-European cultures.

One character, however, does not accept that what has happened is the result of universal divine goodness. The Governor describes his failure in terms of both economic and romantic deceit: he says at the end, "I paid you all, / But fortune has played the slut " (l. 3046–7). He does not accept what the play tries to establish, that a "true God" has exposed a false one and a true "love" has replaced lust. Rather, he says he paid sufficient funds to get what he wanted: Quisara and rule over both islands. But unfortunately his funds were misused: instead of granting the Governor's desire for an enriching love and the acquisition of lands, "fortune" enacted the worst kind of love, becoming a slut. The Governor is of course represented as a truly evil character, so this explanation of what has happened, devoid of real love or decent economics, is thoroughly undercut by being spoken by a despicable person.

The Island Princess thus repeatedly hints at the moral conundrum of mercantile conquest: is it the result of violence and economic manipulation or the superior religious and personal character (i.e. love) of the conquerors? That question also underpins the Shakespeare play that most directly addresses the question of what mercantilism actually is—*The Merchant of Venice*. The central issue in critiques of this play is usually what to make of Shylock: is he an evil figure? Does he represent Shakespeare's view of Jews in general? And these questions seem until the very end to be tending toward a violent solution: either Antonio will be killed, indicating that Shylock is not an evil man but a reasonable merchant, or Shylock will be killed because he is found to be truly alien. But instead, the play avoids violence by the conversion of Shylock—an extremely involuntary conversion, but nonetheless one that can be seen as escaping the threat of physical violence.

The question of whether Shylock is evil turns on a subtler issue: is loaning money at interest immoral? That question can be reframed as the basic question behind the shift from medieval household economics to mercantile economics: should money be used to increase one's wealth or simply to create magnificient displays? The play is caught up in the dilemma of whether to defend the medieval notion that nobles do not need to engage in monetary interactions to increase their wealth or the rising notion that merchants are necessary to increase the wealth of the nation. It is about a nobleman, Bassanio, who does not have a surplus to give away in acts of magnificence: indeed, in order to be magnificent and thereby eligible for winning Portia, he has to borrow money from a merchant, Antonio. Bassanio is essentially not being valued in Venice as he deserves; he is an ignored jewel. We could say, using Romeo's language, that he is a "jewel in a Venetian's ear." His value cannot be seen until he is transported to Belmont, and to reveal that value requires funds from Antonio. So Antonio transforms Bassanio into a product that can be sold at great profit—and that sale is the core of the play. And as in *Romeo and Juliet*, what the trade in goods ultimately does is prop up the older system of nobility: Bassanio is truly himself at the end; mercantilism does not dismantle the medieval household economics but supports it and transforms it, creating an overarching household, the royal center, that includes all the other noble estates. So the play is very much about the new dependency noble and royal status has on trade that is at the core of mercantilism.

At the same time, there is a competition in the play between two men seeking to increase their money—Antonio and Shylock. Because all of Antonio's wealth is at sea, he has to borrow from Shylock to fund Bassanio's trip to Belmont. But Shylock is not really a merchant: he does not have ships; he has money and he gains by lending at interest. So he trades in money and time, not differences of value. In a sense, Shylock is a problem within the evolving system of mercantilism, and in a way he present a problem similar to that of the feuding houses in *Romeo and Juliet*: he seeks to gain by taking from others within the state. As in the competition of Montague and Capulet, Shylock gains only when another person within Venice loses, so his economic enterprise does not contribute to the increase of the wealth of the whole state. He is not a merchant, but a person dividing the internal realm of Venice, and the internal division of the state of Venice is removed by his conversion.

So one way to view the play is that it traces throughout, not merely at the end, the strange conversion of Shylock because that conversion is ultimately an effort at making "domestic" the economic behavior which Shylock brings as a for-eigner—the charging of interest. The crucial first step in Shylock's change is his not asking for interest, which in a way brings him close to saying that he and Antonio are of the same cultural group. According to Jewish law and also according to usual Venetian practice, those who are in the same cultural group do not charge each other interest (a practice that the end of the play will change). So Shylock's shift to an interest-free loan could be seen as a way of declaring himself a domestic subject of Venice, not an agent of a foreign power; we might say he is beginning to convert himself. His later famous speech, "Hath not a Jew eyes?" (3.1.44), emphasizes his claim to identity with the Christian Venetians and thus, I suggest, quite strongly extends this process and at the same time undermines his legal case; if he is identical to a Venetian, then he is not foreign and the bond was an internal contract, irrelevant to Venice's trade and thus has no bearing on one of Shylock's main arguments, that the prince would endanger his international standing by voiding the bond. Furthermore, as Shylock repeatedly demands his bond he starts sounding as if he wants both Antonio and himself to get exactly what is their right, and this too undermines the mercantilism of the entire eco-nomic system: the presumption that there is a single overarching evaluation of what is right for two parties to an economic transaction is precisely the opposite of mercantilist economics, which is based on differing values.

The trickery of Portia's various arguments is that she is in effect trying to stop Shylock from converting himself, trying to restore him to full foreign status by getting him to return to mercantilist principles of difference and unfairness of exchange. Her famous speech about the quality of mercy is of course about the value of inequality in exchanges. Mercy is a religious version of unequal trading: in the trade between the human and the divine, getting mercy from the divine realm when all humans can give is their sins is a superb mercantilist result. When Shylock refuses the logic of unequal trades, Portia tries to show him the absurdity of his position by invoking the logic of precise measurement. Precise measure-ment is not crucial to mercantilist trade. Consider how Portia's analysis about measuring precisely a pound of flesh and not allowing a jot of blood could be applied to any trade: is a bushel of tomatoes exactly a full bushel? What if some juice drips out while you are delivering it? Mercantilist trading is not terribly concerned about such details because the assumption is always that one is going to get far more for the object one is buying than one paid, so whatever small errors might creep into the measurement will be overshadowed by the overall wonderful unfairness of the exchange in the first place. Portia is pointing out the peculiarity of Shylock's demands: they don't fit into any economic logic, either household or mercantile.

One more detail is important: the court case turns on the question of whether or not blood was included in the agreement to forfeit a pound of flesh and whether the measurement of the pound had to be exact. So we might wonder why Portia does not turn to questioning Shylock and Antonio to settle whether or not these conditions were implicit in the original agreement. Given the attitudes of the two, one would expect Antonio to say that he of course expected blood to be spilled and that he did not expect any such precise measurement. But Portia does not turn to the two signatories to settle the meaning of the document they signed; instead, she turns to a section of Venetian law that would seem to have nothing whatsoever to do with such questions: the section about the difference between aliens and citizens. What that section of law says, according to Portia, is that the document was not a contract at all, but rather simply a threat from a foreigner to the body of a citizen, and thus the foreigner is deserving of death. Shylock's insistence on his "bond" is in effect his denying the inequality underlying all mercantile ventures; he is acting as if he is a full citizen, seeking equality under the law. His arguments are in effect denying his foreignness.

Note then that the final result traces a version of the process that Mun proposed for mercantilism to preserve the domestic realm: royalty digests foreignness into domestic wealth. All Shylock's money is delivered to the prince, who then distributes it by giving half to Antonio. But then Antonio gives that half back to Shylock, asking just for the use—for the interest. The prince has thus taken what Shylock as foreigner has extracted from Venice and redistributed it to Venetians, including Shylock as a converted Christian Venetian, but one who now can loan money at interest. So the prince is digesting the foreignness of Shylock while extending the system of using money to increase money, through both foreign trade and money lending. Further, at the end of Shylock's life, whatever he has left will be passed into Venetian-Christian hands through his own daughter, who has voluntarily converted from Judaism and hence has become "domestic" in her marriage to Lorenzo.

The love plots in the play mirror the mercantilist narrative, translating that story from economics to romance. Bassanio's wooing of Portia makes him one of Antonio's ships, indeed the only one that comes in on time. He does not go very far, just to a nearby town in Italy, but what he has to do to win Portia is to treat his trip as if he were engaged in a trip to a foreign land. What he has to do is evaluate which of three coffins contains her image. The play uses the coffins to turn what could have been just a typical wooing of one Italian family by another into a mercantilist venture. The proper choice of coffin involves following a mercantilist way of evaluating things. Two men choose before Bassanio, and they choose the wrong coffin, but what is more important, they choose according to values that do not fit the mercantilist system. The first coffin chosen, a gold one, is interpreted as offering "what many men desire." The man who chooses that coffin, Morocco, interprets that as giving him what is desired in every land (2.7.5). But being equally desirable in all lands is precisely what would make gold useless as a mercantilist import: it won't change value when transported to a new land. To choose gold is to choose something that needs no conversion, and so can only be taken violently or lost violently—and Morocco is essentially condemned to a violent end, no marriage or future family.

The second coffin is silver, and Aragon chooses it to get "as much as he deserves" (2.9.50); this presumes that what he gains will equal in a sense the value he already has, rather than the undeserved excess that is both the reward and the danger of mercantilism. He too fails to recognize the need for conversion; if his merit is recognized by those he is dealing with, he cannot make the unequal trade that underpins mercantilism, so he can only face a form of conquest, and he, like Morocco, is in effect conquered and given that death of his cultural inheritance, no future for his line. Finally, Bassanio describes all the coffins as deceiving and so chooses the one that "rather threaten'st than dost promise aught," the lead coffin (3.2.105). He is performing the crucial mercantile act of entering a realm in which one's own values make no sense, choosing what appears to his eyes dangerous or worthless but actually contains great hidden value that can appear when it is brought back home, when it is converted from foreign values to domestic ones.

The other love plot, Jessica running off with Lorenzo, is also a proper mercantilist transaction. By moving Jessica from Shylock's realm to his, Lorenzo alters her value, converting her from a denizen of what she herself calls "hell" (2.3.2)—in other words, a demon—into a divine creature, an angel. And as in all excellent mercantilist trades, he gains along with her a stockpile of treasure—Shylock's jewels that she takes with her.

At the end of the play there is a final scene where Portia and Nerissa tease Bassanio and Gratiano about the rings the men had received from their beloveds, rings they had turned over to the "men" who solved the court case with Shylock (those "men" being Portia and Nerissa in disguise). This final playing around with rings also explores the strange logic of mercantilist unfair conversions. Of course, the women acquired the rings under false pretences, in other words, by not revealing that those seeking the rings knew their true value. Portia and Nerissa promise to only lie with the men who had taken these rings from Bassanio and Gratiano. From our 20th-century viewpoint we would probably say that the final banter is based on playfully confusing mere rings with the love that binds these couples. But that confusion is at the core of the entire play: the same problem lies at the heart of Shylock's confusing mere economic transactions with the hatred that binds him to Antonio. To separate the emotional meaning of an object from the physical properties it has is to deny the early modern world view. As Douglas Bruster has argued, "Consciously or unconsciously, playwrights connected identity with ownership, rendering the relationship between property and person as one of almost complete interdependence" (xi). Physical properties merge with emotional or even spiritual properties. If the divine can be incarnated as almost anything else (for example, a burning bush), one cannot simply say that the sacrament of marriage is separable from the rings exchanged. And in the mercantilist view, unfair exchanges of objects such as Portia's sneaky acquisition of Bassanio's ring always involve radical conversions of the meanings of those objects, of the values embedded in them. Such unfair conversions of the values in things are not accidents but the central mercantile process for establishing the overall divine value of any social group, whether a nation or a marriage.

The play is shot through as well with transformations that fit the nature of humoral understandings of what a person is. The opening lines set out the basic issue: Antonio has "much ado to know myself" (1.1.7). His methodology for trying to know himself is not to search inside for his "true essence"; rather he focuses on external sources of his emotion of sadness: "how I caught it, found it, or came by it, / What stuff 'tis made of, whereof it is born, / I am to learn" (1.1.3–4). He conceives of his emotion as something that is born elsewhere and made of "stuff" that is simply not part of him (or rather stuff that is now part of him, and therefore he wonders what he is with this stuff added to him). Throughout the play, Antonio is presented as a person who lets others determine what he is and even quite literally what stuff will make up his body: he pledges his "person" along with his wealth to Bassanio, and he is willing to lose a pound of flesh to Shylock. He never feels that he is able to act as a full person: he is a "tainted wether of the flock," a lesser creature (4.1.114). It is possible to see him as in love with Bassanio, in a triangle like that of the speaker to a young boy in the sonnets—encouraging Bassanio to wed Portia but still asserting that "mine be thy love," as the speaker in Sonnet 20 does.

Antonio's uncertainty of where his emotions come from and what he is "made of" is ended by the fiat of the duke, negotiated by Portia. Antonio even makes an independent decision as part of the concluding resolution: the duke having provided the prop which Antonio needed to finally act independently, Antonio then decides to convert Shylock and Shylock's money to Christian "use." We might say that the whole play runs from Antonio's having no sense of himself—and so letting everyone else determine his fate—to his achieving the solid basis on which to be something. In a sense, the duke has secured Antonio's body from being transformed by mercantile ventures, so that Antonio's money at the end does not come from his ships, but from the duke. This basis for solidifying Antonio mirrors the basis for unifying Venice's economics—converting Jewish wealth to Venetian inheritance.

We might say that Portia's role is to find the condition that can stop the endless conversions which make up most of the play—and the condition she finds is the clear distinction between "alien" and "citizen," the distinction that underpins the balance of trade. By reasserting that Shylock is finally an alien, the ethics of balance of trade are finally put into play, and fairness and equity disappear. Shylock does not get what he "deserves," his "bond", rather he gets what is most profitable to Venice from aliens; but the reason this happens is that he has violated the basic terms of trade, bringing in, we might say, trade in body parts (which has never been allowed). At the end of the play, the parallels between the two plots are laid out as both involving trade in body parts, and the ring ends up embodying this trade. Portia says that once the "doctor" "got the jewel that I loved ... I'll not deny him anything I have, / No, not my body nor my husband's bed" (5.1.222–6). Antonio tries to stop her trading her body by saying that his body is actually the one that was mistraded: "I once did lend my body his wealth," but his body was saved by "him that had your husband's ring," so Antonio "dare be bound again, / My soul upon the forfeit" (5.1.246–9), and Portia says, "Then shall you be his surety" (5.1.252). Antonio is now in effect using his own body as surety in a transaction restoring the actual household of Bassanio, no longer devoid of wealth or substance. Thus, the play focuses on the role merchants play in maintaining the older household economics: not only providing wealth to maintain the magnificence of the household, but actually providing substances that maintain the natures of the people so they can hold their households together. Antonio's "surety" of his "soul" upholds the noble household of Bassanio and Portia, as the surety of his pound of flesh upheld the wealth needed to make Bassanio a possible match for Portia. The merchant creates the unity of the state by first dividing himself up into parts that are domestic and parts that are foreign and then being unified by the royal center "digesting" him as well as his foreign wealth. Antonio overcomes his sadness by becoming this crucial part of the household of Bassanio, being "digested" into the role of prop holding up the noble and royal estates.

The interrelationship of love stories and economics is also central to Shakespeare's sonnets: fully a third of the sonnets refer to payments, credit, usury, or even mortgages. This economic language in poems mostly about love may not seem to need much explanation because it is easy to see it as metaphorical: one gains value from a lover, one is in debt for the pleasure one has experienced, etc. What does seem strange to modern readers, though, is that the early sonnets use economic language largely to tell the beloved to go off and make love to someone else. The speaker in the early sonnets is an older man speaking to a beautiful young man, telling him to go have children with some woman. This produces questions about whether the sonnets are homosexual or whether there were different conceptions of sexuality then. But we can arrive at a very different way of understanding what is going on by considering the commercial language used to justify what is being advocated. The sonnets imply that the beauty of the young men is a social value which must be used to serve everyone; as the first line of the first sonnet puts it, "From fairest creatures we desire increase" (1.1)—"we" being everyone in the state because everyone gains from the valuable properties of those in it. The meaning of the term "increase" is different within the household economy and the mercantile economy, and the sonnet hints at both meanings. Within the household, to increase the "fairest creatures" is to reproduce them, to have children that simply repeat the value found in the parents. Within the mercantile economy, as in Mun's essay, the only way to "increase treasure" is from "foreign trade." Foreign trade does not reproduce the same beauties, the same treasure, that is already in the household: rather, it adds new beauties, treasures not available in the household. And of course the goal of foreign sources of treasure is to increase the greatness of the household. So this first sonnet starts with that ambivalent sense of "increase"—is it just maintaining the beauty of the family or adding something new?

Where the young man is being encouraged to go to "increase" himself is to the "realm" of women. In this, Shakespeare is following a commonplace of early modern poetry: women are endlessly described as foreign lands that can be approached as merchants approach such lands. So when the speaker in Shakespeare's early sonnets encourages the young man to have children with a woman, and describes this repeatedly in commercial terms, mercantilist ideas are mixing with older notions of maintaining the household by having children. The young man is told to use his treasure, his beauty, to create more treasure by interacting with others unlike himself, just what Mun recommended merchants do; this method of increasing wealth is a social value: as Sonnet 6 puts it, "treasure thou some place with beauty's treasure … That use is not forbidden usury" (6.3–5). Usury gains a peculiar meaning in this context: it is usually critiqued as money breeding with itself, and in that sense hints that the young man is trying to use his beauty only for his own self. In Sonnet 4 the young man is called a "profitless usurer" for having "traffic with thyself alone" (4.7–9)—he is refusing to "traffic" or trade with others unlike himself. And the question of whether going off to be involved with women is a way to just reproduce himself or a way to trade with those unlike oneself remains a tension in the sonnets. In other words, there is a tension between the household economy and the mercantile one regarding the question of whether pure reproduction of what is already present in the household is the goal or not. The two ideals are perhaps most directly contrasted in Sonnet 20, where the speaker imagines for a moment how pleasant it would have been if the beautiful young man had been a young woman: then the speaker could have had both the pleasure of the young person's beauty and the pleasure of the "treasure" gained from reproducing. But because the young man has to go off with someone else to reproduce, the sonnet ends with a split between two different forms of value in the young man: "Mine be thy love, and thy love's use their treasure" (20.14). The love is what unites the two men, what keeps their realm purely theirs, with no admixture from abroad. This requires what might be considered a failure of the mercantile excursion into the other land of women because the treasure generated by that excursion ends up "theirs" not "ours." This poem has a tone of resignation, but not of total despair: though the gain is lost, the young man's love is still "mine." The distinction between love and treasure marks a tension between household and mercantile notions of value.

The question of what has to remain within the person going off to build value with others and what joins with those others becomes more and more the issue as the sonnets progress. Sonnet 94 presents a distinction between those who are "lords" of their own "faces" and those who are merely "stewards," and this distinction matches that in mercantile theory between the roles of prince and merchant (94.7–8). The sonnet praises those who "while moving others are themselves as stone" (94.3). This describes the ideal prince: able to interact emotionally with others, inspiring their actions, moving them, but not slipping into the feelings or attitudes of those others. That is how the prince transforms foreign wealth into domestic treasure. Those who are changed by those they interact with are "but stewards of their excellence" (94.8). A steward is someone who manages something for someone else. The merchants are stewards of the wealth they gather from foreign lands: it must go through the prince's "stomach" to be safe and supportive of England. Those stewards may "with base infection meet" (94.11)—indeed, Mun's theory implies that so long as the merchants hold onto the wealth they have acquired from foreign lands, they are "infected"; they are like hands refusing to deliver food to the stomach, believing they can feed themselves. Merchants need a lord to digest foreign goods and maintain their domestic biology.

There is a much worse disaster than can happen in a mercantile encounter, when not only the gain from trade is lost but also the love that ties you to your household (or we might say, your homeland). This can happen if the foreign encounter has the effect of completely converting the English values of the merchant. This shadow side of the mercantilist adventure would happen if the foreigner controls the passions that emerge during trade, and so this mercantile disaster can be used to describe a love that drives a man out of his normal personality. This is what Shakespeare examines in the later sonnets. The speaker encounters a woman who is thoroughly "foreign" to the values of the early sonnets but who inspires a passion so great that he is completely transformed. As in the economic treatises of the day, this makes him sick: his love is a "fever"; he is "past cure" and his "thoughts and discourse as madmen's are" (147. 1–11). The results of this transformation are presented in detailed commercial terms, particularly in Sonnet 134. The speaker says, "I myself am mortgaged to thy will" (134.2)—punning on the sense that he does not even own his name, "Will." The woman has also taken that love which the speaker used to call "mine"—in other words, the young man. The speaker proposes a way to get the young man back by giving "himself" in trade: "Myself I'll forfeit, so that other mine/ Thou wilt restore to be my comfort still" (134.4). But that effort fails, and he then suggests reversing the deal, giving up the young man to pay off his "mortgage" and thus free himself. But that too fails: "Him have I lost … He pays the whole; and yet I am not free" (134.13–14). There is no way to pay off the mortgage, to restore either himself or that love which he used to own. In other words, something more than treasure, more than what can be separated from a person and given to someone else, has been lost: part of himself has been lost that will cause him to "pay" forever.

Other sonnets indicate what has been lost, namely the values that defined the speaker in the earlier sonnets. He had valued "fairest creatures" in the first sonnet, but "now black is beauty's successive heir" (127.1–3). The contrast between "fair" and "black" runs through many of the final sonnets, in particular Sonnet 144: "Two loves I have … The better angel is a man right fair, / The worser spirit a woman coloured ill" (144.1–4). The woman colored ill is the embodiment of this new "black" form of beauty. Critics have suggested many interpretations of the woman's blackness, but we do not need to identify some precise meaning: what it represents is simply a different system of values, a foreign set of values. As Roland Greene puts it, "Shakespeare's sonnets to the 'dark lady' are unmistakably anacultural"—they are imagining crossing a cultural line and discovering values very different from those defined as their own. (14). Such a difference of values is what mercantile theory says is the very source of wealth, if what the foreigners value can be converted into a part of the domestic world: in other words, if the "black" can be converted to "fair." What the speaker undergoes in the final sonnets is the reverse: he knows that he is valuing something he knows is valueless—or in other words, he is adopting a value system that is against his own culture, the values that make up his self. Hence he says, "I have sworn thee fair, and thought thee bright, / Who art as black as hell, as dark as night" (147.13–14). Hell and night are images of places unlike his "fair" homeland. He knows that he is betraying what has been his self and the set of values he was raised believing. And he suggests he is separating from the kind of people he used to be part of: "Then will I swear beauty herself is black, / And all they foul that thy complexion lack" (132.12–13). He is even waiting for the complete conquest of his old values, waiting "Till my bad angel fire my good one out" (144.14)—till the dark woman overcomes and elim-inates his original love of what is "fair." This line also draws on commercial notions because an "angel" was a kind of coin; it thus alludes to the economic theory that has become known as "Gresham's Law": bad money drives out good. The pre-sence of "bad angels," bad money, in the monetary system makes it impossible to judge values correctly, and this is the key problem the speaker faces. He now gives credit to persons whom he knows cannot be trusted; as he puts it wryly in Sonnet 137, "Simply I credit her false-speaking tongue" (138.7).

These last sonnets may be reactions to some real change in Shakespeare's love life, or they may simply be his effort to explore the underside of the logic of the early sonnets, the logic that what maintains value in a person, or in a state in the mercantile age, is a balance of trade with those who are decidedly different from oneself, i.e. with foreigners. Shakespeare clearly finds it useful to use this deep logic to describe the effects of passion. It is passion that determines, in economics as in love, whether the valuable properties (beauty, wealth, status) that comprise a person or a state will increase or decrease in exchanges with other persons or states.

Coda

Mercantilism Reappearing in Later Economic Eras: The Endlessly Repeated Story of Pocahontas

Mercantilism does not disappear when new economic theories arise, and one way to see that is to trace the peculiar transformations of one mythic story: the tale of Pocahontas. I am going to trace various versions of this tale as a bit of foreshadowing of what we will see in later chapters, because the story gets transformed as new economic theories emerge. The story began in the 16th century as a tale of an Algonquin princess who marries a British man. What is fascinating about the Pocahontas story is that the tale transforms as the U.S. gets established as a nation: at first it is a tale of British conversion of a foreign jewel—Pocahontas brought to England and her inherited lands becoming part of the colonies. But when the U.S. is established, the tale changes and, as we will see, Britain becomes the "foreign land" that is converted to "domestic" perfection on the American continent—transforming both John Smith and Pocahontas.

This transformation of the tale occurs by changing the person whom Pocahontas loves and joins. In the earliest accounts of Pocahontas, she marries a man named John Rolfe, who apparently was in the Americas at the same time as John Smith. And that seems to be the historical truth: John Rolfe took her to England and inherited land from her. To see how John Smith replaced John Rolfe in later tellings of the tale—after the U.S. separated from Britain—we have to examine multiple versions.

Pocahontas appears in history in the middle of the mercantilist era, and the earliest versions of the Pocahontas story were directly aimed at mercantilist ends, as David Stymeist notes in an article entitled "Strange Wives: Pocahontas in early modern Colonial Advertisement" (3). Pocahontas's marriage to John Rolfe was advertised as the embodiment of the promise of Virginia, of wealth available in foreign lands; for example, a 1615 brochure by Ralphe Hamor indicates the parallelism between the colony and the marriage in its title: "A true discourse of the present estate of Virginia, and the successe of the affaires there ... Together with a relation of ...The christening of *Powhatans* daughter and her marriage with an English-man." Pocahontas's story became a reference in popular dramas, such as the 1605 work *Eastward Ho* by Chapman, Jonson and Marston, in which some taverngoers declare that colonists

> have married with the Indians, and make 'em bring forth as beautiful faces as any we have in England; and therefor the Indians are so in love with 'em that all the treasure they have they lay at their feet.
>
> *(Qtd. in Stymeist, 110)*

While the Indians are described as falling into a love that causes them to give away treasure, the British in these works are presented as always able to control their own emotions. This justifies colonial expansion as the British aren't then "using" the Indians. Walter Raleigh attributes the success of British efforts to convert Indians to this power of self-control, contrasting it to the acts of other colonizers such as the Spanish: he writes, in a semi-fictional account of his ventures in the Americas, that natives

> began to conceive the deceit and purpose of the Spaniards, who indeed (as they confessed) tooke from them both their wives and daughters daily, and

used them for the satisfying of their owne lusts, especially such as they tooke in this maner by strength ... I neither know nor believe, that any of our companie, by violence or otherwise, ever knew any of their women, and yet we saw many hundreds, and had many in our power, and those very yoong, and excelently favored which came among us without deceit, starke naked. Nothing gave us more love among them than this usage, for I suffered not anie man so much as to offer to touch any of their wives or daughters.

(Qtd. in Stymeist, 114)

It might seem then that under such rules John Rolfe could never have married Pocahontas. But Rolfe found a way: he wrote a letter asking permission of the royal governor of the colony, saying that he was in "no way lead ... with the unbridled desire of carnall affection" (qtd. in Stymeist, 113–14); he wanted to marry just to convert her and expand the British nation. Rolfe had to get permission from the ruler to marry in order to make it very clear that he was not acting like the Spaniards, nor was he going native. Rolfe in effect claimed that what seduced Pocahontas was the glory of Britain, not him.

In Rolfe's letter and Hamor's account of the marriage, there is no mention of John Smith, although he had already published an account of his adventures in America. After Hamor's treatise, Smith capitalized on Pocahontas's celebrity, publishing several new versions of his travels highlighting her role. But since he did not marry her or gain any treasure from her, Smith had to develop a different claim to make his role glorious in the story, and what he emphasized is that though Indians admired and even fell in love with him, he was never tempted, though others such as Rolfe clearly were. I suggest that Smith's accounts are efforts to portray himself more as prince than merchant in the drama of mercantilism, and this fits with his overtly stated goal in writing his accounts—he is trying to win himself stature as a gentleman. In Smith's first accounts, he devotes very little to the scene of Pocahontas saving him and much more to a later scene of her being offered to him sexually by the chief along with some thirty other young women—all of whom he refuses.

Needless to say, the story of Pocahontas that has been passed down to today is not this tale of a proposed orgy, nor is it Rolfe's tale of a faithful wife. The transformation of the Pocahontas story happened about the time of the founding of the U.S. The first extended account of the romance of Smith and Pocahontas was published in 1805 by John Davis, over a century after Rolfe's and Smith's encounters, and in Davis's version we can see more fully how Smith has taken over the role of an authority who is the source of the British self-control.

Davis starts his tale with the scene of Smith captured and brought into the Indian camp, where not only Pocahontas but all the Indian women are excited: "When Smith appeared before Powhatan, the first impression he made decided favorably for him on the minds of the women" (44). Pocahontas saves Smith because "The flame of love was now lighted up in the bosom of the Indian maid" (48). She leads Smith into the woods to "endeavour to learn by signs whether he was content to be with her, or again wanted to cross the wide rolling ocean" (49). But Smith's "smiles [were] ... not those of passion. The object of his heart was the colony he had founded" (49). Smith is dreaming of digesting the new land into a proper English colony: he is in effect presented in the role of the ruler in the mercantile venture.

Davis goes on to other scenes showing his power over both Indian and British emotions. There came a day when the colonists were about to die from lack of goods. The British try to save themselves by trading with Powhatan, but Powhatan asks the British to put all their goods out so he can see them, and then he says he will give them just a few cheap things in return. The narrator says this is Powhatan's trick; Powhatan has recognized the intensity of the British need for Indian goods, so treats the colonists as the ones whose passions are out of control. But then Smith plays a trick of his own: he accidentally lets some pretty blue beads slip out of a bag, and instantly, "The imagination of the Indian monarch was inflamed, and he made large offers ... Smith ... at length exchanged a pound of blue beads for five hundred bushels of corn" (76).

Smith's trick saves the colony. Notice the parallels between the incident of the blue beads and the incident of Pocahontas saving Smith's life: in both cases an Indian is "inflamed" with passion by the sight of something unfamiliar to them and Smith thereby gains something while giving nothing or very little in return.

In the account of the blue beads, Smith has to correct the other colonists, restoring their self-control after they have in effect been lured away from Britishness by what they want from the Indians. Smith has to repeatedly perform this function. In another instance, the colonists try to win favor with Powhatan by giving him gifts, but these "present[s] did not meet with the approbation of Captain Smith. With a few gaudy beads he could have levied contribution on Powhatan; whereas a profusion of presents would only increase his pride and insolence" (78). Lavish gifts reveal the colonists' need to please Powhatan: what Smith wants to create is the illusion that the British are self-sufficient and thereby instill a desire in Powhatan to please the British.

What I am saying here is that what Smith represents in this 1805 account by John Davis is the ability to drive Indians out of control and keep the British in control. He represents, then, the crucial function of the ruler of a nation engaging in mercantile exchange. The value of Smith to the history of the U.S. is not his passion but rather his ability to transcend passions in order to support and maintain a colony.

In Davis's account, Rolfe plays the role of the merchant who carries treasure from foreign lands and is thus in danger of losing control of himself: as Davis puts it, upon meeting Pocahontas, "the breast of Rolfe yielded to the empire of his passion" (91). In order to maintain control over himself, Rolfe does not act on his passion until he gains permission from the colonial ruler (no longer Smith at that time). Then he marries Pocahontas and takes her to London, where she sees

Smith again in a poignant climax to the tale: she feels sad, she dies, and Rolfe inherits vast tracts of land. Smith becomes in this tale the impersonal, untouchable object of worship, the image of the nation, while Rolfe is the person who risks getting involved with the foreign and brings home valuable material. In Davis's account, I suggest, Smith is a kind of monumental figure representing the founding of the U.S.

Smith never thought of himself as founding a new nation because of course in the 1600s there was no thought of separating the colony from England. But nonetheless there is in Smith's accounts of his travels much that provided fodder for later readers to see in him the image of a new country, not just a traveling Englishman. For one thing, he presents himself as someone who loses his Britishness in his travels and then regains it in America—and he recommends America as a general cure for Englishmen who have lost their culture because of the infections of travel. America thus becomes not simply an extension of England, but a restored England, a New England.

The attractiveness to women that saves Smith in America is earlier in his career the cause of his loss of Englishness, as Jim Egan traces in an essay about Smith and English-American identity. When Smith was off trying to fight the Turks, a woman named Chratza Tragabigzanda, the sister of the leader of a group of Turks, falls for him and hatches a plan to marry him. But instead of causing her to convert to British culture, her passion causes her to attempt to convert Smith to Turkish culture by dressing him as a Turkish servant in the household of her brother. The brother discovers Smith and makes him a slave, stripped naked with his head shaved, and for a time he is "no more regarded than a beast" (qtd. in Egan, 114). In other words, in this earlier episode where he enflamed a foreigner, it is Smith who gets translated from an object of value into a piece of junk, a trinket, in the other culture.

Smith eventually escapes and proves his Englishness by cutting off the heads of Turks and then later gains his greatest fame by saving his own head from being cut off by enflaming Pochahantas. Smith uses the combination of his Turkish and American adventures to present a way for Englishmen to survive dangerous cultural contacts that threaten to translate Englishness into something else. Egan concludes that in Smith's accounts, "American geographic space harbors the power to restore a body to its rightful, one might even say 'natural', identity" (115). This ability to restore identity is possible only because the "English people have literally transformed the environment" (115), changing the New World from a place "most intemperate and contagious" by cutting down tall trees and draining wetlands, so that "the Sunne hath power to exhale up the moyst vapours of the earth ... which before it could not, being covered with spreading tops of high trees" (qtd. in Egan, 115). In the humoral conceptions of the early modern era, lands and people alike gain their character from the four humors, and adjusting the wetness and heat of the surroundings translates the character of the land from Indian to English. By saying that the land itself changes from "intemperate" to "healthful," Smith implies that the land is being restored to its proper character, and from then on the land functions to restore those who have lost their Englishness in foreign travels. Smith is not at all presenting America as a new country, but his account is easily adapted to become one of the quintessential stories the U.S. tells about itself, that it is a land that can cure Europeans who are sick of their original cultures by restoring them to a New Europeanness that is Americanness.

The John Smith version of the Pocahontas tale thus carries the story into later economic and biological visions, into what becomes crucial in the 19th century: people learning that they have a "natural" core inside them that they can access when they strip off the social mores they have been trained to live out (as we will see in more detail in Chapter 2). That 19th-century vision rejects the necessity of the ruler to digest what merchants or other entrepreneurs gather for themselves.

That 19th-century notion reappears again at the end of the 20th century in neoclassical economic theories such as those of Milton Friedman, who argued that economists should just relearn what was common in the 19th century—that individuals have a natural self that can be relied upon to run the economy. Friedman is rejecting Keynesian theory that in a sense restored the older mercantilist need for a government to intervene and correct what individuals were likely to do on their own. And as neoclassical economics became orthodoxy, two new movie versions of Pocahontas came out: a Disney movie of that name and a Terence Malick art film called *The New World*. In these movies, the conversion in the movie is not presented as a transformation of Pocahontas: rather, it is John Smith who is changed from British to what is implied is simply "natural." One key shift marks this: in both movies, unlike the 17th- and 18th-century versions, John Smith definitely falls in love with Pocahontas and is devastated when they have to separate. These recent movies are thus reversing the sense of what is foreign and what is domestic. These movies present the British John Smith as the foreigner who falls in love with the beautiful non-British woman in the beautiful American land, the foreigner whose passion changes his culture.

In these movies, viewers are encouraged to identify with the land, and with the natives who encounter the "foreign" John Smith, and to expressly reject Smith's justifications for colonization. The theme song of the Disney movie first appears as an answer to John Smith, with what is one of the most common justifications for colonizing: "There is so much we can teach you. We have improved the lives of savages all over the world." Pocahontas responds by singing, "there is so much that you don't know," and then listing wonderful natural things he has never experienced, such as hearing the "wolf cry to the blue corn moon." The song seeks to reveal the value of the "uncivilized" world, telling Smith to "roll in the riches of the world around you." Her song ends with "can you paint with the colors of the wind?," accompanied by leaves blowing past her to surround him. The song is telling him to repaint his world to reap new values.

When he is carried to a ship going back to England at the end of the movie, after getting injured, the feeling is that he is losing what is most valuable—that is, both Pocahontas and the land. As he floats away, leaves are once again carried by the wind past Pocahontas out to Smith's boat, referring back to the theme song. It is a sad ending: a flawed John Smith forced to reinsert himself in the old, staid world.

The American land in this movie is thus not a place which carries history in any form; rather, it is the perfect natural place that inspires passions in everyone and causes them to break with their past and take instead what is present in the American landscape. No matter what culture originally created something or someone, that thing or person actually gains its most valuable, most natural state when brought to the U.S. The movie thus merges the mercantilist origins of the Pocahontas story into U.S. neoconservativism, which posits that if dictators and evil rulers can be removed, all people will just naturally want to become like the U.S. to increase their value. Becoming like the U.S., becoming American in this new version of mercantilism, is not being translated at all; rather it is a process of "untranslating," of stripping off the strange artificial exterior provided by another culture to do just what John Smith promised America would do, restore "a body to its rightful, one might even say 'natural,' identity."

References

Appleby, Joyce Oldham. *Economic Thought and Ideology in Seventeenth-Century England.* Princeton: Princeton University Press, 1978.

Aristotle, *The Ethics of Aristotle.* Tr. J.A.K. Thomson. Harmondsworth: Penguin Books, 1965.

Brooke, Arthur. *Romeus and Juliet.* First published 1562. Newly edited by J. J. Munro. Online at https://archive.org/stream/romeusandjulietb00broouoft/romeusandjulietb00 broouoft_djvu.txt.

Bruster, Douglas. *Drama and the Market in the Age of Shakespeare.* Cambridge: Cambridge University Press, 2004.

Clark, Andy. *Being There: Putting Brain, Body and World Together Again.* Cambridge: MIT Press, 1997.

Cohen, Walter. "*The Merchant of Venice* and the Possibilities of Historical Criticism." *Materialist Shakespeare: A History.* Ed. Ivo Kamps. London and New York: Verso, 1995, pp. 71–92.

Coleman, D.C. "Mercantilism Revisited." *The Historical Journal.* vol. 23, no. 4, 1980, pp. 773–779.

Davis, John. *Captain Smith and Princess Pocahontas, An Indian Tale.* First published 1805. Early American Imprints, 2nd series, no. 8301.

Dixon, Thomas. *From Passions to Emotions: The Creation of a Secular Psychological Category.* Cambridge: Cambridge University Press, 2003.

Dollimore, Jonathan. *Radical Tragedy: Religion, Ideology and Power in the Drama of Shakespeare*, 3rd ed. Durham, NC: Duke University Press, 2004.

Donne, John. *The Complete Poetry and Selected Prose of John Donne.* Ed. Charles M. Coffin. New York: Modern Library, 2001.

Jim Egan. "The East in British-American Writing: English Identity, John Smith's *True Travels*, and Severed Heads." Mary Floyd-Wilson and Garrett A. Sullivan, Jr., *Environment and Embodiment in Early Modern England.* Basingstoke, UK: Palgrave MacMillan, 2007, pp. 103–115.

Ekelund, Robert B., Jr. and Robert D. Tollison. *Politicized Economies: Monarchy, Monopoly, and Mercantilism.* College Station, TX: Texas A&M University Press, 1997.

Engle, Lars. *Shakespearean Pragmatism: Market of his Time.* Chicago: University of Chicago Press, 1993.

Fletcher, John. *The Island Princess.* In Francis Beaumont and John Fletcher, *Comedies and Tragedies.* London: Printed for Humphrey Robinson, at the three Pidgeons, 1647. Online from the Folger Shakespeare Library at https://emed.folger.edu/ip.

Forman, Valerie. "Transformations of Value and the Production of "Investment" in the Early History of the English East India Company." *Journal of Medieval and Early Modern Studies,* vol. 34, no. 3, 2004, pp. 611–641.

Grav, Peter F. *Shakespeare and the Economic Imperative: "What's aught but as 'tis valued?"* New York: Routledge, 2008.

Grav, Peter F. "Taking Stock of Shakespeare and the New Economic Criticism." *Shakespeare,* vol. 8, no. 1, 2012, pp. 111–136.

Greene, Roland *Unrequited Conquests: Love and Empire in the Colonial Americas* Chicago: University of Chicago Press, 1999.

Habib, Imtiaz. "Othello, Sir Peter Negro, and the Blacks of Early Modern England: Colonial Inscription and Postcolonial Excavation." *Literature Interpretation Theory,* vol. 9, no. 1, 1998, pp. 15–30.

Hamor, Ralphe, *A true discourse of the present estate of Virginia: and the successe of the affaires there till the 18 of Iune. 1614. Together with a relation of the seuerall English townes and forts, the assured hopes of that countrie and the peace concluded with the Indians. The christening of Powhatans daughter and her mariage with an English-man.* Printed at London: By Iohn Beale for William Welby dwelling at the signe of the Swanne in Pauls Church yard, 1615.

Hall, Jonathan. *Anxious Pleasures: Shakespearean Comedy and the Nation State.* Madison: Farleigh Dickinson University Press, 1995.

Halpern, Richard. *The Poetics of Primitive Accumulation: English Renaissance Literature and the Genealogy of Capital.* Ithaca, NY: Cornell University Press, 1991.

Harris, Jonathan Gil. *Sick Economies: Drama, Mercantilism and Disease in Shakespeare's England.* Philadelphia, PA: University of Pennsylvania Press, 2003.

Hawkes, David. *Idols of the Marketplace: Idolatry and Commodity Fetishism in English Literature, 1580–1680.* New York: Palgrave, 2001.

Humphrey, Thomas M. "Mercantilists and Classicals: Insights from Doctrinal History." *Economic Quarterly* (Federal Reserve Bank of Richmond), vol. 85, no. 2, 1999, pp. 55–82.

Kantorowicz, Ernst Hartwig. *The King's Two Bodies: A Study in Medieval Political Theology.* Princeton, NJ: Princeton University Press, 1997.

Leinwand, Theodore. *Finance and Society in Early Modern England.* Cambridge: Cambridge University Press, 1999.

Loomba, Ania. "'Break her will, and bruise no bone sir': Colonial and Sexual Mastery in Fletcher's *The Island Princess.*" *Journal for Early Modern Cultural Studies,* vol. 2, no. 1, 2002, pp. 68–108.

Malynes, Gerard. *The Maintenance of Free Trade, According to the Three Essentiall Parts of Traffique; Namely Commodities, Moneys and Exchange of Moneys, by Bills of Exchanges for other Countries. Or answer to a Treatise of Free Trade, or the meanes to make Trade floushish, lately Published.* London: Printed by I.L. for William Shefford, 1622. Online at http://socserv.socsci.mcmaster.ca/oldecon/ugcm/3ll3/malynes/malynes.txt.

Mayr, Otto. *Authority, Liberty and Automatic Machines in Early Modern Europe.* Baltimore, MD: Johns Hopkins University Press, 1986.

Misselden, Edward. *Free Trade or, The Meanes To Make Trade Florish. Wherein, The Causes of the Decay of Trade in this Kingdome, are discovered: And the Remedies also to remoove the same, are represented.* London. Printed by John Legatt, for Simon Waterson, dwelling in Paules Church-yard at the Signe of the Crowne, 1622. Online at http://socserv2.socsci.mcma ster.ca/econ/ugcm/3ll3/misselden/freetrad.txt.

Mun, Thomas. *Englands Treasure by Forraign Trade, or The Ballance of our Forraign Trade is The Rule of our Treasure.* Published for the Common good by his son John Mun of Bearsted in the County of Kent, Esquire. London: Printed by J.G. for Thomas Clark, 1664. Online at http://socserv2.socsci.mcmaster.ca/~econ/ugcm/3ll3/mun/treasure.txt.

Neill, Michael. "Material Flames": The Space of Mercantile Fantasy in John Fletcher's "The Island Princess." *Renaissance Drama*, New Series, vol. 28, 1997, pp. 99–131.

Nocentelli, Carmen. "The Erotics of Mercantile Imperialism: Cross-Cultural Requitedness in the Early Modern Period." *Journal for Early Modern Cultural Studies*, vol. 8, no. 1, 2008, pp. 134–152.

Oser, Jacob and Stanley L.Brue, *The Evolution of Economic Thought*, 4th ed. New York: Harcourt Brace Jovanovich, 1988.

Park, Katherine. "The Organic Soul." *The Cambridge History of Renaissance Philosophy*. Ed. Charles Schmitt and Quentin Skinner. Cambridge: Cambridge University Press, 1988, pp. 464–484.

Paster, Gail Kern, Katherine Rowe and Mary Floyd-Wilson. *Reading the Early Modern Passions: Essays in the Cultural History of Emotion.* Philadelphia, PA: University of Pennsylvania Press, 2004.

Schmidgen, Wolfram. "Robinson Crusoe, Enumeration, and the Mercantile Fetish." *Eighteenth-Century Studies*, vol. 35, no. 1, 2001, pp. 19–39.

Shakespeare, William. *Shakespeare's Sonnets.* Ed. Stephen Booth. New Haven, CT: Yale University Press, 1977.

Shakespeare, William. *The Merchant of Venice: Texts and Context.* Ed. Lindsay Kaplan. Boston: Bedford/St. Martin's, 2002.

Shakespeare, William. *Romeo and Juliet.* Folger Library digital texts. Online at https://shakesp eare.folger.edu/shakespeares-works/romeo-and-juliet/download-romeo-and-juliet/.

Shakespeare, William. *The Tragedy of Othello, The Moor of Venice.* Folger Library digital texts. Online at https://shakespeare.folger.edu/shakespeares-works/othello/download-othello/.

Smith, D. Vance. *Arts of Possession: The Middle English Household Imaginary.* Minneapolis, MN: University of Minnesota Press, 2003.

Spenser, Edmund. *Amoretti and Epithalamion: A Critical Edition.* Ed. Kenneth J. Larsen. Tempe, AZ: Arizona State University Press, 1997.

Starkey, David. "The Age of the Household: Politics, Society and the Arts c.1350–1550." *The Later Middle Ages.* Ed. Stephen Medcalf. New York: Holmes & Meier, 1981, pp. 225–290.

Stymiest, David. "Strange Wives: Pocahontas in Early Modern Colonial Advertisement." *Mosaic: A Journal for the Interdisciplinary Study of Literature*, vol. 35, no. 2, 2002, pp. 109–125.

Sutton, John. *Philosophy and Memory Traces: Descartes to Connectionism.* Cambridge: Cambridge University Press, 2007.

Turner, Frederick. *Shakespeare's Twenty-First Century Economy: The Morality of Love and Money.* New York: Oxford University Press, 1999.

Warley, Christopher. *Sonnet Sequences and Social Distinction in Renaissance England.* Cambridge: Cambridge University Press, 2005.

Wood, Diana. *Medieval Economic Thought.* Cambridge: Cambridge University Press, 2002.

Woodbridge, Linda, Ed. *Money and the Age of Shakespeare.* New York: Palgrave Macmillan, 2003.

2

DISCONNECTING BLOODLINES

Moving to Capitalist Romance

The rise of industrial capitalism changed economics, but it also changed romance. As James Thompson notes, the 18th century marks a transition to "an age confronting money as capital, no longer as treasure, but as money in motion" (9). To conceive of wealth as treasure, as the early modern era did, is to visualize it as glitteringly beautiful, planted on earth as a divine gift, and unchanging; to conceive of wealth as money in motion is to look to the future for what is glitteringly beautiful. Capital is wealth that is not visible at first, but transforms into something tremendously valuable over time: dirty factories, empty swatches of land, and blocks of metal. Similarly, as capitalism emerged, love stories transformed into tales about people who were unattractive but who understood the value of industry, who knew how to labor. Jen Cadwallader notes that "Charlotte Brontë is purported to have once told her sisters that 'they were wrong—even morally wrong—in making their heroines beautiful as a matter of course'" (235). Hence, "plain Jane" Eyre is much less attractive than Blanche Ingram—but Jane labors as a governess, and over time incites a new kind of desire in Rochester. Rochester himself is "more remarkable for character than for beauty" (124). Romeo would never have noticed Jane, and Juliet would have been horrified at being approached by Rochester. Similarly, in *Pride and Prejudice*, Jane is the most beautiful daughter, but Elizabeth is the center of the love story, and she is defined in several ways as connected to the concepts of industry. Darcy first notices her when she has trudged across the grounds to come take care of her sister, when he feels "admiration of the brilliancy which exercise had given to her complexion" (30). And when Mr. Collins proposes to marry her because she is in line to inherit her family's estate, her refusal appears to him as a tease that is supposed to make her more attractive, so she tries to explain, "Do not consider me now as an elegant female intending to plague you, but as a rational creature speaking the truth from her heart." (95). She is proposing a very different sense of value than he is seeking—not just elegance, an external quality, but rationality, an internal quality connected to planning and the future. Love stories gain the structure of a search for the object of desire rather than tracing the magical effects of instantaneous attraction.

Adam Smith defines the economic version of this shift by saying that previous economic treatises have treated "bullion" as the goal of all efforts to gain wealth. Those who have the most bullion, the most gold, the most glittering jewels, were considered the wealthiest. Instead, Smith says that wealth must not be simply stored in valuable treasure, but rather "consecrated to the maintenance of industry" (450). Those whose wealth is invested in the greatest amount of labor will surpass those who have the greatest amount of bullion. Smith even specifies that this new source of value is connected to a change in the way people should think about desires—a change in the conception of the most valuable kind of desire or, in the language of his day, a change in passions. He criticizes the desire for glittering, attractive things—in other words, valuing treasures—which he calls the "passion for present enjoyment" and says is "sometimes violent and very difficult to be restrained." He advocates instead the "desire of bettering our condition," which is "generally calm and dispassionate" (453). This desire he advocates to fuel economics does not look outward at what is attractive or valuable, but rather inward, at one's own "condition"—and not even at the present state of one's condition, but at a future possibility, at a better condition that is possible. The notion of bettering one's condition is a vision of the results of action, of industry, of labor. This desire is based on looking past the surface at hidden potential. And this distinction between what is visible and valuable right now and what is internal, not yet visible, and to be valuable in the future shapes a new structure to the desires presented in love stories and poems.

The shift in the sense of what is valuable that Smith is advocating mirrors what was developing all through the 18th century, a change in the general sense of what is desirable in many realms. After many decades of finding foreign objects attractive, writers in the late 17th century began criticizing that aesthetic. James Bunn notes,

> The polyglot effect of randomly purchasing knickknacks from odd corners of space and time and recomposing them pointlessly in a curio cabinet became so noticeable during the years of mercantilism, from 1688 to 1763, that some English artists and thinkers commented upon an aesthetic that was developing out of their hands.
>
> *(303)*

The excessive love of foreign objects starts seeming to have consequences even for government, as Pitt the Elder states on 22 January 1770:

For some years past, there has been an influx of wealth in this country, which has been attended with many fatal consequences, because it has not been the regular, natural produce of labor and industry. The riches of Asia have been poured in upon us, and have brought with them not only Asiatic luxury but Asiatic principles of government.

(Qtd. in Bunn, 317)

What Pitt calls "Asiatic" could be called "exotic" or simply "other," and implies that instead of the objects being transformed into domestic wealth, as mercantile theory postulates, domestic houses and even governments have been transformed into foreign forms. What Pitt advocates instead is a variant of what Smith advocates: recognizing that the only real wealth is wealth that is the "natural produce of labor and industry."

The mockery of mercantilist aesthetics is captured in Alexander Pope's "The Rape of the Lock." The poem opens by describing Belinda's dressing table, upon which "Unnumber'd Treasures ope at once, and here, / The various Off'rings of the World appear (II.129–30)." Her maid then uses these treasures to adorn Belinda's beauty,

From each she nicely culls with curious Toil,
And decks the Goddess with the glitt'ring Spoil
This Casket *India's* glowing Gems unlocks
And all *Arabia* breathes from yonder box.
(II.131–4)

The poem even notes that when fully adorned, she will be "prais'd for labors not her own" (I.149). The poem suggests as Smith does that what should be valued is labor, not treasure.

The plot of the poem turns on a baron seeking to take her treasure, "By Force to ravish, or by Fraud betray … For when Success a Lover's toil attends / Few ask if Fraud or Force attained his Ends" (II.33–6). In other words, the poem sets it up that the Baron and Belinda are operating in the mercantile system that defines beauty as akin to (or in this case created by) the treasure from foreign lands and wooing as adventure and assault and exploitation. But of course the poem is undermining this whole system. I suggest that Pope is ultimately denying that something can be simply taken away from its "ground" and retain its value. As Pope wrote in the introduction to his Epistle to Burlington, "all must be adapted to the *Genius* and *Use* of the Place, and the Beauties not forced into, but resulting from it" (qtd. in Bunn, 311). The Baron and Belinda both believe that her value derives from what is "forced into" her and her world, not what results from the "ground" of her self. But the Baron makes a mistake in his own mercantile aesthetics and seeks to take precisely that which grows directly from Belinda, her hair. The lock of hair is not part of the "glittering spoil" which bedecks Belinda, not a "jewel" in the ear that can be removed as Romeo seeks to remove Juliet from the "ground" of her family. The poem makes much of the mechanics of removing the hair and the impossibility of rejoining it to the head—the hair is not transportable like jewels. The Baron is thus mistaken when he treats Belinda as a foreign culture whose beauties can be sneakily removed. What the new aesthetic proposed by Smith would advocate is to view Belinda's hair as an image of land to be cultivated by investment: hence, the act the new capitalist aesthetic would promote would be for the Baron to give Belinda some expensive hair care products rather than clip off even a lock. This would keep the value of the hair growing. But he and Belinda would have to value what grows from her rather than what simply adorns her.

One could see the poem as saying in a satiric way that what each person has should be under that person's own control. And Smith's economics is usually presented as a vision of quite separate individuals each pursuing their own interest. The Wealth of Nations is unquestionably a defense of the liberty of the individual, but the book does not start by presenting free individuals as the source of wealth; rather, it starts by tracing the source of modern wealth to the division of labor. Indeed, the very idea of persons being able to improve their lives derives in Smith's theory from the presumption of a division of labor. What Smith focuses on as the way individuals can improve their lives is "improvement in the productive powers of labor" (17). Seeking the causes of such improvement is the stated goal of Smith's whole treatise. And he finds the most immediate source of improvement in the "division of labor," which allows ten men working together to create "forty-eight thousand" pins, whereas if they each had to cover the whole process, they "could not each of them have made twenty" (19). The division of labor also seems to create the talents, even the genius, which workers seem to have; Smith says:

> The …very different genius which appears to distinguish men of different professions, when grown up to maturity, is not upon many occasions so much the cause, as the effect of the division of labour. The difference between the most dissimilar characters, between a philosopher and a common street porter, for example, seems to arise not so much from nature, as from habit, custom, and education and wealth of a society.
>
> (32)

But though Smith gives so much credit to division of labor, it is not the end of his search: he seeks a source for that division and finds it: "labour can be more and more subdivided in proportion only as stock is previously more and more accumulated" (361). He concludes that "The quantity of industry, therefore, not only increases in every country with the increase of the stock which employs it, but, in consequence of that increase, the same quantity of industry produces a much greater quantity of work" (362). Stock that is devoted to increasing the value of industry is "capital," so we can see why Smith's economics is called "capitalism" even though he declares labor the source of all value: it is capital which makes labor valuable.

But even capital is not the ultimate source because he goes on to find a cause for the "increase of capital" itself, and that is the final, deepest cause Smith identifies. And what is that first cause? Smith calls it "parsimony." It might seem odd to claim that "parsimony" is at the core of all of Adam Smith's economics, but he emphasizes that "Parsimony, and not industry, is the immediate cause of the increase of capital" (448)—and hence of the division of labor and hence of the improvement in the productive powers of labor and hence of the wealth of nations.

Now what is "parsimony" for Smith? To understand, let me quote a somewhat longer passage where he defines it by contrasting it to its opposites:

> Capitals are increased by parsimony, and diminished by prodigality and misconduct ... The prodigal perverts in this manner. By not confining his expense within his income, he encroaches upon his capital. Like him who perverts the revenues of some pious foundation to profane purposes, he pays the wages of idleness with those funds which the frugality of his forefathers had, as it were, consecrated to the maintenance of industry.
>
> *(448–9)*

Note the religious tone: capital is "consecrated," value is "bestowed," and the prodigal is compared to someone who "perverts" a "pious foundation." There is more than a hint that devoting wealth to the maintenance of industry is a sacred function, transforming what otherwise would be of little value into something wonderful and hence akin to God's bestowal of grace upon humans. The word "perverts" also suggests that the prodigal is not merely distorting wealth but also distorting his own nature, his own character. Smith carries that sense further by saying that "the effects of misconduct are often the same as those of prodigality" (452). Misconduct is not only wrong, it is mistaken, it is a misunderstanding of what one's conduct can accomplish, and a misunderstanding of one's core self, of what is valuable inside oneself. Those characters in 19th-century love stories who are glitteringly attractive, such as Wickham and Blanche Ingram, are ultimately exposed as "perverting" true values, possibly just by displaying their value in their bodies. Belinda's soul is perverted by the "glittering Spoil" from India and Arabia which "decks" her out so she appears to be a "Goddess."

Modern readers might read a sexual connotation in the word "perverts," a connotation that seems only to have emerged much later in the 19th century, However, the sense that resisting the temptations of money is akin to resisting the temptations of sexuality as a fundamental feature of capitalist theory perhaps becomes more evident in the work of an economist who followed Smith. Nassau Senior extended Smith's theory that parsimony is the source of capital by literally replacing the word "Capital" in his economic theory with the term "Abstinence"

(3.106). It is not, in his view, money that constitutes capital, but rather the will to resist temptation. And when Senior goes on to explain what he means by "abstinence," he turns to "abstinence in marriage" as the prime example. What he means by this is not avoiding marriage entirely, but rather putting off marriage until one has enough wealth to support a good lifestyle. As he puts it, abstinence in marriage is "the hope to acquire, by the accumulation of a longer celibacy, the means of purchasing the decencies which give a higher social rank" (3.39). A person contemplating such an action "stands hesitating between love and prudence" (3.39). Senior is elaborating on the shift from one kind of desire to another, in the realms of both love and economics, from the pursuit of what appears immediately satisfying and visibly valuable to the investment in potential.

But to change from one kind of desire, one sense of what is most valuable, to another is not easy. Adam Smith provides a striking metaphor for this transition in a critique of the mercantilist system:

> The monopoly of the colony trade ... by forcing towards it a much greater proportion of the capital of Great Britain than what would naturally have gone to it, seems to have broken altogether that natural balance which would otherwise have taken place among all the different branches of British industry.... . In her present condition, Great Britain resembles one of those unwholesome bodies in which some of the vital parts are overgrown, and which, upon that account, are liable to many dangerous disorders scarce incident to those in which all the parts are more properly proportioned. A small stop in that great blood-vessel, which has been artificially swelled beyond its natural dimensions, and through which an unnatural proportion of the industry and commerce of the country has been forced to circulate, is very likely to bring on the most dangerous disorders upon the whole body politic. The expectation of a rupture with the colonies, accordingly, has struck the people of Great Britain with more terror than they ever felt for a Spanish armada, or a French invasion.
>
> *(801)*

Smith's metaphor for the "body" of England is that of a person with a swollen blood vessel, and even stranger, a blood vessel connecting that body to another body. What he proposes is disconnecting that blood vessel from the external source and reconnecting it internally in the body of England. The image of cutting and reattaching a blood vessel is disturbing, but it fits what we see in many Victorian works: characters from wealthy families are cut off from their inheritance or from their mercantilist source of wealth and undergo what is often a fairly violent process of learning some new way of surviving economically.

This process of disconnecting and redirecting the flow of wealth is of course also a process of transforming the individuals who have that wealth. Many Victorian novels trace such a process, showing aristocrats disconnected from their families and thrust into the world of domestic labor, and eventually returned after they have been transformed by their encounter with labor. Howard Horwitz, writing about 19th-century American novels, notes similar transformations and summarizes the strangeness of the process by asking, "How does it feel … to be yourself by relinquishing yourself?" (244). The act of being expelled from their families appears at first rather horrific and leads them to be badly treated by wealthy persons. Think of Jane Eyre, stripped of her wealthy background and put into a school for the poor. Or John Harmon in *Our Mutual Friend*, who is declared dead and forced to become the "Secretary" for those who seem to have the fortune he should have inherited. As a result of their disconnection from their familial sources, these displaced wealthy persons begin to do labor themselves, using skills that emerge within them.

But Victorian novels rarely leave characters on their own: at the ends of most novels, those who were displaced are returned to being a part of wealthy families. The novels could be seen then as ultimately restoring aristocratic values, with characters undergoing "reabsorption into the system of inheritance and primogeniture," as Nancy Pell argues (418). But to try to place 19th-century novels into either capitalist or aristocratic systems distorts the particular way Smith connects his vision of capitalism to the aristocracy. His capitalism is not an economics aiming at creating a world entirely of separate individuals, entrepreneurs, and laborers. Rather it is an economics of teaching the wealthy to connect their wealth to industry, to laborers, as a way of increasing that wealth. Smith's capitalist theory focuses on how to use wealth one already has, wealth deeply tied to land and inheritance, not how to generate wealth from nothing. What the novels are tracing is the transformation of aristocrats and mercantilists into aristocratic capitalists by the recognition of the increased value that arises when wealth (and wealthy persons) are connected to domestic labor. And these transformations transform both the economic system and the nature of romance.

Jane Eyre traces two conversions of rich persons: Jane and Rochester. The process involves violent disconnections from what are presented as corrupting sources of wealth. Jane Eyre is violently disconnected from her family's wealth, shipped off to an aunt's house where she is told that her relatives "will have a great deal of money and you will have none; it is your place to be humble" (7). She is at first furious, out of control, screaming that her cousins are "like … slave-driver[s] … like the Roman emperors!" (5). She is thus given a vision of the relationship of the wealthy to the working class that Smith seeks to alter. Jane's relatives do not see any value in "investing" in those without money, even if they are their own relatives. Jane also finds herself sharing that view, but hinting at what the book will carry her later to think: she describes herself at that early state as having "not much idea of industrious, working, respectable poverty … poverty for me was synonymous with degradation" (20). That hints at what she will learn through the book—the value of industry—and what she will teach the other wealthy people she meets.

She is sent to a school where she is treated badly until a terrible disease sweeps through the valley where the school is located and many die. The disease transforms the school from a place that sucks the life out of those who are there into a place that trains the poor in methods of production. Jane becomes a fine student and much happier, though not rich at all. The school prepares her for domestic labor, and she goes off to become a governess in a rich man's house. But Jane does not remain simply a governess, an employee: eventually she is restored to her family fortune and marries a rich man. But she does not end up returning to the aristocratic version of what a woman should be in a wealthy household—part of the "magnificence" of the household, acquired for her beauty. She becomes, as Jen Cadwallader puts it, one of "a new order of women, interesting and valuable because of their characters and actions rather than their good looks" (245). Character is a version of potential that can be realized by actions; and actions are a version of industry or labor. So she becomes a rich woman whose life and actions are, in Adam Smith's terms, "consecrated to the maintenance of industry," creating value rather than simply embodying it (450).

Rochester at first is the embodiment of everything Smith says has to change: his wealth flows to him through a vessel tying him to a British colony: marriage to a Jamaican woman, Bertha Mason. Bertha is described as "intemperate and unchaste" (325), and the book implies that she has infected Rochester with these qualities; he is what Smith calls a 'prodigal'; he says, "I tried dissipation," wandering the world, having mistresses (330). But the novel suggests that Rochester remains aware that he is losing himself: he says his dissipation never became "debauchery" because "that was my Indian Messalina's attribute" (330). He is in effect distinguishing between England and "Indian" forms of degradation, and he holds himself back from falling into this "foreign" form of immorality. He tries mistresses, but rejects them because "Hiring a mistress is the next worse thing to buying a slave" (331), a hint that he is not fully wrapped up in the older feudal vision of class relations—only the newer capitalist vision would call such relations slavery. He has a young girl, Adele, living with him who is the daughter of a French opera singer who is too busy to care for her. Adele represents the "offspring" of prodigality: she is described as having roots "which nothing but gold dust can manure" (146). This is an image of the perversion of growth and of investment: putting gold dust into the soil around a plant would not cause the plant to grow, but would "pervert" it; gold dust is leading Adele to become a prodigal like Rochester.

Rochester in a sense tries to perform the transformation of mercantile wealth into domestic wealth by boxing Bertha up in his attic—a perverse version of putting the capital from foreign exploitation into domestic structures. But Bertha's presence does not increase the value of the house, but rather destroys it. She is not converted into domestic value, but rather remains an inflaming irritant.

Jane brings the perspective of industriousness into the Rochester household. She can see that Rochester has "excellent materials in him, though for the present they hung together somewhat spoiled and tangled." (154): he has been twisted like Adele, his "roots" watered with gold dust as hers were. And those excellent materials are an internal potential, not an external value: his looks are "more remarkable for character than beauty" (124).

The novel traces the dual transformations of Rochester and Jane into proper subjects of the new Smithian capitalist order. They learn to resist what appearances tell them and in effect not even to accept themselves as they appear, but rather to join a process of production with others—a division of labor. And it requires quite violent chastening to accomplish this transformation. Each lives through the destruction of an inherited "household" full of violent passions which are equated to money acquired without having learned to work and improve that money. In other words, their early life and family ties, such as they were, taught them to view money as treasure. In Jane's childhood in her aunt's house, there is a distinction between "domestic and foreign" that assigns Jane to the "foreign" and subjects her to deprivations and a position akin to slavery—to which she responds with "fierce speaking" and no self-control.

Jane is sent to Lowood School, where she eventually learns to govern her passions. She speaks of the "wholesome discipline to which I had thus forced my feelings to submit" and credits this discipline with allowing her to survive Rochester's onslaught (169). Rochester eventually says he will "try violence" to seduce her, but she is not afraid because she "felt an inward power ... The crisis was perilous, but not without its charm: such as the Indian, perhaps, feels when he slips over the rapid in his canoe" (321). This is a striking image: she still identifies herself as the "foreign," but now it is a foreign figure in control, in its own environment, and Rochester, the Englishman seeking to enslave the Indian, is reduced to a "rapid" that Jane can easily travel over without losing control of herself.

Jane leaves Rochester, surviving the temptation that he succumbed to, the temptation of the passion inspired by visible wealth. But the novel puts her through two more temptations—from St. John and from her own family's wealth—both of which she has to resist to become a fully self-controlled, dispassionate person. She is tempted by St. John, who seeks a different kind of mercantilist goal: going to Hindustan to convert heathens. He wants to marry her for this goal, not because the two of them will grow together. His very person is a temptation, like a beautiful woman; indeed, he is described as "nearly as beautiful for a man" as the most beautiful woman (388). His beauty contrasts with Rochester's "character" in terms that precisely define the difference between production and mere glitter: after Jane describes St. John, Rochester says, "Your words have delineated very prettily a graceful Apollo ... tall, fair, blue-eyed, and with a Grecian profile. Your eyes dwell on a Vulcan—a real blacksmith, brown, broad-shouldered" (473). Jane agrees he is like a Vulcan. This sets out the difference in values between the mercantile age and the Smithian capitalist—people are more valued if they are shaped for labor than if they are beautiful.

But it is not really as hard workers—as blacksmith and governess—that Jane and Rochester join together; rather it is as aristocratic capitalists, understanding how to invest wealth they have not themselves directly earned by their labors. He has great wealth, so he does not really have to earn his money; but he is better as a blacksmith than an Apollo because this implies he will increase his wealth, hammer it into "use." Jane seems purely a worker, but when she gives up her job and loses everything, she stumbles into her family relations and acquires an inheritance from an uncle in Madeira: in effect, she too gets foreign, mercantile wealth, but unlike Rochester she gets it after she has learned how to use foreign wealth, how to convert it into domestic industry. When she gets the gold, her reaction is quite different from Rochester's; instead of feeling free to do anything she wants, to become a prodigal, she finds that "ponderous gift of gold is ... sobering from its weight" (411). She contrasts that gift to what she gets when she realizes she has relatives who love her: a "mine of pure, genial affections" which in contrast to the gold is a "blessing" (411). She can invest her money in that quintessentially domestic "mine," using it to extract more wealth. So long as her wealth is just sitting there as something disconnected from her domestic world, it is disturbing. Jane says, "One does not jump, and spring, and shout hurrah! at hearing one has got a fortune; one begins to consider responsibilities, and to ponder business" (407–8). This is precisely a Smithian response: wealth is only valuable insofar as it leads one to set up a domestic business to make that wealth grow. So Jane takes her foreign wealth and consecrates it to her domestic realm: she divides up the wealth so that each member of her family "is possessed of a competency" (415). As Chris Vanden Bossche summarizes, Jane draws on both aristocratic and middle-class discourses and values: "rather than identifying with one or the other of these potential ruling classes, Jane strategically alternates between them" (47).

And with her wealth and her sense of business, Jane is able to return to Rochester, who has been converted by the ultimate inflammatory power of Bertha's mercantilist roots: Bertha sets fire to the house, killing herself and maiming Rochester. One hand and his eyes are hurt, and Jane takes charge of healing him: metaphorically and somewhat literally giving him new eyes that are connected to hands, to labor, to industry. At the end, Rochester and Jane do not end up supporting any particular industry except the workings of their new household, Ferndean. So in a sense their wealth seems at the end to be returned to the aristocratic world. But that fits with Smith's claim that capital must ultimately be grounded in the "cultivation of land." The transformation of Aristocrats into capitalists is not that they leave their estates and go set up factories; rather it is in how they view their estates and their money as something to be cultivated and carefully managed.

Critics often see another well-known novel by a Brontë sister, *Wuthering Heights* by Emily, as a rejection of capitalism, though for a remarkable range of contradictory reasons. Neville F. Newman argues that the novel remains thoroughly a vision of the old, aristocratic, feudal world, having little to do with 19th-century industrial England (316). Terry Eagleton sees the novel as a proto-Marxist rejection of capitalism and at the same time a desire for the world before capitalism: he calls "The love between Heathcliff's and Catherine ... a revolutionary refusal of the given language of social roles and values" (108), and says Heathcliffe's "true commitment is an outdated one, to a past, increasingly mythical realm of absolute personal value which capitalist social relations cancel ... a passionate human protest against the marriage-market values" (113).

Instead of considering the book as reactionary or revolutionary, I suggest we can get a more nuanced view if we consider its relationship to the transitional era of mercantilism between the feudal and the capitalist periods. The central plot element—the introduction of Heathcliff into a region of large estates—is precisely the introduction of an "alien" whose origins and ethnicity are never identified. Lockwood says he is a "dark-skinned gypsy in aspect, in dress and manners a gentleman" (5), immediately creating suspicion that he has somehow acquired gentlemanly status through some process other than inheritance; his blood is not gentleman's blood, his darkness a marker of foreignness. Maja-Lisa Von Sneidern calls Heathcliff "an irregular black, a mongrel, a source of great anxiety for the mid-nineteenth-century Victorian" (172) and says he is identified with Liverpool and the slave trade. Ivan Kreilkamp suggests Heathcliff is so alien that he is beyond any social or ethnic realm:

> To assign Heathcliff a 'racial' status is potentially to attach him to human history, lineage, and parentage, but what seems fundamental to his being is precisely its failure to attach to such traditions or grounds of social identity. Heathcliff is a 'cuckoo' or 'animal' in his outsider status to human categories of being and belonging.
>
> *(98)*

But for all the mystery of his origins and social identity, Heathcliff succeeds in becoming a landowner and hence seeming to become a part of English society. His success raises the crucial question about the "foreign" which ends up having a role in the English economy: was it an English core of value that allowed that success and which transformed the earlier apparent foreignness? Catherine clearly sees such a core, but she does not believe it can simply grow from its poverty-stricken state into visible value. She feels she needs to acquire wealth from the Lintons that she can then give to Heathcliffe to raise him up. She is planning then on doing what Adam Smith said was the problem of Mercantilism: that ties to the "foreign" lands were like blood vessels circulating English blood into the colonies in hopes of getting large returns. Smith said this process would result in the sapping of English value, not its increase. Catherine doesn't get to complete her plan, but the result of her marrying Linton to pursue such a dream is what Smith said would happen: the draining of the strength of the English blood (both hers and the Lintons'), represented by the rather peculiar weakening and sinking to death of her and Linton.

But while Catherine's dream of using Linton's wealth to raise Heathcliff never comes true, Heathcliff finds another way to achieve the status of an English gentleman. His rise in status begins with a mysterious period away from the estates, after which he returns with considerable funds. He appears in many ways an English gentleman. However, he does not contribute to the value of the English community; rather his funds operate the way Mercantilism fears foreign funds could operate, deceitfully converting English wealth to foreign: having no last name, no "household" to bring others to join, he destroys the heritage and the nobility of both Earnshaw and Linton estates.

The economic transactions Heathcliff uses to acquire the English estates are presented as illicit: gambling (with Earnshaw) and deception (with Isabel Linton). He turns to these methods of raising himself up rather than being industrious largely because his beloved Catherine had rejected the potential strength in him in favor of the graceful but weak qualities of Linton. Catherine says looking at Heathcliff makes her think of "bleak, hilly coal country" in contrast to Edgar who makes her think of a "beautiful fertile valley" (69). In a sense, then, Catherine's rejection of Heathcliffe is essentially a rejection of the value of coal, of industrialism, of internal potential, and in response to her rejection he too shifts from building himself up to manipulating others to gain wealth. His rise to ownership of two estates isn't via industry; rather it is essentially via finance: he is a manipulater of money and of human desires. Note that the basis on which Heathcliff takes possession of the Heights is that "Earnshaw had mortgaged every piece of land he owned for cash to supply his mania for gaming, and he, Heathcliff, was the mortgagee" (184). Heathcliff succeeds as a moneylender rather than as a laborer or Smithian capitalist: he does not grow wealth but manipulates it into his possession. The book traces Catherine's becoming seduced by older aristocratic values: it starts when he stays with the Lintons for a time. When she returns, Heathcliff sulks because she has become a "graceful damsel ... instead of a rough-headed counterpart of himself' (53). She not only loses her roughness but becomes less able to see its value: roughness is a value useful for hard labor, and so she loses her ability to see the potential in Heathcliff's roughness. Heathcliff too becomes unable to see his own value. He compares himself to Edgar Linton and feels worthless. Ellen Dean tries to show him what he has that Linton doesn't: "you are taller and twice as broad across the shoulders; you could knock him down in a twinkling" (57); in other words, he has strength that could do hard labor. But his response shows him losing his sense of the pleasure and value of his roughness:

> Nelly, if I knocked him down twenty times, that wouldn't make him less handsome or me more so. I wish I had light hair and a fair skin and was dressed and behaved as well and had a chance of being a rich as he will be.
>
> (57)

Heathcliff will of course become as rich as Linton, not because of fair skin and good behavior but because of his will and his intelligence, applied in ways that are ultimately corrupt but nonetheless reveal the potential that he could have used to create wealth through industry.

The crucial flaw in Catherine's adopting aristocratic values is embodied in the way she describes her decision to marry Edgar Linton. Ellen Dean says that Catherine is marrying him because he is "handsome and young, and cheerful, and rich." Catherine agrees, saying, "I should only pity him—hate him, perhaps, if he were ugly, and a clown." Ellen then says, "he won't always be handsome, and young, and may not always be rich." Catherine's response to this projection of the future is crucial; she says, "He is now, and I have only to do with the present" (78). Ellen mocks Catherine's logic, saying she is "Perfectly right, if people be right to marry only for the present." Ellen's is not generally the voice the book supports, but the disaster that follows Catherine's marriage clearly shows this way of deciding to marry to be wrong. The book indicates that one should consider what the person one is marrying will develop into, what increase in value that person can provide. Edgar is valuable, but will not increase the value he embodies and owns. Catherine is marrying for the older feudal, household economics of *present* value. She uses the same logic to say she cannot marry Heathcliff even though she loves him because "it would degrade me to marry Heathcliff now" (80). Once again she only sees what is "now" visible. She fails to see that Heathcliff has more potential to increase economic value than Edgar has. The distinction between an internality of potential versus visible glitter is crucial here: she is following the older set of values rather than the newly emerging capitalist ones.

Isabel's decision to marry Heathcliff is presented as based on similarly flawed reasoning, on choosing older, aristocratic values. Heathcliff himself says Isabel married him "under a delusion … picturing in me a hero of romance, and expecting unlimited indulgences from my chivalrous devotion" (149). Chivalric heroes are figures in feudal love stories, heroes who live to maintain beauty and the magnificence of nobility, not to support industry. Heathcliff further says of Isabel, "I can hardly regard her in the light of a rational creature, so obstinately has she persisted in forming a fabulous notion of my character." Isabel cannot see "character" because she is living in a world of fables, looking for what is fabulous. Rationality is a tool for recognizing potential, not succumbing to fabulous glitter. Rationality moves from premises to conclusions, from what is visible to what follows from what is visible. Isabel, like Catherine, acts on the basis of the premises she can see, on the basis of the "present," not on what she could "reason" would follow from what is present.

So the two marriages that wreck the estates occur because of people choosing older aristocratic values over the new capitalist ones. The book replaces those faulty older values with the newer capitalist ones by moving to a second plot that traces a version of the same pattern I have suggested is in the other 19th-century novels I am examining. The second plot is the tale of Hareton, who begins, as Jane Eyre and Elizabeth Bennett and John Harmon also begin, as a disinherited aristocrat forced into the role of "common laborer." When Hareton first appears, he is "a young man without coat, and shouldering a pitchfork" (8) and his "dress and speech were ... entirely devoid of the superiority observable in Mr. and Mrs. Heathcliff ... his hands were embrowned like those a common labourer" (10). But though Hareton appears "devoid of superiority," the novel points out potential within him. Lockwood eventually describes him as having "wealthy soil" inside him "that might yield luxuriant crops under other and favorable circumstances" (193). Heathcliff overtly aims to suppress the potential in Hareton, even though he recognizes it. Heathcliff says Hareton is like "is gold put to the use of paving-stones" and contrasts him to his own son Linton, who is like

> tin polished to ape a service of silver. *Mine* has nothing valuable about it; yet I shall have the merit of making it go as far as such poor stuff can go. *His* had first-rate qualities, and they are lost; rendered worse than unavailing.
>
> *(214)*

Heathcliff recognizes that Hareton has "gold" inside him, but seeks to ensure that such gold will never be developed; in contrast, Linton's inner metal (or should we say "mettle") is worthless, both because it is derived from Heathcliff's alien "blood" and because it has been pampered and polished rather than developed via labor. Heathcliff understands but perverts the process of developing internal value. In contrast, when the second Cathy takes over Hareton's development later in the novel, her "sincere commendations acted as a spur to his industry" (311). She stimulates industry, while Heathcliff had made Hareton's labor at worthless task, turning his gold to mere paving stones.

Hareton's transformation leads to his marriage to Cathy, which is in a sense a restoration of the values that could have led the first Catherine to marry Heathcliff. And Heathcliff himself recognizes this: he says Hareton seems "a personification of my youth" and even that "Hareton's aspect was the ghost of my immortal love" (312–13). In a sense, watching Hareton grow out of the surliness Heathcliff forced on him is like watching what could have happened if the first Catherine had not chosen Linton. At that late point in the novel, Heathcliff loses his desire to "demolish the two houses" (312); instead, he sinks as so many others have into a dying lethargy, but what he is sinking into is a dream of rejoining Catherine. It ends his efforts to destroy the English country world, and so it is also in a sense the completion of the conversion of his foreignness: he and Catherine have become mystical additions to the wonder and value of the English countryside.

Hareton ends up master of the two estates, so the book concludes with the disinherited aristocrat who learned to labor restored to aristocratic possession. The servant Joseph does not recognize how Hareton is a transformation of old aristocratic qualities, concluding that the old feudal ways had returned: Joseph "fell on his knees, and raised his hands, and returned thanks that the lawful master and ancient stock were restored" (324). Unlike Joseph, the novel seems to recognize the new values of capitalism, the values of industry and strength, and even contains a dream of uniting those values with the old beauty and grace of the aristocratic world—which could be a way of interpreting the uniting of the rough but skilled alien, Heathcliffe, and the elegant Catherine, as ghosts.

The characters who are disconnected from their inheritance in the two Brontë novels I have discussed turn to labor to learn their new values. But some other works suggest that entering the world of the market, the world of business, is equally a way to break out of the limitations of the older feudal world. A strange version of this process takes place in *Goblin Market*, by Christina Rossetti. As in *Jane Eyre*, the process of transforming the cultivation of land involves a seductive vision of foreignness entering the English world, bringing goods that "inflame" desires extremely. The poem begins with two sisters living self-sufficiently in a version of the old household economy: as Terence Holt comments, they "have no need to resort to the market to trade for someone else's wares" (53). But when Laura hears the goblin men's cry, she is drawn away from her family's land and into the market. What she hears is the phrase, "Come buy" (3–4), which is a sexual pun, promising both value and intense pleasure. And it is the bodily response that the goblin men seek far more than money: they seek to convert those in this domestic realm as Shakespeare's sonneteer was converted by the Dark Lady, to make the sisters "alien" to themselves and to their land. The goblin men are described as so foreign that their products are of a kind that "men sell not such in any town" (101). The phrase could imply that those who sell these things are not men or that men who sell them do not sell them in any known town. Both meanings are apt: the goblin men are described as entirely animal-like: "one had a cat's face / One whisk'd a tail / One tramp'd at a rat's pace / One craw'ld like a snail" (73–4). And what they sell comes from beyond any human society. What they offer is entirely sensuous pleasure, precisely what Smith says a "prodigal" seeks. And what prodigals end up doing is "perverting" their own character, and that is what we see happening when Laura goes shopping. What Laura gives is described in the same terms Othello uses to describe what he gave up: "she clipp'd a precious golden lock, / She dropp'd a tear more rare than pearl" (126–7). Laura is repeating what we saw Pochahontas and Jessica do in the last chapter, acquiring such a passion for foreign things that they give up their cultural identity, their family identity.

But Laura does not become one of the goblins; rather, what she was living on before they came no longer feeds her. She is described as "knocking at Death's door" (321), but she undergoes a resurrection when her sister Lizzie goes to the market and treats it just as a market, seeking goods, not something marvelous. Lizzie is a good Smithian, approaching the market in a calculated way, only offering a silver coin, not golden locks or tears. The goblin men try very hard to inflame Lizzie and get her to give more than a mere silver coin, but she stands "Like a royal virgin town" (418). She defends her town against these men who come from no town and is strong in her "dispassionate" desire for economic trade, never succumbing to inflamed passion for the extremely attractive fruit. The goblin men are finally "Worn out by her resistance" (438).

It is Lizzie's "abstinence," an active process of stridently resisting temptation, resisting the desire to give in to one's own pleasure, that produces capital. Lizzie offers a simple coin, a small price, but that won't buy the exotic pleasures the goblin men offer. She is not resisting spending money, merely being parsimonious. But this poem shows that the act of abstaining is actually difficult and tiring. And the poem goes on to show that this tiring, hard act produces capital, which Lizzie then takes back and uses to restore the ability of her sister to "produce."

Lizzie tells Laura to lick off the juices left by the goblin men: in effect, these juices are what Lizzie acquired by her active abstinence, and Lizzie is bestowing them upon Laura, thereby converting her "labor" into something that can produce great value. Her strident resistance to temptation transforms the very foreign substances that would have destroyed her body. The goblin men pressed their fruits onto Lizzie's body, so when she leaves she is covered with juices from those fruits. But those juices were not acquired by giving in to an intense passion, but rather by holding firm to her economics—it was the goblin men who lost control and smeared their "goods" all over her in their attempt to inflame her passion. By acquiring the juices without passion, Lizzie transforms them from dangerous foreign substances into something that can be used to restore production in the domestic realm, to restore her sister's body.

Lizzie tells Laura to "suck my juices / Squeez'd from goblin fruits for you" (468–9). The juices produce an intense, painful result, nearly killing Laura. Laura falls "Like a watch-tower of a town / Which an earthquake shatters down" (514–15). The juices operate deep inside her: a "Swift fire spread through her veins, knock'd at her heart / Met the fire smouldering there / And overbore its lesser flame" (507–9). The juices, transformed by Lizzie's abstinence, have become the antidote to the pleasure that Laura pursued in sucking the fruits.

Once Laura is restored to health, the poem leaps to the goal of this restoration, and this is "labor" of a particular kind. Immediately after Laura "awoke as from a dream ... And light danced in her eyes" (537–42), the poem shifts in time—"Days, weeks, months, years /Afterwards, when both were wives/ With children of their own" (543–4). Laura and Lizzie are then able to produce something that increases the value of the domestic realm: children. Foreign importation has been converted into domestic production. And the goblin men have been replaced by domestic men: the two women are "wives."

The final lines elaborate a moral message that seems to exclude men: "there is no friend like a sister / In calm or stormy weather" (562–3). These lines even suggest an answer to Shakespeare's early sonnets. In those sonnets, the other sex seems a "foreign" land that can provide riches if one just trades the right way, but this poem suggests that the trade one has to make, the trade of part of one's body to someone unlike oneself, will only result in destruction of the self. But the poem can be seen as tracing something necessary for allowing these women to have children. It is not simply that they would have been happy mothers if they had never met the goblin men: rather, the goblin men seem part of the process of developing the power to produce families. Remaining entirely in their farm-like world, a world much like aristocratic estates, would not allow them to have that "increase" which Shakespeare's sonnets imply requires going to the other sex. So one might say that the poem is about the need to engage with the market side of society and then return to the land-based economy, in order to allow the original domestic world to expand, to grow. One might even suggest that the juices the goblin men spread all over Lizzie were what the two women need to have children: but they must convert those juices from foreign wealth to domestic capital in a very violent process. The poem thus also revises a very old myth, that the seed which produces a child is entirely from the father, the mother being just the ground in which the seed grows. In this poem, women radically transform what men provide. The process of that transformation is a process of acquiring the "juices" men provide without succumbing to an uncontrollable passion, and then using those juices to connect women to each other. The domestic realm is coded as purely female in this poem, but it requires this substance from men to be re-productive. Laura moves from a foreign connection that is destructive to her and her land to a domestic connection that merely expands what the land can pro-vide. Lizzie accomplishes that transformation because she understands how to have a limited, purely economic and dispassionate connection to the "other." Laura learns from her sister that there is value in a woman having strength, resolve, and the ability to participate in a purely economic transaction with men.

Another novel that traces a subtle version of that transformation is *Pride and Prejudice*. Critics have seen this novel either as a defense of aristocracy (Butler) or as revolutionary and joining in the spirit of romanticism (Auerbach; Morgan). But I will try to show rather that it is akin to novels such as *Jane Eyre* in reframing the way the aristocracy makes use of its wealth and understands what makes people valuable. And as such the novel joins in the development of aristocratic capitalism as Smith recommends.

To see in more detail the distinctive economics in this novel, I want to tie it clo-sely to an economic treatise written just a few years earlier: Henry Thornton's *Reflections on Paper Credit in Great Britain*. Thornton brings out the relationship of capital and character that I am tracing in Victorian novels. He says that the entire economic system runs on what he calls "commercial credit," which he defines as "confidence," a belief in what others will do—in other words, an aspect of character:

> Commercial credit may be defined to be that confidence which subsists among commercial men in respect to their mercantile affairs. That con-fidence operates in several ways. It disposes them to lend money to each

other, to bring themselves under various pecuniary engagements by the acceptance and indorsement of bills, and also to sell and deliver goods in consideration of an equivalent promised to be given at a subsequent period.

(75)

In other words, the confidence of commercial credit is a belief about what will emerge in the future from what is not totally visible now. Confidence derives from believing that the person one is dealing with has potential wealth that is not directly visible as one makes deals with that person. It presumes that those making deals are dispassionate, are capable of holding back and not spending some of the wealth they have. Jane Eyre directly invokes the concept of "confidence" as what she values more than wealth. When Rochester offers her "half his estate" if she would become his lover, she replies, "Do you think I am a Jew usurer, seeking good investment in land? I would much rather have your confidence. You will not exclude me from your confidence, if you admit me to your heart" (277). The Jew usurer is a figure of a foreign person seeking to exploit the wealth of others—an image of mercantile advantage. Instead, Jane wants to see in Rochester an internal quality, something in his heart that would allow her to feel "confidence" in him far more than his having any amount of land or wealth.

Pride and Prejudice is all about how much confidence people can have in each other and about mistakes made in evaluating the internal qualities that would inspire confidence. For example, Bingley's dropping of Jane Bennett derives not from his sense that she is not valuable, but from his inability to read her intentions: her inexpressiveness leaves him with a lack of confidence in her commitment to him. He can read her external value—she is the most beautiful woman in the novel—but cannot be confident of what she will be worth in the future, what her character will lead her to become.

Of course, the most dramatic event in the novel is the crisis of confidence created by Wickham's running off with Lydia. The result of that escapade is that he is exposed as failing to base his acts on confidence in two different senses: he is a gambler, someone who risks and causes others to risk investments that are not backed by sufficient confidence in the outcome, and he is someone who is willing to engage in sexual liaisons without any assurance of the future promised by such a liaison—namely, marriage. The cure to both problems is the infusion of money provided by Darcy, which provides the "backing," the resources not present at the moment when Wickham and Lydia run off, and so in effect restores "confidence" in Wickham.

The problem with Wickham is described in terms that mix economic and characterological meanings: his "general unreserve" (119) promises much more than is actually there—he does not have "reserves" to back up his appearance of being such a valuable person. The very large emotional credit which he draws to himself by his attractive demeanor is in effect a speculative bubble; to love him is to gamble. Further, Wickham is defined by his surface, not any hidden depths: "there was truth in his looks" (75). In Victorian literature and economics, the surface does not reflect what is real. The assurance provided by Wickham's looks should actually create doubt about what is there; as Thornton notes, sometimes "a great quantity of individual dealings is … carried on by persons having comparatively little property," and he concludes that "under such circumstances" regardless of what are "ostensible riches," there is the "delusive appearance of wealth" (78). Wickham is all "ostensible" value, and as such is presenting a delusive appearance. The process of discovering who really deserves love or credit is a process of uncovering what is invisible, uncovering the "grounds" standing behind a current appearance, and so it makes sense that Elizabeth says that she first loved Darcy when she in a sense snuck behind his back to see his "beautiful grounds at Pemberley" (314). Elizabeth sees then what was not visible in Darcy, what stands behind his appearance of wealth. That contrasts with Wickham because what is hidden in Wickham is that there is nothing hidden. He is all surface, as the goblin fruits are all delicious surface, providing no real nourishment.

Darcy is of course all hidden value: he appears rather unpleasant, not at all as delightful as Wickham. But behind his unpleasant exterior, there is true depth, true reserves—and a great deal of wealth. The contrast between Darcy and Wickham is mirrored in the contrast of Pemberley and Rosings. Rosings seems on the surface to have even greater wealth than Pemberley, but as Elizabeth interacts with the DeBurghs she gradually loses confidence in them and the estate seems less and less valuable. What inspires confidence is the way an estate is cultivated, its potential for increase in value, its ability to be used as capital. Pemberley inspires love of Darcy because it reveals his managerial skills. Elizabeth marvels at what he has done with his grounds: "She had never seen a place for which nature had done more, or where natural beauty had been so little counteracted by an awkward taste" (204). He has maintained the natural beauty—and more, he has actually increased its value: for example, a stream "of some natural importance was swelled into greater but without any artificial appearance" (204). This peculiar detail is important because it reveals a subtle economic virtue crucial to the age in which Austen lived, an uncertain era between aristocratic and capitalist economics, when the source of value was shifting from the seeming stability of well-bounded estates (as of national states) to the mobility of market exchange. The slight swelling of the stream is an act of increasing the value of its natural beauty, adding something that is generated by labor, a slight addition of value which is to the "credit" of the owner. Delighted by what Darcy has done with the grounds, she thinks, "to be mistress of Pemberley might be something!"(204). She is imagining herself as joining in the management of this estate.

Elizabeth is also moved by the way Darcy treats his employees: she asks them about him and finds their words are "very much to his credit" (207). She elaborates,

What praise is more valuable than the praise of an intelligent servant? As a brother, a landlord, a master, she considered how many people's happiness were in his guardianship!—How much of pleasure or pain it was in his power to bestow!

(209)

These terms of praise straddle the line between the values of aristocracy and capitalism: Darcy gains credit from what he has "bestowed" upon those who work there, and he has found ways to increase the value of their labor in "producing" the estate. Sheryl Craig notes that Austen sets Darcy's estate in Derbyshire, a region "financially stimulated by the Industrial Revolution" and a "Whig stronghold," concluding that the novel "encouraged Whig readers to be generous to laboring classes" (65). The novel is advocating the transformation that brings wealth to be consecrated to industry.

And just as Elizabeth sees Darcy's value in his treatment of others, so he sees her value in the way she comes to care for her sick sister. To get to the house where her sister has fallen ill, Elizabeth walks through mud, staining her skirts, reducing the visible elegance of her dress, but her walk causes Darcy to admire "the brilliancy which exercise had given to her complexion" (30). Darcy is glimpsing what is within Elizabeth and ignoring the surface she presents. Similarly, what allows the two to finally recognize each other is a letter he sends: words, not his visible presence, words that reveal what is inner and what is potential. And of course he demonstrates his willingness to use his money to increase the value of his relationship to Elizabeth by giving money to Lydia and Wickham so they can marry: he is investing in the family he is creating.

In contrast to Pemberley, Rosings does not inspire confidence in those who visit because those who own its wealth are not reserved and thus do not appear able to do what is necessary to increase the value of their estate. When Elizabeth is given a tour, what she is told is the exact value of everything, and she "could not be in such raptures as Mr. Collins expected ... and was but slightly affected by his ... relation of what the glazing altogether had originally cost Sir Lewis de Bourgh" (138). When Lady Catherine takes over, she does no better, narrating in "so authoritative a tone as marked her self-importance and brought Mr. Wickham immediately to mind" (139). The comparison to Wickham might seem surprising, since Elizabeth at this point in the novel admires him but clearly finds Lady Catherine pompous. But it foreshadows what will be revealed: that such a style does not imply untapped reserves, but instead reveals the "mere stateliness of money and rank" (138). Lady Catherine is claiming she has worth due entirely to the money and rank she has. But money that is simply visible as wealth is not capital. Essentially, Mr. Collins and Lady Catherine (and Wickham) are relying on money and visible status rather than commercial credit to create belief in them. Thornton writes about moments in economic history when money becomes more important than credit, and those moments occur when there is a failure of confidence, when people are afraid of what will happen in the economy. Thornton says that in "a state of distrust, ... a greater quantity of money will be wanted in order to effect only the same" transaction (99). Mr. Collins and Lady Catherine are acting as if they are in a moment of economic uncertainty, presenting their estate as merely money, not potential, and so they inspire distrust in others.

Charlotte Lucas's decision to marry Mr. Collins is similarly based on a lack of confidence in human relations: she chooses the visible presence of money as security because she cannot believe she can recognize a deeper, hidden basis of security—human character. She is quite precise in saying that she does not believe anyone can know what a person's character will be in the future. And it is this inability to have confidence in what a person will be in the future that leads her to marry entirely for money. She says,

> Happiness in marriage is entirely a matter of chance. If the dispositions of the parties are ever so well known to each other, or ever so similar beforehand, it does not advance their felicity in the least. They always continue to grow sufficiently unlike afterwards to have their share of vexations, and it is better to know as little as possible of the defects of the person with whom you are to pass your life.
>
> *(21)*

She does not trust that she can recognize a person who deserves credit, one whose value will increase, so she wants someone whose value is completely visible. She says that she will marry for money, even though it may be "uncertain of giving happiness, [it] must be the pleasantest preservative from want" (107). She marries, then, someone with no depth, a show-off who has funds. Her marriage is a form of gambling, of relying on luck, parallel to Wickham's story. Of course, Mr. Collins is also a man incapable of recognizing character and so unable to make good investments of his money as well. When Collins proposes to Elizabeth, her refusal focuses on the fact that she is more than what she seems, and he is addressing only the surface. He claims that her refusal is "merely words" because she needs the kind of wealth he will inherit—her family estate. So he says she is merely toying with him. She pleads with him, as I quoted before, that she is not trying to increase her attractiveness, to be "elegant," but rather to be "rational" (95). She is proposing a very different sense of value than he is seeking—not just external wealth or beauty but internal qualities that could be developed. By preferring rationality to elegance, Elizabeth is moving toward capitalist values, towards a sense of what is inside, rather than what appears as treasure on the surface. As Nina Auerbach concludes, Austen wrote to "subvert the conventional picture of the 'elegant female'" (126).

The members of Elizabeth's family do not generate either credit or confidence. As the narrator says about Mrs. Bennett, "it was certain that her manner would be equally ill-adapted to do credit to her sense" (315). The description has a certain convoluted irony: it suggests she does have some "sense" but her manner makes it seem she has less than she has. She does then have some quality that is not visible, but she does not know how to make use of that quality in her "manners," in what she presents to other people. In general, the actions of the Bennett family hurt their "credit", as Elizabeth notes in thinking about what Lydia's behavior does for Elizabeth and Jane, "how materially the credit of both must be hurt by such impropriety or conduct" (177). Impropriety is a failure of restraint, giving in to those passions Adam Smith said "pervert" value.

This issue of what is visible as people present themselves to others and what is hidden redounds to the voice of the book itself: the narration implies more than it reveals. The realism of this novel is not the realism of accurate representation: that would be something like Wickham's "truth in his looks" or money's accurate statement on its surface of exactly what it is worth. We can then consider in economic terms the value created by Austen's ironic style: she is seeking to create confidence and credit. And what she is giving credit to is a way of running estates and a way of loving. By not directly revealing the values it represents, her ironic style can give credit to love and to estates and put that credit into circulation with the novel, but at the same time keep love and estates "private." Thus, consider this description of Darcy's declaration of love: he "expressed himself on the occasion as sensibly and as warmly as a man violently in love can be supposed to do" (307). Austin's words assume that we already know how a man in love is supposed to speak, but it does not show us his actual words, and I think it is obvious why: because the words would never actually make visible the "violence" of love. The words would always be inadequate because they are just serving as markers pointing to something invisible. Darcy is given credit for acting like a lover without our actually seeing his actions; such visibility would only be necessary if we had a crisis of confidence in his love or in Austen's narrator.

Note how differently Austin gives us Collin's declaration of love: after a lengthy speech about the value of his bestowing his love upon Elizabeth, he says "And now nothing remains but to assure you in the most animated language of the violence of my affection" (93). As in all his other quotes, he attempts to make visible what he is pointing to that should reside inside him; he believes that the animatedness of his language will make visible the violence of his affections, completely bestowing all value in the words themselves: they are to be valuable objects given to her, like dollar bills, rather than markers of something in him which cannot be seen—his inner capital, his character, which can be intuited but is never simply "there."

Austin's irony is a way to avoid what Collins is doing. An authoritative tone that sought to accurately put into words the true character and value of love would transform what Austen believes is the deep, inexpressible, unshareable value of love and of estates into something like the liquidity and self-importance of money that can pass through everyone's hands. *Pride and Prejudice* thus seeks to direct us to what is hidden or buried, economically, personally, and literarily.

One 19th-century novel—*Our Mutual Friend*, by Charles Dickens—turns the metaphor of buried value I have been exploring into literal piles of dirt, or dust, in which the treasure of a wealthy man is apparently hidden. His wealth has somehow become stored inside huge piles of dust, while multiple characters seek ways of turning it back into usable value. And his will requires his son to marry a woman regardless of their feelings for each other—forcing people to do for money what they do not choose, in effect killing their characters.

But the plot the will suggests is transformed and, rather strikingly, what sets it in motion is the recovering of dead bodies. The book opens with a man fishing dead bodies out of a river in hope of converting them into cash. And it appears that John Harmon, the son of the rich man who should have inherited the buried wealth in all those dust piles, is one of those bodies. So it appears some new family will get the money. But the transformation this book traces is not the passing of money to a new family: rather, it turns out that the son is not dead, but the mistaken body gives him an opportunity to transform himself and those around him by his assuming a new name and becoming Secretary—always capitalized—to a working-class couple, the Boffins, who were put in charge of the inherited money. Harmon becomes the "mutual friend" who brings about the reform of several people so that he can inherit the money without joining in the will's effort to corrupt everyone. In this novel, both bodies and older forms of wealth have to be metaphorically destroyed, turned to dust, to corpses, and then resurrected in new forms in order to escape the corrupting effects of the older economic system. Catherine Gallagher describes the central issue of the plot as the main character John Harmon seeking what is necessary to "render possible his possession of (instead of by) his money" (Gallagher, *The Body*: 87). Borrowing a term from John Ruskin, Gallagher describes money that possesses people as "illth"—and says the novel traces the change from "illth" to "wealth" (Gallagher, *The Body*: 87). "Illth" is a term close to "filth," and fits a novel tracing the process of extracting money and people from piles of waste.

Money becomes illth when it is not used to support industry. As Adam Smith argues, what makes wealth useful are acts of bestowal of capital on workers. The novel supports Smith's theory quite precisely by distinguishing between workers whose labor is supported by wealth and those who just work hard. The book presents an extreme example of the disaster of hard work without the benefit of capital in the figure of Bradley Headstone. Bradley has worked his way up from poverty to a position as a teacher, without any help from anyone investing capital in him. And it seems that despite all his efforts he can never establish a firm basis for his status or even his seemingly educated personality: he has no self-command and succumbs to thoroughly violent passions. His name points to the problem: what is overseeing his rise, the "head" that lies behind all his actions, is not a stockpile of capital, but a marker of a grave. What he has stored in his brain has died and been buried. His acquired knowledge, the fruit of his labor, is not growing like capital, precisely because no capital has been invested in him.

In contrast to Bradley there is a young woman, Lizzie, who is also educated out of her working-class status. But her education is paid for by a wealthy man, Eugene Wrayburn (who seems to be doing so to try to seduce her). Her rise in personal capital is contrasted to Bradley Headstone's: she becomes an elegant person; he becomes bitter. Both Bradley and Lizzie gain cultural capital from their education, but Bradley's increase in what is valuable within him is much less because he is building on a small base of capital in the first place. So what the novel suggests is that there needs to be transfer of wealth from the upper class to the lower class in the form of investment in labor to increase the value of that labor. As Smith puts it, wealth needs to be consecrated to the maintenance of labor. No wealth is consecrated to Bradley's labor.

As Lizzie rises in personal capital, she also becomes the object of Bradley Headstone's desire. However, her desires are all directed at Wrayburn; she rejects Bradley. Bradley Headstone becomes wildly jealous of Wrayburn's interest in Lizzie—perhaps because she represents the results of successful, financed education, results Bradley cannot achieve on his own. Bradley becomes so enraged he attacks and nearly kills Wrayburn—and then wanders off in such a daze that he dies a violent and mistaken death. Wrayburn does not die, although he is left unconscious in the river. He is saved by Lizzie, making use of the precise skill she learned from her father before being educated by Wrayburn: the skill to use a boat to retrieve bodies from the river (her father had been making his living fishing up corpses). So the book rather neatly presents the way that the bestowal of money on a worker makes the labor that worker was doing far more valuable: Lizzie's working-class skill has become literally life-saving for the wealthy Wrayburn. After being rescued by Lizzie, Wrayburn is transformed, and instead of seducing Lizzie, he marries her and turns into a devoted husband. It is then not simply the dazzling wealth Wrayburn bestows on Lizzie that creates what eventually makes them a good family: rather, it is quintessentially what the two classes contribute to each other. Wrayburn quite literally needs Lizzie's working-class skills to stay alive and continue making use of his inherited wealth.

The novel contains another plot of the transformation of an aristocrat, a plot that is more central to the novel. This is the story of John Harmon, the son of the rich man whose buried inheritance everyone is seeking. Harmon cannot simply take the money because his father set up various conditions that would have required him to become as corrupt as his father; in particular he had to marry a poor but money-hungry woman, Bella Wilfer. As in *Jane Eyre*, to accept money from older economic systems boxes one into a corrupt lifestyle and personality. To free oneself and one's money from that corrupt system requires violent and strange acts. John Harmon is able to recreate himself because of the dead body that was mistaken for him, so he is able to adopt a new name, John Rokesmith, and become a "man of business" (181) who demonstrates a Smithian attitude toward money: "He showed no love of patronage or command of money ... If, in his limited sphere, he sought power, it was the power of knowledge; the power derivable from a perfect comprehension of his business" (193). The novel presents as contrast to Rokesmith numerous persons who see in money the power to harm or take from others. The attack on the power of money to corrupt has led critics such as Daniel Scoggins and Howard W. Fulweiler to see this novel as a critique of capitalism or political economy in general. I think such conclusions are excessive: the novel is against what Harmon/Rokesmith says that the will is aiming at, "the old perverted uses of the misery-making money" (373). But there is another way to use money, not to make others miserable by taking away what they value, but rather by using money to increase the value of what others can do, in other words, to increase the value of labor. Rokesmith describes his whole project as manager of the estate's money to

> live the same quiet Secretary life ... until the great swarm of swindlers under many names shall have found newer prey. By that time, the methods I am establishing through all the affairs ... will be, I may hope, a machine in such working order as that they can keep it going.
>
> *(367)*

In other words, he is trying to make his inherited wealth into a "machine," a mechanical operation, a kind of factory, that turns the money into useful products and keeps away the "swindlers" who wish only to pervert the money.

The book traces the transformation of the greedy excessive valuing of money for itself into the capitalist use of money as investment in labor—in the working class—through the way Rokesmith uses his role as money-manager to change the money-hungry Bella. She comes from a middle-class family, and when she hears about the will that would have given her wealth if Harmon had lived, she feels deprived and horrified: "I hate to be poor, and we are degradingly poor, offensively poor, miserably poor, beastly poor" (45). She recognizes that the will would have turned marriage to John Harmon into a heartless financial transaction: she would have been "left to him in a will, like a dozen of spoons," but she would have accepted her position, "for I love money and want money" (45).

John Harmon also recognizes that the will would have corrupted him, making him into a "Sultan buying a slave" (367). Along with working to change his own inherited views, he struggles to change Bella's views, to bring her to see that character is more important than mere money in those one associates with or marries. His method of changing her is to create around her the very world of corrupting wealth that she said she would have accepted. She comes to live with the Boffins, who had worked for Harmon's father and who the will said should have the inheritance if the son was declared dead. John has the Boffins treat him, in the role of their Secretary, very badly. Eventually, Bella finds herself siding with Rokesmith against his cruel bosses: she recognizes that he is industrious and respectable even though he seems just an employee. As a result she gives up her plan to marry a rich man and falls in love with and marries Rokesmith. Her transformation even leads her to start acquiring skills; she consults "The Complete British Family Housewife" to become a proper manager of a household and suddenly discovers she can do needlework. The novel explains this discovery by saying, "Love is an all things a wonderful teacher and perhaps love ... had been teaching this branch of needlework to Mrs. John Rokesmith" (724). Love is thus rather mystically connected to learning how to use one's labor to increase value: she falls in love because she recognizes John's work ethic, and this magically leads her to seek her own industriousness. John and Bella then become "economical and orderly" (663), a productive merger of wealth and labor—both of them actively doing things to make value.

The transformation of Bella allows John Rokesmith/Harmon to satisfy the requirements of his father's will without a marriage that would make him essentially a slave-owner, but there is another step necessary before he inherits his family's money. While he was pretending to be a mere Secretary, a will appeared giving everything to the Boffins no matter what John did. But when the Harmons are so efficiently and industriously living in their new house with a new baby, the Boffins decide to give the money to them anyway, concluding that it is as if the old man's "money had turned bright again, after a long, long rust in the dark" (757). In other words, the overall plot of the novel is about the transformation of money from something that corrodes people by keeping those people from working into something that gives people incentive to work. It is striking that in this novel it is ultimately working-class people who bestow wealth on those who can manage it best. The Boffins giving money to Harmon is not simply returning wealth to the corrupt aristocrats who stole it from the working class in the first place; rather it is recognizing that Harmon knows best how to manage and invest money—in work—because he has become a worker.

The novel goes further than *Jane Eyre* by actually including working-class characters such as Lizzie Hexam, Bradley Headstone, and the Boffins; the novel implies that what is crucial in improving their lives is not taking money away from the wealthy but rather having the wealthy learn that wealth actually derives from work and will turn to dust if it isn't used for work, invested in workers. The last chapter is a discussion of the value of such investment, a discussion of whether Eugene Wrayburn was wise to marry the poor Lizzie. That chapter is entitled "The Voice of Society," and most of the voices we hear condemn the marriage as a mistake, as Eugene failing to see the true source of value in people, which is their ties to inherited wealth. But one character in the discussion, Twemlow, who is the only one to actually come from an aristocratic family, praises the marriage, saying of Eugene that "he is the greater gentleman for the action, and makes her the greater lady" (796). The statement is quite precise in expressing the novel's values: it does not say that the marriage made Lizzie a lady; though from a working-class background, she was already a lady; Eugene just made her a "greater lady." And Eugene did not lose his status as a gentleman by marrying a working-class woman; rather, he also became greater. Lizzie and Eugene both increased in value by this marriage, and that final line points up the final vision of the novel: it is the marriage of the working class and the aristocrats—or at least their becoming mutual friends—that will make everyone "greater."

References

Auerbach, Nina. "O Brave New World: Evolution and Revolution in Persuasion." *ELH* 39, 1972, pp. 112–128.
Austen, Jane. *Pride and Prejudice*. New York: New American Library, 1961.
Brontë, Charlotte. *Jane Eyre*. New York: Tom Doherty Associates, 1994.
Brontë, Emily. *Wuthering Heights*. New York: Barnes & Noble Classics, 2004.
Bunn, James H. "The Aesthetics of British Mercantilism." *New Literary History*, vol. 11, no. 2, 1980, pp. 303–321.
Butler, Marilyn. *Jane Austen and the War of Ideas*. Oxford: Clarendon, 1976.
Cadwallader, Jen. "Formed for labour, not for love: Plain Jane and the Limits of Female Beauty." *Brontë Studies*, vol. 34, no. 3, 2009, pp. 234–246.
Cheadle, Brian. "Work in *Our Mutual Friend*." *Essays in Criticism*, vol. 51, no. 3, 2001, pp. 308–329.
Craig, Sheryl, *"Pride and Prejudice* and Poor Laws." *Persuasions: The Jane Austen Journal*, vol. 35, 2013, pp. 64–74.
Dickens, Charles. *Our Mutual Friend*. Ed. Adrian Poole. Penguin Books, 1865/1997.
Eagleton, Terry. *Myths of Power: A Marxist Study of the Brontës*. Basingstoke, UK: Macmillan Press, 1975.
Fulweiler, Howard W. "'A Dismal Swamp': Darwin, Design and Evolution in *Our Mutual Friend*." *Nineteenth-Century Literature*, 'vol. 49, no.1, 1994, pp. 50–74.
Gallagher, Catherine. *The Industrial Reformation of English Fiction: Social Discourse and Narrative Form, 1832–1867*. Chicago: University of Chicago Press, 1985.
Gallagher, Catherine. *The Body Economic: Life, Death and Sensation in Political Economy and the Victorian Novel*. Princeton, NJ: Princeton University Press, 2009.
Garofalo, Daniela. "Impossible Love and Commodity Culture in Emily Brontë's Wuthering Heights." *ELH*, vol. 75, no. 4, 2008, pp. 819–840.
Holt, Terence. "'Men Sell Not Such in Any Town': Exchange in 'Goblin Market'." *Victorian Poetry*, vol. 28, no. 1, 1990, pp. 51–67.
Horwitz, Howard. *By the Law of Nature: Form and Value in Nineteenth-Century America*. Oxford: Oxford University Press, 1991.
House, Humphrey. *The Dickens World*. London: Oxford University Press, 1960.
Kreilkamp, Ivan. "Petted Things: Wuthering Heights and the Animal." *Yale Journal of Criticism*, vol. 18, 2005.
Morgan, Susan. *In the Meantime: Character and Perception in Jane Austin's Fiction*. Chicago: University of Chicago Press, 1980.
Newman, Neville F. "Workers, Gentlemen and Landowners: Identifying Social Class in *The Professor* and *Wuthering Heights*." *Brontë Studies*, vol 38, no. 4, 2013, pp. 313–319.
O'Gorman, Francis. *Victorian Literature and Finance*. Oxford: Oxford University Press, 2007.
Pell, Nancy. "Resistance, Rebellion and Marriage: The Economics of *Jane Eyre*." *Nineteenth-Century Fiction*, vol. 31, 1977, pp. 397–410.
Pocock, J.G.A. *Virtue, Commerce, and History: Essays on Political Thought and History, Chiefly in the Eighteenth Century*. Cambridge: Cambridge University Press, 1985.
Politi, Jina. "*Jane Eyre* Class-ified." *Literature and History*, vol. 8, 1982, pp. 56–66.

Pope, Alexander. *The Rape of the Lock*. Sanctuary Press edition published 2004, based on the edition originally published by Leonard Smithers, London, 1896. Online at www.93beast.fea.st/files/section2/The%20Rape%20of%20the%20Lock.pdf.

Rossetti, Christina. *Goblin Market and Other Poems*. Cambridge: Macmillan, 1862. Online at http://rpo.library.utoronto.ca/poems/goblin-market.

Scoggins, Daniel. 2002. "A Speculative Resurrection: Death, Money and the Vampiric Economy of *Our Mutual Friend*." *Victorian Literature and Culture*, vol. 30, no. 1, pp. 99–125.

Senior, Nassau. *Political Economy*. London: Richard Griffin, 1854, 3rd edition. Online at www.econlib.org/library/Senior/snP.html.

Smith, Adam. *An Inquiry into the Nature and Causes of the Wealth of Nations*. First published 1776. London: Electric Book Company, 2001. Online at https://ebookcentral.proquest.com/lib/brynmawr/detail.action?docID=3008435.

Thomas, Sue. "The Tropical Extravagance of Bertha Mason." *Victorian Literature and Culture*, vol. 27, no. 1, 1999, pp. 1–17.

Thompson, James. *Models of Value: Eighteenth Century Political Economy and the Novel*. Durham, NC: Duke University Press, 1996.

Thornton, Henry. *An Enquiry into the Nature and Effects of the Paper Credit of Great Britain*. Ed. F.A. Hayek. New York: Augustus M. Kelley, 1962. First published 1802.

Vanden Bossche, Chris R. "What Did 'Jane Eyre' Do? Ideology, Agency, Class and the Novel." *Narrative*, vol. 13, no. 1, 2005, pp. 46–66.

Von Sneidern, Maja-Lisa. "*Wuthering Heights* and the Liverpool Slave Trade." *ELH*, vol. 62, no. 1, 1995, pp. 171–196.

Watt, Ian. *The Rise of the Novel: Studies in Defoe, Richardson, and Fielding*. Berkeley, CA: University of California Press, 2001.

3

USURY IN THE BEDROOM

Financing Desire

The 19th-century vision of love and money seemed ready to produce an idyllic future. Society would be full of well-regulated, self-controlled individuals, using their wealth rationally to produce future wealth and loving other well-regulated, self-controlled individuals. Everyone would be freed of ties to old sources of wealth and old class and status rules on what and whom to desire. But as the century ended, people seemed to be acting in all sorts of strange ways, not buying the wonderful things being produced for them and not remaining devoted to normative forms of sexuality. There developed a broad sense that people's desires had been altered, repressed, or blocked—and all their desires, around both love and money. People found themselves "inhibited" so strongly that they did not even know what they would desire if their inhibitions were removed.

A whole conglomeration of new theories emerged to explain what had happened. Darwin, Freud, Marx, and then, a bit later, Keynes proposed that people were moved by forces they were not aware of. Human desires—for wealth, for happiness, for love—came to seem shaped by social, material and instinctual forces. Self-control was perhaps impossible, and toward the beginning of the 20th century, the effort to control the self even began to seem inhibiting rather than liberating. New ways of understanding human desires emerged and permeated those texts attempting to represent and shape human desires—the literature of love and economic treatises.

Karl Marx makes perhaps the broadest and most overt claim, arguing that consciousness is not controlling much of anything in the lives of individuals. He writes, "It is not the consciousness of men that determines their existence but, on the contrary, their social existence that determines their consciousness" (43). And Marx defines "social existence" as the "sum total of these relations of production [which] constitutes the economic structure of society—the real foundation ... to which correspond definite forms of social consciousness" (43). Marx points to a material structure which he says constructs consciousness—and so shapes what people pursue in all parts of their lives. Ideas, philosophy, metaphysics, all that constitutes the mental universe, are results of physical forces, and economics is at the core of those physical forces. So all human behaviors and desires are shaped by economic forces.

Darwin provides another theory, that bodies and minds are products of a process that has little to do with anyone's current intentions: rather, a very long history has shaped people's desires through genetic structures that are instinctual. Darwin shares with Marx the sense that a long history is embedded inside people: they are not simply thinking about their lives, but functioning as part of a vast system.

Freud is perhaps the most influential of late-19th-century theorist arguing that humans are not consciously in control of their own actions. He proposes that unconscious, instinctual parts of the brain and body provide the basic desires humans pursue, and conscious acts are shaped and sometimes disrupted by those unconscious desires. Freud changes the language of love, shifting the emphasis away from character as the ground of love toward a vision of bodies and unconscious forces bringing lovers together.

The core of all three of these theories is that material processes shape consciousness, though they differ in what they focus on as the material base of human thought—the entire economic structure of the society or the instincts bred by evolution. But in all these theories the physical shapes the mental, and the surrounding environment has a significant role in shaping behavior, regardless of how a person tries to control their actions.

The economist who developed the dominant orthodoxy of the 20th century until the 1970s—John Maynard Keynes—invokes a mixture of Marxist, Darwinian, and Freudian language. He argues that "instincts" are shaping the economic system: "the essential characteristic of capitalism" is "the dependence upon an intense appeal to the money-making and money-loving instincts of individuals as the main motive of the economic machine" (Keynes, *Essays*: 319). And Keynes concludes that the intense appeal to money-loving instincts has caused "The duty of 'saving'" to become "nine-tenths of virtue ...and ... the object of true religion," leading to "unstable psychological conditions" that are "not natural" (Keynes, *Economic Consequences*: 20–1). Saving is in essence what Smith advocated—"parsimony"—but in Keynes's view the value of parsimony has become wildly exaggerated, distorting human behavior and in essence wrecking other desires. Keynes uses language that in effect mixes the Darwinian model of physical instincts and the Marxist model of social structures shaping human behaviors. Keynes describes the effects of social structures as entwined with and modifying instincts. He says that locking away money in savings derives from "the love of money as a possession—as distinguished from the love of money as a means to the enjoyments and realities of life," and concludes that such a love of money "is a somewhat disgusting morbidity, one of those semi-criminal, semi-pathological propensities which one hands over with a shudder to the specialists in mental disease" (Keynes, "Economic Possibilities": 24). Keynes is suggesting that the instinctual desire for enjoyment and love is transformed by the social order into a pathological mental disease. The desire for pleasure, which underlies the pursuit of love, becomes instead a desire for money. A similar idea appears in Ezra Pound's *Cantos*: he writes that "the perverts ... have set money-lust/ Before the pleasures of the senses" (61). He says this is a result of what he calls "Usura," or usury, which then brings "palsey to bed" between lovers. That economics can affect what happens in bed may seem a rather strange idea, but it was actually implied in the writings of numerous writers, as I explored in an earlier work, *Deficits and Desires: Economics and Sexuality in Twentieth-Century Literature*. In that book, I argued that what occurred in the 20th century in reaction to the new conceptions of desire was a general movement toward greater freedom economically and sexually. I wish to modify that argument now: the move to consumption as the core driver of the economy and the move to pleasure as a driver of sexuality is not in the early 20th century a move toward freedom. It is a move toward more varied forms of action, but it is also a move toward recognizing that the individual is being driven by social forces or internal instincts to those varied forms of action, and is not actually free to control the self either economically or sexually.

Keynes's entire economic theory is an effort to produce governmental policies that would transform what he calls "demand," which is in effect the aggregate of all the desires of people. The unstable psychological condition created by capitalism leads to excessive saving, which disrupts the circulation of money and makes it impossible for all that is produced to be sold. Keynes calls this a situation of "pent-up demand" (a concept that bears striking similarity to the Freudian notion of "pent-up desire"). Keynes puts demand—or desire—in place of production as the core driver of the economy. Keynes' proposed polices are designed to create new "canals" by changing the economic atmosphere to allow emotional energy inside people to flow in new ways, thereby changing individual psychologies in dramatic ways.

In the "Concluding Notes" to his *General Theory of Employment, Interest and Money*, Keynes writes that

> dangerous human proclivities can be canalized into comparatively harmless channels by the existence of opportunities for money-making and private wealth, which, if they cannot be satisfied this way, may find their outlet in cruelty, the reckless pursuit of personal power and authority, and other forms of self-aggrandisement.
>
> *(374)*

Keynes suggests that there are "dangerous human proclivities" inherent in everyone, and those proclivities become active when the social order inhibits "opportunities for money-making." This bears similarity to Freud's view of society repressing sexual desires, but Keynes suggests that the desires people have instinctually in themselves can be dangerous, not merely because they are repressed. And instead of proposing psychotherapy to cure dangerous human proclivities, Keynes proposes changing the economic environment that is limiting the opportunities for allowing desires to be satisfied. Deficit spending can "stimulate demand," in effect altering inherent desires in ways that reduce their danger. Keynes hopes for such a radical transformations of human psychology that he even fears the results might not be controllable:

> I think with dread of the readjustments of the habits and instincts of the ordinary man, bred into him for countless generations, which he may be asked to discard ... To use the language of today, must we not expect a general 'nervous breakdown'?
>
> (Keynes, "Economic Possibilities": 22)

Though Keynes says he is drawing on "the language of today" in talking about "nervous breakdowns" and "instincts," he actually turns to a much older term to describe the basic stuff that drives human behavior: "animal spirits." Tracing where Keynes found that term, Roger Koppl writes that "Keynes seems to have borrowed it from Descartes. The earliest use, however, is apparently by Galen in the second century" (207). D.E. Moggridge provides more specific details of how Keynes came to the term: while an undergraduate, Keynes attended a lecture on Descartes and copied down in his notes that "The body is moved by animal spirits—the fiery particles of the blood distilled by the heart" (208). Then Keynes added a note of his own: "unconscious mental action." Animal spirits are part of the system of humoral biology of the early modern era that I discussed in Chapter 1: they are forces carried in the blood that move people quite separately from the way their minds or souls dictate. So Keynes is mixing into biological and psychological theories of his own age a concept from hundreds of years earlier. His rejection of Smith's economics is not entirely a move into a new age, but in part a move back to an earlier one.

Keynes's concept of animal spirits also follows a development in early 20th-century physiology that implies that the mind is deeply shaped by the body and is indeed itself rather more a bodily organ than something transcending the body. And not just one organ: the brain came to seem not a coherent whole at all, but a collection of separate parts. The theory came to be known as "localization"; Anne Stiles summarizes the heyday of localization in her book, *Neurology and Literature, 1860–1920*:

> Beginning in the early 1860s, neurology and the study of language collided dramatically when French neurologist Paul Broca (1824–1880) linked the third frontal convolution of the left brain hemisphere to linguistic ability.

Broca's findings immediately inspired his scientific peers to trace other mental faculties back to discrete cerebral locations, ushering in a period of biological determinism and physiological reductionism that reigned until shortly after the First World War, when Sigmund Freud's psychoanalytic approach gained broader currency throughout Europe and America … During the six previous decades, therefore, biological explanations of psychological states held sway.

(1)

The move to localization implies that consciousness does not emerge from a "self" or a "soul" or any other coherent non-physical entity. The brain itself comes to seem a body part—or a congerie of body parts.

At about the same time that localization within the brain came to prominence, there grew a sense as well that other parts of the body could in part control the way the brain and the nervous system worked. One influential source for this vision of the body was William James's 1884 definition of emotions as "felt awarenesses of visceral activity" (qtd. in Dixon, 24). This notion that emotions come to the brain from the "viscera", from the body, also contributed to redefining how humans connect to the external world—instead of assuming that the mind perceives and then reacts to external things, there developed a notion that external things could directly interact with the "viscera" or with subsections of the brain and produce reactions quite independent of the overall "self."

Keynes's notion of animal spirits builds on these notions of the viscera shaping consciousness. As Jack Amariglio and David Ruccio point out, "The idea of 'animal spirits' … points not to the mind—and thus to processes of intellection, decisions to follow conventions, and the formation of conscious expectations … but, instead, to the body" (72). Drawing on notions of the bodily influence on thought, Keynes argues that animal spirits are often more important that rational calculations in economic decisions. He writes,

individual initiative will only be adequate when reasonable calculation is supplemented and supported by animal spirits, so that the thought of ultimate loss which often overtakes pioneers, as experience undoubtedly tells us and them, is put aside as a healthy man puts aside the expectation of death.

(Keynes, The General: 161)

It is striking that Keynes equates the role of animal spirits to that which allows pioneers to go into the wilderness, the unknown, where death could follow some unpredictable and unexpected act. Keynes suggests that some of the most important initiatives people undertake—ones that truly expand the economics of a business and indeed of the whole economy—are in part forays into such an unknown, and no matter how well thought out, can only be pursued if there are these irrational animal spirits to overcome rational fears.

The role of animal spirits in allowing people to pursue their hopes for the future, their desires, causes behaviors that are clearly not rational, and indeed involve reactions to all sorts of things besides overt economics. Hence, he concludes,

> If the fear of a Labour Government or a New Deal depresses enterprise, this need not be the result either of a reasonable calculation or of a plot with political intent;—it is the mere consequence of upsetting the delicate balance of spontaneous optimism. In estimating the prospects of investment, we must have regard, therefore, to the nerves and hysteria and even the digestions and reactions to the weather of those upon whose spontaneous activity it largely depends.
>
> *(Keynes,* The General: *162)*

Keynes is suggesting that what can appear a response to an economic action of the government such as a New Deal can rather be a reaction to things that seem not at all economic, such as "nerves ... digestions and ... the weather"—in other words, to those animal spirits that are active along with conscious calculation.

Keynes's policies are designed to interact with animal spirits, to counter their tendency to create instability, and thereby allow individuals to successfully pursue their own initiatives, to do what Smith proposes. While Keynes is focused on changing the psychology of individuals, he does not propose doing this by directly addressing individuals. It is in the social order, not in the individual, that Keynes finds the source of economic problems and economic solutions, because the individual's psychology is a function of the overall social order. As the economic historian Thomas Francis puts it, "the 'foundation' of Keynes's thought" is that "Society is not the fluctuating interactions of individuals with a 'natural liberty' to property, etcetera but a *thing* in itself. It is not a timeless artifact but something that is malleable and fluctuating" (271). And it is by acting upon the malleable social order that human desires can be changed and thereby alter the operation of the whole economic system.

So Keynes proposes that government actions can alter the direction that the overall array of animal spirits are going. To do so, the government has to engage in countercyclic policies: when people are scared of spending money and products go unsold and businesses retreat from expansion, the government spends as a deficit and thereby modifies the overall "social atmosphere" to make people feel that spending and investment are likely to bring rewards.

One crucial way that Keynes' and Marxist theories differ is that Keynes does not base his theory on the premise that some social group has been controlling and distorting the social atmosphere. Rather, economic problems derive from irrational elements in all sorts of individuals, and policies need to counter the varied forms of irrationality, not simply eliminate or remove from power some single group. Irrational reactions derive from animal spirits, and those are bodily reactions, which vary across the social order. As Jack Amariglio and David F. Ruccio note in an analysis of Keynes' use of the term:

> In addition to the body's being the site of 'nonrational' motives and inspirations, its 'situatedness'—the extent to which the body is often conceived to respond to fundamentally local and specific stimuli—also serves to disrupt the presumed universality of the motivating causes and reasons that … are often presumed to lend order to the outcomes of individual actions.
>
> *(72)*

Keynes is thus seeking to understand an economy that is not universal, not formed of persons all alike, but rather formed of persons reacting rather differently to the local stimuli around them. As a result, economics requires consideration of how the general attitudes of a community are formed. As Piero Mini puts it: "The General Theory injects into the economy the unfamiliar viewpoint of 'community' in which we have detailed and intimate knowledge of attitudes, likes, dislikes, hysterias and propensities, and within which not calculations but mutual adjustments will produce harmony" (107). As a corollary to the multiplicity of the social order, the individual is also not a unified whole, but rather influenced by the various groups and situations to have a whole congerie of animal spirits influencing consciousness.

Keynes gained much of his influence because of fear of Marxist movements, fear that the Depression in particular would lead to communism—or to another rising non-individualist vision of the social order, fascism. Both communism and fascism proposed that a form of non-individual agency could become more powerful and more satisfying than the individualism of Smithian capitalism. As Adolf Hitler put it, when individuals who feel "very small" in a "little workshop or big factory" enter a mass meeting, they feel the "magic influence of what we designate as mass-suggestion" and then feel that "the power of thousands are accumulated in every individual" (478–9).

When the Depression hit, so many felt cast out of the possibility of individual success that communism and fascism both seemed to have the potential to overthrow capitalism. But then capitalism developed its own "magic influence" that also allowed individuals to feel that they could draw on the accumulated power of thousands, and the method used in capitalist countries is macroeconomics: the provision by the government of funds to counter oppressive effects of the overall economic structure. Keynes' macroeconomic policies allow the individual to borrow power from thousands of other persons via the mechanism of government spending. The government in Keynes' theories performs an action similar in some ways to what the mercantilist Thomas Mun proposed for the royal center: it digests elements that threaten to wreck the overall system. In Mun, these elements were the foreign treasures that merchants brought in, which if left "undigested" would corrupt and wreck those very merchants who brought them in. In

Keynes, there is similarly a sense that individual economic actions are being corrupted, but not by foreign things; rather, in Keynes it is the very economic system created by Smithian capitalism that is driving people to make bad economic decisions, to hold their money too long, to be too parsimonious. Keynes proposes that the government can change the "atmosphere" in which individuals act and think and thereby change those behaviors, keeping the economy running.

In conceiving of the possibility that government action can change the psychology of individuals, Keynes implies that consciousness is not simply a process deriving from a single center, the self; rather it is something like a collage produced by multiple artists (the body, the social atmosphere, the weather). And visions of such a form of consciousness are very much what appear in modernist literary works. As Franco Moretti has described James Joyce's style:

> In *Ulysses*'s stream of consciousness the individual is split … The illusion that he could be an autonomous and independent subject collapses. Far from being the expression of an 'interior freedom,'… [the] stream of consciousness indicates that the individual is enslaved by arcane and uncontrollable forces.
>
> *(195)*

Moretti goes on to connect the external control of internal mental processes to economic change by noting the profession of the main character Leopold Bloom, in *Ulysses*, who makes his money selling ads: "Stream of consciousness and the crisis of the ideology of the free individual meet under the ensign of advertising … And this is so because advertising is the myth of the commodity." It is the shift to an economy of commodities, of consumption, that brings with it the sense that internal thoughts and desires are shaped by external forces.

But even as the consciousnesses of characters in novels are moved by all sorts of forces, there is often a sense that the artist creating the work is still able to exert some control. Indeed, modernist artists often seem to be standing apart from the chaos shaping everything, including consciousness, in the worlds they portray, and in the worlds around them. As T.S. Eliot wrote, Joyce in *Ulysses* by imposing a mythic structure on his novel is "giving a shape and a significance to the immense panorama of futility and anarchy which is contemporary history" (Eliot, *Selected Prose*: 177). The novel thus both presents the chaos of forces shaping thought and history and provides something that stands apart from that chaos and gives "shape" to it.

I suggest then that modernism and Keynesian economics remain suspended between the recognition that individual consciousness is shaped by social forces and the possibility that some individuals and some social institutions could in some sense stand apart from and at times counter the effects of those social forces. Tamar Katz has explored this tension within modernism more generally, arguing that it stages a "negotiation between models of subjectivity," between a "self as "abstracted from the world, autonomous or transcendent" and an "all-too-malleable openness to impressions or conventions" that marks "the absence of any autonomy, signaling instead the subject's thorough implication in cultural stories" (233). She concludes that modernism "persistently explores" this dichotomy "not by choosing one model or another as an anchor, but by enacting this very contradiction within its texts in order to explore its implications" (233). Many critics have landed on one side or the other of the dichotomy Katz sees in modernism: there are critics who describe modernism as a literature of deep interiority of geniuses who reject the surrounding social order, maintaining their autonomy. Such a view lends itself to regarding modernists as politically conservative (Lukács) or as quite radical (Adorno). Others have seen modernism as deeply imbedded in social forces and even deeply tied to popular culture (Kershner; Graham). I want to explore the possibility that this very tension between what is individual and what is social is at the core of early 20th-century modernism and early 20th-century macroeconomics, and marks a perhaps impossible effort to maintain a connection to the Smithian belief in individual freedom while recognizing the force of irrational social and bodily influences.

The key element of Keynesian economics—the importance of consumption—lends itself to such an ambivalent view. If stimulating consumption is the key method for reducing the inhibiting effects of the previous economic system, then paradoxically it is by taking in what is surrounding the individual, by consuming what is socially available, that the individual can be "freer" to follow their own desires. Interiority requires consumption, and what sits behind and around consciousness is not merely a Freudian inheritance of eternal instincts, but a socially structured set of drives and habits that can be "adjusted" by social acts, particularly economic ones. Quite a number of modernists overtly present such a view of the power of economics in relation to individual psychology and interiority.

The writer who shows the connection between economics, the depths of human psychology, and modernism most vividly is Ezra Pound, who declares himself a fascist. But Pound's *Cantos* present a strange version of fascism that is actually close to Keynsian macroeconomics: he equates fascism to an economic theory known as "social credit," though Mussolini and Hitler, so far as I know, never made that equation. Social credit is the creation of C.H. Douglas, an early 20th-century economic theorist who argues that the social order has been distorted because the government and banks and certain rich people have restricted access to money by restricting credit, creating a blockage that doesn't allow most people to be able to buy the things they want. As Pound puts it in Canto XXXVIII,

there is and must be therefore a clog
and the power to purchase can never
(under the present system) catch up
with prices at large.

(190)

The "power to purchase" is a version of what Keynes would call "demand," so we can see Pound's sense that there is a "clog" blocking purchasing is similar to Keynes's sense of "pent-up demand." And Pound goes on to recommend a

Keynesian solution: government distribution of money beyond what is currently available, and even beyond what the government takes in as tax. Citing Douglas, Pound writes in *The Cantos*, "any government worth a damn can/ pay dividends ... instead of collectin' taxes" (231). Pound suggests then that the government can simply distribute credit to everyone to buy things and thereby release people from the blockages in the current social order. Pound argues that fascist governments are doing this, saying in an essay,

> Douglas proposed to bring up the TOTAL purchasing power of the whole people by a *per capita* issue of tickets ... Mussolini and Hitler wasted very little time PROPOSING. They started and DO distribute BOTH tickets and actual goods.
>
> *(Pound,* Selected Prose*: 294)*

When the people have "TOTAL purchasing power" they are free of social restrictions, and society becomes a paradise.

Pound is quite explicit in indicating the connection between what is deep inside individuals and the overall economic system by saying that what is generally regarded as the most private part of private life—sexuality—is in fact shaped by the system of credit. In his most famous Canto, number XLV, he calls the bad system of credit he sees around him in the U.S. and Britain "usury" (or in Latin, "usura"), and says that

> Usura slayeth the child in the womb
> It stayeth the young man's courting
> It hath brought palsey to bed, lyeth
> between the young bride and her bridegroom.
>
> *(230)*

For both Keynes and Pound, human psychology has been powerfully shaped by the economic system, creating a hell on earth.

Pound thinks that artists and poets have a role in countering the effects of usury, though not as great a role as the government. He believes some artists can maintain contact with the natural world inside their bodies and thereby find something to counter the effects of the socioeconomic system. Most people, though, essentially have their consciousness entirely controlled by the surrounding social environment: "Their minds are, that is, circumvolved about them like soap-bubbles reflecting sundry patches of the macro-cosmos" (*The Spirit*: 92). Alec Marsh notes that the term "bubble" suggests "the traditional image of financial speculation, where hollow artificial values are allowed to expand until they burst" (112). In contrast to those whose minds are full of artificial values, Pound argues that

> with certain others their conscious is 'germinal.' Their thoughts are in them as the thought of the tree is in the seed, or in the grass, or the grain, or the blossom. And these minds are the more poetic, and they affect mind about them and transmute it.
>
> *(The Spirit: 92)*

While the germinal poetic mind may be embedded in nature, its function is to transmute the "macro-cosmos" and perhaps break through the bubbles in which so many minds float. Pound implies the poet is free of the false beliefs created by the macro-cosmos, or at least is capable of free action in modifying those beliefs. But at the same time, his image of the poet is as a seed in that structure of the macro-cosmos, a part growing from it. The image embodies the ambivalence between individual autonomy of the artist and his existence as rooted and grow- ing from the "macro-cosmos." Pound similarly states the goal of his poetry is to "to record the precise instant when a thing outward and objective transforms itself, or darts into a thing inward and subjective" (Sieburth, 146). Is the poet remaking the world into something "inward" or is the outer world reconstructing the insides of the poet?

Douglas is quite clear about whether the individual or the social order is the main creator of economic value: "The factor transcending all others in impor- tance in the modern world is the cultural inheritance by the aid of which wealth in practically unlimited quantity can be produced by a small and diminishing amount of human labour" (188–9). If we apply Douglas's theory to art, then we can say that the value of a poem derives more from the cultural inheritance—from its connection to the vast macro-cosmos of thought—than from individual labor. Pound's *Cantos* follow that view, being built out of an extensive list of cultural references—writings from early America, from Renaissance Italy, from many eras of Chinese history, from multiple languages, from politics, economics, and political treatises as well as numerous literary works. The poems seem to have no single central voice or imagery. But within these extensive allusions, Pound glorifies certain great men—Confucius, Mala- testa, Mussolini, Jefferson—for their ability to control and shape the overall economic order. The artist, seeking like Pound to alter the economic system and to thereby change human consciousness, casts himself in a role similar to those government figures who can control the chaos of the social order, and in particular can act counter-cyclically, resisting the mass tendencies that produce psychological distortions as well as economic cycles.

William Carlos Williams joined Pound in advocating Douglas's social credit but did not at all agree with Pound that Douglas's vision was embodied in fas- cism; rather Williams believed that Douglas's theory could work in the U.S. so that government-provided credit could free up the economic system without turning to fascism. Williams also finds Douglas's own writings to be a form of poetry. In an essay on Pound's Cantos, Williams writes, "And so, when a light breaks and penetrates the blinding chaos in which we are sweltering—a name such as that of Douglas in England—it is poetry and Pound hails it not from a spirit of partisanship but as it is, a light from heaven" (Williams, *Selected Essays*: 169). Williams is almost quoting Pound in reaching that conclusion, because in Canto number 38, after the explanation of Douglas's theory which I cited earlier—

there is and must be a clog
and the power to purchase can never
(under the present system) catch up with
prices at large

Pound immediately writes,

And the light became so bright and so blindin'
in this layer of paradise
that the mind of man was bewildered.

(190)

When Williams says that Douglas's theory is poetry it is not of course because of its style or form, but because for Williams poetry is a breakthrough in both experience and expression—it is, in Pound's terms, a "germinal" act disrupting the "macro-cosmos," the hell created by the economic system. In *Spring and All,* Williams writes, "So most of my life has been lived in hell—a hell of repression lit by flashes of inspiration, when a poem such as this or that would appear" (Williams, *The Collected*: 203). Williams connects the hell of repression to economic issues by saying it was particularly due to "the futility of acquisitive understanding" (Williams, *The Collected*: 202). In other words, people become "acquisitive," seeking to hold things and in particular to hold money, and that is a central cause of repression that is both economic (i.e. the Depression) and sexual. And like Pound, Williams ties sexual issues to usury:

> That sex will be accomplished in sin, is the blind behind which venality has worked to undo the world. Kids may go masturbating into asylums but profits must be preserved. But, if the poet has always seen through the absurdity, today he sees more clearly than formerly. Love versus usury, the living hell-stink of today.
>
> *(Williams,* Selected Essays*: 168)*

Thus, both Pound and Williams conclude that there is a deep structure in society that has kept people repressed, kept them from being themselves, and that structure is economic at its core. And the poet has "always seen through this absurdity"; indeed, in the era when poetry seems to be far more obscure than ever before, Williams says the poet "sees more clearly than formerly." Poetic clarity is in the creation of works that will ostensibly change the distorted consciousness of everyone else. But it cannot appear as a coherent text or a distinct narrative voice: the text presents a vision of the social multiplicity and chaos, but implies that there is an individual standing behind that vision.

Williams's early poems contain vivid images of the repression due to economic suffering. For example, in poem XVIII of *Spring and All*, a poem beginning "The pure products of America/ go crazy," he presents a series of images of distorted personalities of impoverished persons because Americans have "… no / peasant traditions to give them / character" (Williams, *The Collected*: 217). A desolate young woman ends up "expressing with broken / brain the truth about us" (218). But within this vision of people destroyed by money and lust, Williams finds

> It is only in isolate flecks that
> something
> is given off
> No one
> to witness
> and adjust, no one to drive the car.
> *(219)*

Those isolate flecks are images of poetic inspiration, but there is no way to make use of those flecks because there is no one to turn them into something that adjusts the system and changes the way that things are "driven."

The inability to adjust and change the way things are driven is very much what is wrong with communism in Williams's view: the point of social credit versus communism is that it does not need to restructure all the way things are done, does not need to change the whole way businesses run. It is a system for releasing what is repressed by the system but does not require controlling everything. Williams describes the problem that communism presents in another short poem, one that again suggests that poetry itself is the answer to the economic issues communism is trying to address:

> Walk on the delicate parts
> of necessary mechanisms
> and you will pretty soon have
> neither food, clothing, nor
> even Communism itself,
> Comrades. Read good poetry!
> *(Williams, The Collected: 370)*

Douglas's treatise is part of the "good poetry," which would not walk all over the necessary mechanisms, but rather release the divine light that can alter the way people can pursue their desires.

Later, Williams writes a long poem, *Paterson*, which makes as explicit as Pound does the belief that credit is the key to undoing repression in all its forms, particularly sexual. He includes some direct quotes from Douglasite economic tracts, for example, citing the Federal Reserve System: "They create money from nothing … In other words, the Federal Reserve Banks constitute a Legalized National Usury System" (73–4).

He goes on to represent the system of producing money as a perverse sexual act:

> While in the tall
> buildings (sliding up and down) is where
> the money's made
> up and down
> […]
> predatory minds, un–
> affected
> UNINCONVENIENCED
> unsexed, up
> and down (without wing motion) This is how
> the money's made . using such plugs.
>
> *(165)*

The "blockage" that Douglas, Pound and Keynes theorize as distorting the circulation of money becomes here the entire system, plugging up desires and unsexing people. Williams, like Pound, focuses on banks as the key element in this distorted economic system. Williams says the U.S. is suffering from

> the cancer, usury. Let credit
> out . out from between the bars
> before the bank windows.
> . credit, stalled
> in money, conceals the generative
> that thwarts art …
>
> *(183)*

Usury is the charging of excessive interest, which limits people's ability to borrow and thereby start up businesses without already having cash. Usury in Williams and Pound is what limits opportunity, vision, and "thwarts art." Usury is a disease, rotting things that money could maintain, such as houses and businesses—and individuals themselves. Williams contrasts the effects of usury with a vision of paradise that could be created if credit were unleashed, describing the "Difference between squalor of spreading slums / and splendor of renaissance cities":

> Credit makes solid
> is related directly to the effort,
> work: value created and received,
> "the radiant gist" against all that
> scants our lives.
>
> *(185)*

The new economic theory—social credit—could restore a very old socio-economic structure, the splendor of renaissance cities, the era before capitalism. Williams' poetry aims doubly at this move into the future and into the past. I suggest that texts such as *Paterson* and Pound's *Cantos*, texts full of allusions and sudden jumps from one thing to another, represent a double relationship of elements in the social order to individuals: 1) they are representations of the social disorder and fragmentation that is blocking and repressing the individual; 2) they are representations of the "credit" that must be made available from the social order and that individuals must accept as part of the self in order to turn their lives from "squalor" to "splendor."

Williams and Pound both imply that turning the world from squalor to splendor also releases what is deepest and most distinctive in individuals. Those deep parts of people are in a sense what the person finds in the surrounding world to "invest" in—or we might say, to love. Pound thus writes in a section of the *Cantos* with the refrain "Pull down they vanity" that

> What thou lov'st well shall not be reft from thee
> What thou lov'st well is thy true heritage
> Whose world, or mine or theirs
> or is it of none?
>
> *(535–6)*

The rejection of vanity is the rejection of the notion that one loves only what is in one's own body and private possessions; what Pound is advocating is loving something out there in the world that will then become part of the self and so can never be separated, or "reft from," that person. The world is neither one's own nor "theirs"; no one singly owns anything and no one is completely separate from what everyone else owns. Pound ends this section with a summary:

> To have gathered from the air a live tradition
> or from a fine old eye the unconquered flame
> This is not vanity.
>
> *(536)*

Gathering from traditions or gathering the flame from someone else's eyes to build one's own poetry is not vanity, is not just claiming to be such a genius that one has already the essence of everything one finds; rather, it is joining with the world, letting the culture surrounding one create through the person.

Pound and Williams both include images of nearly superhuman figures who stand beyond or upon the chaos that is the image of the world in their poems. Pound glorifies numerous government leaders and sages—Malatesta, Jefferson, Mussolini, Confucius, John Adams—but in a strange way: we never see them with any clarity; they do not stand apart from everything else in the poems; they tend to appear only in fragments—a few words, a partial description, an allusion to something they did—and those fragments blend into fragments from other persons and other ages. They are deeply entwined with the social chaos around them, but still somehow standing above it. Most dramatically, Pound imagines these men as mating with goddesses. He envisions himself that way:

> By prong have I entered these hills:
> That the grass grow from my body,
> That I hear the roots speaking together
> The air is new on my leaf.
>
> *(238)*

In this passage, Pound envisions a sexual act between the poet and the earth. Creation is not then extracting from the soul and expressing oneself freely, but rather implanting oneself inside the world, joining with the earth and the heavens to cause growth that can be distributed to others. Williams too regards the land as the source of inspiration and even the self—in his poem *Paterson*, he imagines "one man—like a city" (7). The equations of the man and the city is emblematized through a waterfall next to the town, a waterfall that washes over the man and also seems to emerge from inside him. Thus, Williams and Pound both present the need for the individual to borrow from the social world and then become the agent shaping that social world. Williams sees that world as the geography and history surrounding one city, a local social world; Pound feels the need to borrow from all sorts of global traditions in order to break out of the hellish American system he feels trapped within. This double vision of the individual as both a part of and apart from the overall socioeconomic system could be called a "macroeconomic" form of poetry, which for Pound and Williams also includes calls for a macroeconomic solution to current social problems.

Louis Zukofsky, in his long poem "A," also traces the horrors of the modern world to economic structure, and he too sees its most extreme result in the distortion or destruction of love. But he also presents love as the method for undoing the horrors of the modern world. In "A-9" he sets up a set of contrasts of the effects of alienating labor and the effects of love: the section sets up two sets of five sonnets each, the first five on the abstraction and alienation of labor due to its turn into exchange, the second on love as the counter to that abstraction. The abstraction is the reduction of the body to money, to gold, so that the physical labor is lost in the object. Love restores the pleasure of labor, restores the sense that what is valuable is the labor, not the product produced.

Section "A-9" of the poem begins by tracing the process of distortion that ruins what the laborer has put into things, turning objects into mere abstractions, making the world a meaningless place:

The measure all use is time congealed labor
In which abstraction things keep no resemblance
To goods created: integrated all hues
Hide their natural use.

(106)

The stanza argues that the turning of labor into abstract value—money—erases the human source and puts all "hues" together, hiding what is natural or usable or human. In direct contrast to that stanza about the way "congealed labor" becomes the measure of everything is another measure, derived from love:

The measure all use who conceive love, labor
Men see, abstraction they feel, the resemblance
(Part, self-created, integrated) all hues
Show to natural use.

(108)

Unlike the way that using "congealed labor" as a measure hides the true "hues" of everything, love provides another measure—labor itself. By viewing labor, "all hues show to natural use."

The second stanzas of the two parallel sections of "A-9" are parallel sonnets, one about economics and one about love creates the effect that love is the antidote to the "congealing" effects of labor. Consider for example the first few lines of these parallel sonnets:

Values in series taking on as real	Such need may see reason, the perfect real
We affect ready gold a steady token	A body ready as love's steady token
Flows in unbroken circuit and induces	Fed thought unbroken as pleasure induces
Our being, wearies of us as ideal	True to thought wearies never its ideal

(106–9)

The first describes illusions created, things "taking on as real" and gold being the "token" that then our being gets weary of us because we have covered up the ideal, hiding it behind the crass existence of money. The second shows a "perfect real" which takes the "body" as the "token" not of "value" but of "love" itself, and thus the "ideal" never wearies. That second stanza goes on to say that thought is not abstracted or separated from the real, because thought derives from the body and is "induced" by "pleasure." So bodily pleasure replaces gold as the experience of the real.

The third set of paralleled stanzas present love as an active antidote to the deadening effects of "congealed labor," the deadening effects of abstraction. The opening lines speak of the contrast between "value" and "love" as the goals of human action:

Hands, heart, not value made us, and of any   Virtue flames value, merriment love—any

(107–9)

The two opening lines both oppose qualities of love and qualities of "value," but they do so in reverse order. The first stanza leads from "hands, heart" to "value" the second from "virtue" and "value" to "love." The first in effect traces the process of distortion, of hands and heart being lost in the turning of everything to abstract value. The second traces the process of undoing that distortion, of merriment overcoming virtue and turning value into love. These lines highlight the notion that one can find merriment in the action of the hands and the heart—the notion that labor can be pleasurable, can be a form of love.

At the end of the two sonnet sequences there are shorter sections about the goal of the poem itself: in the first half about labor:

> ... rhyme now how song's exaction
> Forces abstraction to turn from equated
> Values to labor we have approximated.

In the second half, about love:

> ... rhyme now how song's exaction
> Is your distraction—related is equated,
> How else is love's distance approximated.

In the first version, rhyme, a key element of poetry, forces "abstraction" to turn to "labor," to the real physical processes that can be, in an ideal world, a source of pleasure. And in the second version, rhyme gets us approximately to "love's distance." Abstraction is what labor turns into in the capitalist system, and abstraction is what words turn into when we separate some abstract meaning from the structure of the words, from the "rhyme" and visible arrangement of words. The poem makes us aware of the labor that has gone into constructing the poem, with its intricate structure of paralleling stanzas. The poem aims to help people remember the labor that constructed every object we have, and love is deeply integrated into labor. We tend to pay attention to the residues of labor and love, objects and feelings and memories, and we then take these things as themselves possessing value. So we desire things and thoughts rather than the human actions, bodily experiences—merriment, pleasure, love, labor—which constructed those things. We repeatedly congeal labor and love into abstractions.

Zukofsky implies that the belief that we need to delay pleasure to perform labor has distorted everything. Labor, which we engage in so much of the day, should be a central part of the pleasure, the love, of life. Zukofksy notes that we tend to become "wholly /Dead labor ... Assumed things of labor powers extorted" (107)—instead of seeing ourselves as labor in process, we see ourselves as dead labor, as things that now contain what labor constructed, but that sense that we are fully just "things" not things in process "extorts" the power of labor. The result is "labor speeded while our worth decreases" (107). Everyone works (and writes) faster while having less pleasure in the process because they see no pleasure in the process and instead think that value and pleasure lies only in the final product.

In contrast to this loss of pleasure in labor is the answer in sonnet 2 in the second half, "This sole lee is love: from it offenses / To self or others die, and the extorted / Word" (109). The "extorted Word," which is the word separated from the labor of speaking or writing that word, the word as purely abstract thing, is saved by love. Love is the sole cure for the structures which have turned labor to dead labor, made labor into things which "extort" labor power; love undoes the extortion, and causes all the "offenses" to the self to "die": the self that thinks it exists separate from labor is returned to a self that exists in action, in labor, and it is love that brings the self to that awareness. The mind ends up "Well-sorted by imagination speeded" (109)—an active thing, a laboring entity, sorting and arranging, not merely "being." And as a result of love's restoration of the pleasure of action, of labor, "error ceases" (110).

While A-9 presents the restoration by love as the core of the revolution that will cure the destruction and distortions of labor, A-8 traces a more direct macroeconomic solution to the problems of the current economic system. But Zukofsky's macro-economics starts from a very different place than the macroeconomics of Pound, Williams, or Keynes. Zukofsky paraphrases Marx, saying that "war of the classes / Springs from the means of production" (61). He highlights the suffering of laborers, who exist in a "death-like sleep / Bathed in the fire of labor" producing the "rage of an age" (62). A-8 is all about what "labor" might be able to create. The opening and ending lines both contain the phrase, "labor light lights" (43 and 105). After that set-up, the poem opens with a vision of a chorus "employed" to sing Bach (43). He is imagining a form of communal art, communal creation, a vision of communal labor as enlightenment. Zukofsky states that all labor should be like music, like art, creative:

What distinguishes any worker from the best
of the bees
Is that the worker builds a cell in his head
before he constructs it in wax.
The labor process ends in the creation of a thing.
[...]
And he realizes his own purpose

(61)

However, the economic system has forced workers to do labor that does not let them be expressive, warping the self: "But the less attractive he finds the work in itself, the less it frees him body and mind" (61).

Zukofsky ends "A-8" with several verses suggesting the hope of some revolutionary change to restore the meaning lost in the abstract value. These verses mix together allusions to choral singing as in the opening of A-8, and each verse ends with the phrase from the beginning of A-8, "Labor light lights" (103). The verses at first suggest lovely springtime: "A pretty May note ...we are singing of gardens—March / Days ... May is, Airs wreathe." But then the next-to last verse turns to images of revolutionary violence:

> ... Shirt rags imbue
> A red, free blood. Men ...
> ... the attacker dogs will not stop you.
> *(104)*

The final verse then starts by calling itself "Coda" and mixes the springtime and the violence: "May is red blossom ... blood reads the wounds" (105); it then adds music to the mix before returning to the repeated last line:

> Luteclavicembalo—bullets pursue:
> Labor light lights in earth, in air, on earth.
> *(105)*

Zukofsky is calling for a musical revolution to rip through the mental curtains that block individual expression. The ending is a dream, but in the middle of the poem Zukofsky provides some indication of the economic change he believes is necessary. This analysis starts by suggesting that the turning of individual labor into abstract value is part of an increasing centralization of power, which Zukofsky equates to the rise of corporations:

> The old maxim of the common law,
> That corporations have no souls.
> Corporate life and corporate power
> [...]
> It tends always to development.
> Always to consolidation.
> Even threatens the central government.
> *(76)*

The sense that the corporations stand against the central government could, Zukofsky fears, lead workers to turn to an authoritarian government as the answer to corporate power:

The people . . seek protection against it . .
Look for such protection, significantly enough,
Not to their . . legislature,
But to the single autocratic feature
. . of government, -
The veto by . . Executive . . this . .
Something more imperial than republican.
[...]
And put Caesarism
At once in control of the corporation and of the
proletariat.

(77)

When Zukofsky tries to imagine a counter to the rise of an imperial—or fascist—government, he does not simply turn to the possibility of the end of government after the dictatorship of the proletariat, as his quotes from Marx might
suggest; rather, what he says sounds much more like the prescriptions of Douglas
and Keynes:

It is not by the consolidation
Or concentration of powers (corporate bodies)
But by their distribution,
That good government is effected.

(90)

Zukofsky presents a macroeconomic solution: that the government can counter the consolidation and concentration hurting the masses by creating a new
distribution of powers, allowing all who labor to have power and not merely be
commanded by others.

Not all modernist writers end up suggesting macroeconomic policies as Pound,
Williams, and Zukofsky do. Gertrude Stein resolutely opposes the very idea of
the government distributing money or trying to adjust the economic system, but
by examining how she includes such opposition in her art, we can nonetheless
gain a sense of some ways that modernist techniques are tied to a macroeconomic
vision. In a work entitled *The Geographical History of America Or the Relation of
Human Nature to the Human Mind*, Stein asks, "Is Franklin Roosevelt trying to get
rid of money," and goes on to say, "it would be interesting to try to get rid of
money by destroying it" (189). Luke Carson provides an explanation of what
Stein might mean: "To destroy money, as Stein thought Roosevelt was trying to
do, is to destroy the social bonds constituted by the deferred and disavowed debt"
(71). Carson argues that for Stein, money has its meaning from the bonds it creates by having people realize they are indebted to others; that they owe and are
owed and so feel tied to others. Money is the glue that ties all the intersecting

debts of one person to another specific person. Money thus carries with it a sense of people who can benefit from each other, and that is its core meaning. If instead money derives from the government, from that abstract and non-individual institutional source, it loses its meaning. Hence Stein writes, "Perhaps Franklin Roosevelt wants to get rid of money by making it a thing having no meaning" (194). Stein similarly regards taxes as draining away the meaning of money, as she writes in another work:

> everybody who earns it and spends it every day in order to live knows that money is money, anybody who votes it to be gathered in as taxes knows money is not money. That is what makes everybody go crazy.
>
> *(Stein,* How Writing*: 106)*

The public provision of money wrecks the basis of private life and thus the basis of thought: it makes everybody go crazy.

Stein quite strongly disagrees with Pound and Williams on the role of money from the government, but she shares with them the sense that economic structures have a crucial role in supporting—or distorting—individual thinking. And like Pound and Williams, Stein suggests that the distortion of economics wrecks love. Throughout the *Geographical History* she presents a strong parallel between feelings about money and feelings about love: "Now anybody who loves money and anybody who loves loves money anybody who loves loves to have money" (20). Money allows individuals to show their love by creating private lives. But the government providing more money from an institution destroys this connection of money to love: "More money is not what money is. / Do you see its connection with romanticism" (185). Money and romanticism are inherently connected together, immediately calling each other up; they imply each other like the relationship of a question and an answer; as she puts it, "question and answer is like romanticism and money" (202).

The Geographical History of America has a second half to its title: *Or the Relation of Human Nature to the Human Mind.* Her examination of American history from a "geographical" point of view aims to distinguish between human nature and human mind, and mostly she is seeking to understand how human mind transcends human nature. Human nature is what is there already in humans, while human mind is undefined, unlimited, allowing desire to operate—and desire is what I have argued is central to the Macroeconomic sense of the source of value. The equation of money and romanticism is repeatedly invoked in Stein's work as two crucial elements which create the openness and undefined quality of the human mind: "What is money and what is romanticism it is not like human nature because it is not finishing it is not like a master-piece because it has no existing" (194).

Neither existing nor finishing, money and romanticism are equally ethereal, unconfined by either space or time: "money and romanticism they do not end and they do not begin but they do not exist and therefor they are not anything"

(195). But these nonexisting nothings actually provide something for humans: "scenery." "It is an obligation to have money connect itself with romanticism because that too is not human nature but scenery" (184). For a playwright, scenery is what sits behind humans acting, what allows action to become meaningful, to go beyond "human nature." As she epigrammatically puts it:

> Money one.
> Romanticism one.
> Scenery one.
> Human nature not one.
> *(186)*

Understanding the physical world entirely as "scenery" helps explain why Stein focuses on the "geographical": not because geography is determinate, but because it is the backdrop, the scenery, for human minds to write and act and create things that have never existed.

Writing books and poems and plays is a way to engage in romanticism and a way to engage with money in a liberating way, a way that expands what there is in the world. Hence Stein equates money and words:

> Money is what words are.
> Words are what money is.
> Is money what words are
> Are words what money is.
> *(165)*

Money and words both expand the value found in things, adding value by allowing those things to have roles in the interactions of individuals. In another of her books, *Useful Knowledge*, Stein creates in an "advertisement" for the book that is placed before the text an unusual description of American economic practices:

> in America the best material is used in the cheapest things ... it is really that it has come to be a romantic thing that has been so added to the history of living for a whole generation ... Romance is everything and the very best material should make the cheapest thing is making into living the romance of human being.

As an advertisement for the book, Stein is suggesting that the "best materials" are in her book, but the book ends up one of the "cheapest things." Books can carry inside them extremely valuable "materials" but by making the books relatively cheap, those materials can be used by many people in many different relationships: the "romantic" value of cheap things is due to their ability to create relationships among people. Her vision of using things—money, words—to unite people is her vision of America. As she puts it in the advertisement,

> This is the American something that makes romance everything. And romance is Useful Knowledge. Useful knowledge is pleasant and therefore it is very much to be enjoyed. Where there are many Americans and there are there is a great deal of pleasure in knowing.

Spreading pleasure is one of the goals of her art, and of economics in general.

Stein's rejection of Franklin Roosevelt's monetary policies and her general rejection of taxes seek to release money from institutions such as the government so that they can become widespread and cheaply distributed. However, she cannot just ignore the institutions and history that have made money something to hoard or something to rely on the government for. Stein dreams of freeing humans from the sense of being shaped and controlled by money and words and government. So she writes a presentation of the vast system to counter the effects of that very system which has destroyed meaning, and hence she writes *The Geographical History of America*. This is a complex, modernist text, mixing historical passages from many eras with small scenes of people identified by first names that almost seem to float unmoored through history. The text shows that Stein cannot simply ignore the macroeconomic view and present visions of the social bonds she wishes existed: rather, she has to create a vision of the macroeconomic system in order to break it.

Even modernist works that appeared before the Great Depression were driven to present impersonal, systemic, "macro" views of the world. *The Waste Land* is almost completely a vision of spaces, geographies, and buildings that largely interfere with or destroy individual thought and feeling. The poem is usually treated as referring to the death of culture, of religion and mythology, having little to do with economics, yet a number of critics have connected Eliot's images of a destroyed landscape to his reading of one of Keynes' essays, *The Economic Consequences of the Peace*. Tom Paulin argues that

> Any account of the poem has to face the fact and take on board the proven historical fact that Eliot read and digested John Maynard Keynes's *The Economic Consequences of the Peace*, his great attack on the Versailles Peace Treaty of 1919 … Keynes's vision of a derelict Europe, the hot, dry atmosphere in the chamber where the negotiations were conducted, the destruction of industry and the exhaustion of the soil all feed Eliot's vision of the European wasteland.
>
> *(para. 13–14)*

Eleanor Cook agrees that Keynes' essay "entered into the making of *The Waste Land*," and also establishes that Eliot was acutely aware of Keynes' essay because he was Lloyd's representative, "in charge of settling all the pre-war Debts between the Bank and the Germans," and he wrote his mother in 1929 that he was kept busy "trying to elucidate knotty points in that appalling document the Peace Treaty" (347–8). Michael Levenson claims even more broadly that "More than Jessie Weston, more than *The Golden Bough, The Economic Consequences of the Peace* anticipates the ghostly modality of *The Waste Land*, the spectral insight into the fictions of modernity" (3). And Lawrence Rainey states that Eliot was a "firm believer in the thesis articulated by Maynard Keynes in *The Economic Consequences of the Peace*" and notes that Eliot "recommended Keynes' book warmly to his brother in early 1920" (205 note 11).

The influence of Keynes' essay on the composing of *The Waste Land* suggests that economics plays a significant role in the poem itself. One section, "Death by Water," is rather directly about those who control the money in society. That section addresses those who think of "the profit and loss" and specifies them as "Gentile or Jew" (46). The juxtaposition of Jews to profit and loss hints at anti-Semitic ideas, but by including Gentiles along with Jews in this warning, Eliot suggests that the problem includes all who are involved with profit and loss. The section of the poem implies that those who think of profit and loss are in danger of death by water, in particular due to the way they "turn the wheel and look to windward" (47). It seems then that the poem associates thinking of profit and loss with trying to control a ship across waters—making this section seem to be about those who are directing the economic ship of state, warning that their directions are leading to death by water. This section thus hints at governmental policies that lead to people piling up money, in a sense drowning in it. Such policies fail to see Keynes' central argument, that money needs to be distributed widely to avoid economic crises such as the one Keynes predicted would happen in Germany if the peace terms were enforced. Keynes recommended that the recovery of Europe, including Germany, after World War I required a vast loan, probably from the U.S., to avoid a deep depression. Money needed to be distributed by the victors, not taken away from the losers of the war, as the Peace Treaty required.

Toward the end of the poem another part that alludes directly to economic issues is the explanation of the commands of the God of Thunder. The first command, "Datta" or "give", is explained quite explicity as a rejection of saving: the poem says that what allows people to "exist" is not found "under seals broken by the lean solicitor" (49): in other words, an individual life does not exist or find its value in the wealth that has been accumulated; rather, the poem asks "what have we given" in a moment of "surrender which an age of prudence can never retract" (49). The rejection of an entire "age of prudence" seems very much what Keynes was calling for in all his writings, the rejection of the age of Adam Smith in which wealth needed to be stored up and desires restrained, with no surrendering to them.

Keynes seeks to unleash desires that have been held in check, and Eliot's poem begins with a vision of such an action. April releases "Memory and desire" which were buried under the "forgetful snow" of a long winter (37). That opening can be understood as breaking free of an age of prudence when desire remained buried. The poem envisions a dead land, but with repeated images of the possibility of something growing from it. It is considering how to bring back to life a land as destroyed as Europe after World War I—and it suggests that releasing desire, ending an age of prudence and giving instead of saving, is the way to start that process.

The last command of the God of Thunder returns to the metaphor of directing a ship, the metaphor connected to "those who think of profit and loss" in the "Death by Water" section. The God commands "Damyatta" or "control" (49). To explain that command, Eliot writes,

> The Boat responded
> Gaily, to the hand expert with sail and oar
> The sea was calm, you heart would have responded
> Gaily, when invited, beating obedient
> To controlling hands.
>
> *(49–50)*

Here is another boat being controlled, but in this part of the poem the boat is moving "gaily" and the sea is calm; there is no fear of drowning. And here the control of the boat is equated to the control of hearts. This is very much what Keynes says government stimuli do: acting rather magically on the animal spirits inside individuals, on their beating hearts, on demand, which is composed of the desires of everyone. During economic depressions, people repress their desires, stopping their hearts from beating gaily, and government stimuli can get those hearts beating again and so move the ship of state forward across the waters of the economy.

It may be difficult to believe that *The Waste Land* is really very much about a need for a changed economic policy. But if we return to C.H. Douglas's claim that the "cultural inheritance" is the most important element in producing value, we can certainly see that *The Waste Land* is built by mining that cultural inheritance, in particular seeking out valuable materials that have been buried in libraries and expensive houses but are not currently circulating. The stony rubbish that needs rain to grow is both dead vegetation and, as the poem puts it, a "heap of broken images" (38), fragments of art. To bring art as well as the economy back to life requires a stimulus, a source of sustenance, a source of refreshing liquid (or should we say "liquidity"?) for a dried-up world. This poem is in effect trying to start a Keynesian stimulus, bringing into view potential cultural treasures buried in libraries and blocked from current circulation.

The poem of course does not seek to circulate those treasures to the masses, as Keynes sought to circulate government money. Eliot is seeking rather to restore buried parts of the cultural inheritance to an elite, those who Eliot felt could guide the ship of state. Culture locked away is as useless and valueless as money buried in the ground. The elite is failing to see that culture, like money, is not valuable when stored away, but rather produces value when circulated. Eliot focuses on obscure references to give even those who are well-educated literary scholars the experience of discovering hidden, buried sources of value that could be released. We who study the poem are tasked with uncovering these values, tasked to find the blocked values that could restore the Waste Land of modern culture. But this poem does not attempt to reach minds at every level, perhaps because it was written at a moment when Eliot felt there was no such possibility. At the end of World War I, the cultures of Europe may have seemed isolated and disconnected, like the parts of the poem itself; nothing was circulating with anything else. The poem is in a sense a vision of the total absence of an economy, a horror beyond even Keynes' imagining.

Another modernist who saw in war the image of the horrors of the economic system is Virginia Woolf, in *Three Guineas*. The essay aims at ending war, but she stridently refuses to join any anti-war movement, or indeed any movement for any cause. What she proposes instead as a way to help end war is to change the way money is distributed: the title refers to three guineas that she gives to three organizations, essentially without specifying what should happen with that money. It is the sheer change of the distribution of money that she proposes could possibly change unconscious attitudes sufficiently to end war. And the crucial reason that a change in economics can change war is that the change she proposes would change the very nature of genders, what men and women think they are . Woolf implies that love itself is distorted by the economic system, making it lead to just one kind of marriage and family. The channeling of all desires into the heterosexual family is at the core of what she says leads to war, and the process is deeply economic. Suggesting that economic redistribution across multiple social structures could change human psychology, allowing new forms of love, is very much a macroeconomic theory.

Woolf's essay presents as the cause of war the way men are trained. First she focuses on the fact that considerable money is spent educating men, making them feel dominant over the women in their lives, and causing them to join in the economic dance of society: "Here we go round the mulberry tree, the mulberry tree, the mulberry tree. Give it all to me, give it all to me, all to me. Three hundred millions spent upon war" (59). Then she argues that men are further distorted by the professions they enter:

> If people are highly successful in the professions they lose their senses ... Money making becomes so important that they work by night as well as by day. Health goes. And so competitive do they become that they will not share their work with others though they have more than they can do themselves. What then remains of a human being who has lost sight, and sound, and sense of proportion? Only a cripple in a cave.

> That of course is a figure, and fanciful; but that it has some connection
> with figures that are statistical and not fanciful—with the three hundred
> millions spent upon arms—seems possible.
>
> *(72)*

The term "cripple" denigrates disabled persons, and Woolf means to denigrate
those she is describing, so we might wish she had chosen a different word, but
ironically Woolf is using this term to describe the most successful persons. And
what she outlines is a cure for this disabling disease brought about by the current
structure of gender. Her description of what happens to the most successful persons
mirrors what Keynes and Pound argue, that love of money destroys sensual
experience, but she draws a further conclusion: that it leads to violence, to war.
Woolf's solution is to give "one guinea" to women's colleges and "one guinea" to
an organization devoted to helping women enter the professions. She tries to
describe how colleges and professions should change so they don't promote war,
but she repeatedly falls back on recognizing that all she can really do is give money
with the purpose of bringing women into those institutions in the hope that
women will keep the values they have and not be transformed into the kind of
person those institutions make men into. It is the redistribution of money across
society—a macroeconomic change—that, she implies, would ultimately end war.

Woolf further concludes that the economy devoted to male dominance leads
to an unconscious structure in men, which she calls an "infantile fixation" (127).
But unlike Freudian theories of "infantile fixations," she believes this one can be
changed: "must we not, and do we not, change this unalterable nature?"(140)
The entire essay is devoted to saying that the redistribution of money can alter
even the "infantile fixations" of men. The effect on women she imagines as
equally drastic: "It was the lady who could not earn money; therefore the lady
must be killed" (133). Woolf herself was raised to be a lady, but she found ways
to make money—by writing and by running the Hogarth Press— so she killed
the "lady" she had been. She writes as a person who has been reconstructed by a
change in economics, which is just what she hopes her redistribution of money
could accomplish for everyone.

Woolf presents a vision of the change necessary to allow a woman to have a
career in her most personal novel, *To the Lighthouse*. What the novel traces is the
way the Ramsay family, which seems based on Woolf's childhood family, is
situated in the surrounding socioeconomic world, and in particular the effect of
that overall structure upon an artist visiting the family, Lily Briscoe. While Mrs.
Ramsay orchestrates an elegant dinner party, Lily hears underneath it all, "women
can't write, women can't paint" (130).

Mrs. Ramsay herself has an impossible dream, that "she would cease to be a
private woman ... and become what ... she greatly admired, an investigator,
elucidating the social problem" (18). But Mrs. Ramsay is trapped in a marriage
that drains her of the energy she could have turned to social causes. The sense of

her being drained is presented in a scene when Mr. Ramsay is upset, feeling that he is a failure in his profession, and Mrs. Ramsay comforts him simply by looking up at him as his face pleads for help. The text then describes metaphorically the exchange between them:

> Mrs. Ramsay, seemed to raise herself with an effort, and at once to pour erect into the air a rain of energy, a column of spray ... and into this delicious fecundity, this fountain and spray of life, the fatal sterility of the male plunged itself, like a beak of brass, barren and bare ... all her strength flaring up to be drunk and quenched by the beak of brass, the arid scimitar of the male, which smote mercilessly, again and again, demanding sympathy.
>
> (58–9)

The description is full of sexual imagery, but this is a thoroughly destructive sexuality. Mrs. Ramsay offers a "rain of energy" which could be "delicious": a potentially pleasurable encounter between two people. But what drinks up her delicious rain is a "a beak of brass, barren and bare" which "smote mercilessly." Pleasure offered is turned into a warlike act of violence. The metaphoric description encapsulates what *Three Guineas* argues, that the pleasures of the senses are destroyed in men by the structure of the normative family, and in particular by the way it is used to support male success in professions.

The novel traces a change in the socioeconomic order which allows a woman, Lily Briscoe, to not get trapped in such a draining marriage and instead have something like her own profession. As Woolf argued in *Three Guineas*, to bring about such a change the lady who cannot earn money must be killed, so the death of Mrs. Ramsay is necessary to alter the environment of the house enough to allow Lily to create her painting. Mrs. Ramsay's death is coincident with World War I, and while the war lasts the family does not return to this vacation home, but immediately after the war, working-class men and women enter the house to repair and essentially reconstruct it; thus, when Lily and the remaining Ramsay family members return, they are in a new environment. Instead of a dinner party overseen by Mrs. Ramsay, the climax of this section is a trip by the family members out to the lighthouse in a boat skippered by a working-class youth. The upper-class family is no longer envisioned as an enclosed structure supporting itself, but rather as part of the entire economic structure. And Lily finds herself in a new kind of space, an open field, looking at the Ramsays in the boat and at the reconstructed house with no one in it. She is thus in the position Woolf advocates at the end of *Three Guineas*: outside all particular social organizations and yet still part of the overall human world. From her outside position she finds she can finish her painting, which involves a revised structure of gender roles and of love. She turns the Ramsay family into an abstract triangle and concludes that "she would move the tree to the middle, and need never marry anybody" (262). Escaping the draining role of a married woman allows Lily to pour her soul into art and to experience and express strong desires. As Lily thinks about her painting, she feels she "wants and not to have Mrs. R." and feels it so intensely that she is crying as she paints. This intense desire could be seen as homosexual or as a desire to share with Mrs. Ramsay parts of the two of them that were repressed in the pre-war world. The novel ends with words that seem both Lily's and Woolf's: "I have had my vision" (310)—a vision of a change in economics and in love which frees women (and by implication men as well) to release the "rain" of emotions within them without being beaten down by "arid scimitars." Passions do not all lead to war in this new vision.

In a later novel, *Orlando,* Woolf imagines the historical processes that have allowed her and others to imagine different forms of love and different ways of living besides traditional marriage, and as in *Three Guineas,* those changes are connected to escaping the centrality of war to the entire system. The book begins in the Elizabethan era, where Woolf creates a male character, Orlando, who is trained for war but wishes he could be a writer: he can slash with a sword but he cannot write well at all. This character then lives through the ages up to the present, while aging just some 36 years, and along the way changes sex. That change is seen as releasing a part of the character that was always present. The narration states quite directly,

> In every human being a vacillation from one sex to the other takes place, and often it is only the clothes that keep the male or female likeness, while underneath the sex is the very opposite of what it is above.
>
> *(189)*

The violence presented in *To the Lighthouse* between male and female in the relations of Mr. and Mrs. Ramsay is thus a violence within everyone, created by the surrounding social order that demands part of oneself—the "other sex" besides the one assigned by the social order—be violently suppressed.

Freed from being restricted to one sex, Orlando "enjoyed the love of both sexes equally" (221). Her freedom to do so is crucial to her finally being able to write well. Woolf argues in *A Room of One's Own* that all great writers rely on both sexes within them. So Orlando can finally complete the work begun four hundred years before. But she is at the same time unable to maintain her noble estate because women can't inherit property. Like Lily Briscoe, Orlando is a character freed of the ties that turn emotions into warlike acts, freed to think for herself (i.e. write), but she has very limited power to change anything else because she has no economic base. She chooses then to marry a man, Shelmerdine Bonthorp, but they do not remain divided as two separate sexes. They surprise each other, so that Shelmerdine asks Orlando, "'Are you positive you aren't a man?' ... [and] she would echo, 'Can it be possible you're not a woman?' and then they must put it to the proof without more ado" (258). They can prove their separate sexes, but each one still contains elements of both sexes. And even though Shelmerdine transcends masculinity, he still goes off to engage in warlike acts. The novel thus quite precisely distinguishes between two elements that are central to the argument in *Three Guineas*: the ability of persons to transcend their assigned sex and the ability to end war. In *Orlando*, the first is represented as somewhat possible, due to historical developments, but the second depends on economic change to significantly alter the way professions and educational institutions and houses function. Orlando cannot own her house, cannot really have her own income, and Shelmerdine cannot quite give up turning to warlike acts.

Another of Woolf's novels, *The Waves*, presents quite powerfully but in somewhat obscure ways the deep, unconscious connections between violence and the gender structure of education and professions. The novel is divided into two parts: descriptions of natural settings that progress through a day and interior monologues of six characters who age through their life. The descriptions of natural settings have come to be called "interludes," but they are not merely breaks in the interior monologues: rather, they are metaphoric representations of the unconscious forms created within the characters by the social structures they are placed within. The characters start as six intertwined persons, but then in two chapters they are divided into gender groups, first going to different kinds of secondary school, then the males going to college in one chapter and entering professions in the next, while the females go back to their homes or enter into relationships. In these chapters about education, the gender division is emphasized by the text putting all the monologues of one gender together, separated by white space from the monologues of the other gender. And in the interludes when the characters go to school, there are images of violence that mirror the gender violence presented in the scene of Mrs. Ramsay supporting her husband's profession. Following the first section of gender-divided schools, the interlude has a bird which "accurately alighting, spiked the soft monstrous body of the defenceless worm, pecked again and yet again, and left it to fester" (74). And there is a whole area under the plants where

> yellow excretions were exuded by slugs and now and again an amorphous body with a head at either end swayed slowly from side to side. The gold-eyed birds ... observed that purulence ... Now and then they plunged the tips of their beaks savagely into the sticky mixture.
>
> *(75)*

These metaphoric images suggest that some creatures are allowed into the air while others are forced to live in the dark, and those in the air then violently take what they need to survive from those in the dark. These images reappear in the interludes leading into sections where the men are elevated into higher levels of education and professions, while the women are pressed into homes with no means of rising up the higher rungs of the social order. I suggest that these images of birds plunging their beaks into the bodies of worms are visions akin to what

Woolf used to metaphorically represent what Mr. Ramsay extracted from Mrs. Ramsay, destroying the "delicious rain" she flung up to soothe him and support his sense of himself as a successful professional. Both novels thus imply what *Three Guineas* explicates, that men gain the power to succeed in professions by feeding on the repression of women.

In *The Waves*, the beaks are of birds, not directly identified as male, and what they are plunging into is "purulence" and horrible rotting, not "delicious fecundity" as in *To the Lighthouse*. I suggest that in *The Waves* we are seeing the mutual destruction of young males and females by the educational experiences they have and by the economic distinctions created by those educational differences. We hear extensively of the females feeling nearly destroyed by their school experience: Rhoda is repeatedly terrified that she has "no face" and retreats to images of hidden lakes; Susan feels a hard knot forming in her and hates school; Jinny survives by repeatedly seeking out male companions, largely ignoring her schooling. The school system for young women removes the very basis of identity for Rhoda, causes pain to Susan, and drives Jinny to rely on male companions for a sense of her own power. All three are turned into supports for male dominance, and that process involves draining something from those women. The males feel themselves growing larger, rising into positions with status, becoming important writers, bankers, or professors. I suggest that the division in the interlude into those who fly and those who are rotting in the dark is the distinction between male and female, and that structure is deeply tied to an economics of extraction of value from one group and possession of that value by another group. Woolf's imagery provides a way of understanding how such an economic distinction between groups is deeply tied to violence. For one group to profit while another is purely supportive of the profiting group is to be trained to violently remove what one wants or needs from others.

The metaphoric violence that the interludes suggest separates men and women turns to international violence following the education of the characters. The most idealized male, Percival, becomes a military figure, and all the characters gather to send him off to India. In doing so they feel like "soldiers in the presence of their captain" (123). They imagine that Percival will succeed gloriously "by using the violent language that is natural to him" (136). As they gather round Percival, celebrating him and his mission, Rhoda says, "There is a dancing and drumming, like the dancing and the drumming of naked men with assegais" (140). These elegant upper-class characters are getting ready to kill. The sharp beaks of the metaphoric birds in earlier interludes have become metaphoric spears. The novel thus traces the way that the system that sends men into schools and professions eventually turns those men into soldiers ready to conquer foreign others.

But there is a turn in the plot that hints at a different future: in India, in an absurd gesture, Percival dies, falling off a horse. The English effort to violently control India fails, and then something new appears in the subsequent interludes: there are domestic, non-threatening scenes of non-English parts of the world. There is a "smooth gilt mosque ... and the long-breasted, white-haired women who knelt in the river bed beating wrinkled cloths upon stones" (148). If, as I have argued, the interludes represent the unconscious structures of thought of the characters, then their unconscious world has expanded beyond their own country, and the violence that was bred into them, the violence first directed against women and then directed against the "Orient," has been replaced by images of female others. The violence that appeared repeatedly in earlier interludes is gone.

The interlude leading into the very last chapter of the book ends with an image of foreign females, "girls sitting on verandahs" in snowy mountains, the last thing seen before darkness covers everything (237). This final chapter leads to a change in the arrangement of voices in the novel: it is entirely spoken by Bernard, but he says that he cannot tell himself apart from any of the other characters. He is thus on the way to becoming an androgynous voice, a new possibility that could be an answer to the unfair division of male and female that Woolf seeks to end. However, he cannot fully move into a new vision of himself, possibly because that would mean the death of the self he has been shaped to be by the socioeconomic structures of England. At the very end he imagines himself going to war against death, imagining himself becoming Percival, able to "ride with my spear couched and my hair flying back like a young man, like Percival's, when he galloped in India" (297). The image reads as a return of the earlier images of spear-like violence against all that is dark and hidden inside the English domestic world—a repeat of the effort of the dominant group to keep to itself all that is valuable and remove it from lesser groups. After Bernard imagines himself in that violent posture, the book ends with a single sentence interlude, "The waves broke on the shore" (297). A liquid medium is left, and it is unclear if that represents the end of all structure or a hint of something that could be different in the future, a social order where no group is empowered to extract value from other groups, where all value is fluidly circulating and flowing across all social differences. I suggest it is a vision of unbounded liquidity, a flow crossing all parts of the social order and all countries of the world. It is a vision of a change in the distribution of opportunities, of wealth, a change in desires and the ability to satisfy desires. The previous system that channeled desires into conquest (of one gender by another, of one nation by another) is potentially going to be replaced with the pleasure of allowing waves of sensation and possibility and value to flow over and into many different people in many different ways.

The novel that is usually considered most closely connected to *Three Guineas* is *The Years*, because Woolf set out to write the two works as one intertwined novel-essay structure. But she eventually separated the two. *The Years* retraces the period from 1880 through World War I to the 1930s, showing "daughters of gentlemen" moving out of their restricted roles, fighting for rights and the vote and entering professions. The book traces moments when the economic and social structures separating genders and classes are dissolving, creating temporary visions of some alternative possibility such as she delineates in *Three Guineas*. The most powerful such moment in the book occurs when many family members gather in a bomb shelter during a raid, where the common threat to everyone breaks through usual distinctions among groups. As Paul Saint-Amour puts it: "The lattice of resilient social ties necessary to transcend war can only be formed in war, when sexual mores and partitions of nation, class and generation lose their 'surface hardness' enough to permit new combinations to form" (124). But though the possibility of new combinations floats behind that scene, the book ends with divisions still in place. In the final scene, the main characters meet a group of children whom they ask to "sing a song for sixpence" (429). The children sing, and "Not a word was recognizable." Woolf includes verses that are in no language (e.g. "Fanno to par, etto to mar"). After they sing, the narrator says, "there was something horrible in the noise they made. It was so shrill, so discordant, and so meaningless" (430). The listeners speculate that it is due to the children's "cockney accent" and what "they teach 'em in school" (430). As in *Three Guineas*, the educational system has separated society into those who rule and those who cannot even be heard or understood by those who rule. This scene is about class differences, rather than gender differences, yet it highlights the same problems that *Three Guineas* says lead to war: relationships of power and money and what can be expressed by whom

At the same time, Eleanor, the eldest member of the family listening, says that the children's song is "beautiful" (431). Eleanor is the character most identified with searching for some solution to war, and she joins a man, Brown, who is homosexual, in trying to envision some new psychology for humans: "The soul— the whole being ... It wishes to expand, to adventure, to form—new combinations" (296). She has a close but non-sexual relationship with Brown, and I suggest that what they share is a step out of the social order that defines marriage and war as the ultimate results of the norms of love. She feels transformed by Brown's words: "He seemed to have released something in her ... a new space of time ... new powers, something unknown within her" (296–7). The book never defines this new possibility; it remains a vague beauty on the horizon, like the final lines in the novel: "The sun had risen, and the sky above the houses wore an air of extraordinary beauty, simplicity and peace" (434). The peace that Woolf seeks in *Three Guineas* is an ethereal vision, still in the sky, unable to settle on earth because of economic divisions that create the drive for power and the inability of those in power to hear or understand what those excluded say or feel.

In all of these novels, Woolf extends Keynes' analysis of the effects of maldistribution of money, suggesting that those with wealth and power have extracted it, violently, from others in society, and so are unconsciously trained in attitudes that inevitably lead to war. And that extraction is also a distortion of sexuality, of desire, the draining of women to make men successful. Woolf's novels and her essay on ending war all trace the intersection of economics and desires and seek an alternative that allows pleasures without their being used to support the economic success of individuals or of the entire country. Woolf dreams of a far more extensive change in the distribution of money and in the

ر

structures of desire than Keynes does, but the core justification of that change is
the same for all the modernists I have discussed—namely, that the way money is
corralled into certain parts of the economic system is distorting and corrupting the
desires of everyone.

References

Adorno, Theodor. *Aesthetic Theory*. Tr. Robert Hullot-Kentor. New York: Continuum, 2002.

Amariglio, Jack and David F. Ruccio. *Postmodern Moments in Modern Economics*. Princeton, NJ: Princeton University Press, 2003.

Bederman, Gail, *Manliness and Civilization: A Cultural History of Gender and Race in the United States, 1880–1917*. Chicago: University of Chicago Press, 1995.

Lawrence Birken, *Consuming Desire: Sexual Science and the Emergence of a Culture of Abundance, 1871–1914*. Ithaca, NY: Cornell University Press, 1988.

Carson, Luke. *Consumption and Depression in Louis Zukofsky, Gertrude Stein, and Ezra Pound*. Basingstoke, UK: Macmillan, 1999.

Cook, Eleanor. "T. S. Eliot and the Carthaginian Peace." *ELH*, vol. 46, no. 2, 1979, pp. 341–355.

Dixon, Thomas, *From Passions to Emotions: The Creation of a Secular Psychological Category*. Cambridge: Cambridge University Press, 2003.

Douglas, C.H. *Social Credit*. New York: Norton, 1933.

Eliot, T.S. "A Commentary." *Criterion*, vol. 12, July, 1933, pp. 644–646.

Eliot, T.S. *The Complete Poems and Plays, 1909–1950*. New York: Harcourt, Brace & World, 1971.

Eliot, T.S. *Selected Prose of T. S. Eliot*. Ed. Frank Kermode. New York: Harcourt Brace Jovanovich, 1975, pp. 175–178.

Esty, Jed. *A Shrinking Island: Modernism and National Culture in England*. Princeton, NJ: Princeton University Press, 2004.

Francis, Thomas, "Keynes and Macroeconomics after 70 Years." *Philosophy of the Social Sciences*, vol. 41, no. 2, 2011, pp. 269–277.

Gordon, Craig A. *Literary Modernism, Bioscience and Community in Early Twentieth-Century Britain*. New York: Palgrave Macmillan, 2007.

Graham, T. Austin. *The Great American Songbooks: Musical Texts, Modernism, and the Value of Popular Culture*. New York: Oxford University Press, 2013.

Gross, Charles G. *Brain, Vision, Memory: Tales in the History of Neuroscience*. Cambridge, MA: MIT Press, 1998.

Joyce, James, *Ulysses*. New York: The Modern Library, 1961.

Katz, Tamar. "Modernism, Subjectivity and Narrative Form: Abstraction in *The Waves*." *Narrative*, vol. 3, no. 3, 1995, pp. 232–251.

Kershner, R. Brandon. *The Culture of Joyce's Ulysses*. New York: Palgrave Macmillan, 2010.

Keynes, John Maynard. *The Economic Consequences of the Peace*. London: Harcourt, Brace & Howe, 1920.

Keynes, John Maynard. "Economic Possibilities for our Grandchildren." *Nation and Athenaeum*, vol. 48, October, 1930. In *Revisiting Keynes: Economic Possibilities for Our Grandchildren*, ed. Lorenzo Pecchi, and Gustavo Piga, MIT Press, 2008. Online at http://ebookcentral.proquest.com/lib/brynmawr/detail.action?docID=3338920.

Keynes, John Maynard. *A Treatise on Money*. New York: Harcourt, Brace & Co., 1930.

Keynes, John Maynard. *Essays in Persuasion*. New York: W.W. Norton, 1963.

Keynes, John Maynard. *The General Theory of Unemployment, Interest and Money*. New York: Harcourt, 1964.

Koppl, Roger. "Retrospective: Animal Spirits." *Journal of Economic Perspectives*, vol. 5, no. 3, 1991, pp. 203–210.

Lewis, Pericles. *Modernism, Nationalism and the Novel*. Cambridge: Cambridge University Press, 2000.

Lukács, György. *The Meaning of Contemporary Realism*. London: Merlin Press, 1962.

Marsh, Alec. *Money and Modernity: Pound, Williams and the Spirit of Jefferson*. Tuscaloosa: University of Alabama Press, 1998.

Marx, Karl and Karl Engels. *Marx and Engels: Basic Writings on Politics and Philosophy*. Ed. Lewis S. Feuer. Garden City, New York: Anchor Books, 1959.

Mini, Piero. *Keynes, Bloomsbury and the General Theory*. London: Palgrave Macmillan, 1991.

Moggridge, D.E. "Correspondence." *Journal of Economic Perspectives*, vol. 6, no. 3, 1992, p. 208.

Moretti, Franco. *Signs Taken for Wonders: Essays in the Sociology of Literary Forms*. Tr. Susan Fischer, David Forgacs, and David Miller. New York: Verso, 1988.

Nickels, Joel. *The Poetry of the Possible: Spontaneity, Modernism and the Multitude*. Minneapolis, MN: University of Minnesota Press, 2012.

Osteen, Mark. *The Economy of Ulysses: Making Both Ends Meet*. Syracuse, NY: Syracuse University Press, 1995.

Paulin, Tom. "Review: All at sea in the Waste Land." *The Observer*, January 7, 2007.

Pound, Ezra. *The Cantos of Ezra Pound*. New York: New Directions, 1986.

Pound, Ezra. *Selected Prose, 1909–1965*. Ed. William Cookson. New York: New Directions, 1973.

Pound, Ezra. *The Spirit of Romance*. New York: New Directions, 2005.

Rainey, Lawrence, Ed. *The Annotated Wasteland with Eliot's Contemporary Prose*. New Haven, CT: Yale University Press, 2006.

Saint-Amour, Paul. *Tense Future: Modernism, Total War, Encyclopedic Form*. Oxford: Oxford University Press, 2015.

Segel, Harold. *Body Ascendant: Modernism and the Physical Imperative*. Baltimore, MD: Johns Hopkins University Press, 1998.

Sieburth, Richard. "In Pound We Trust: The Economy of Poetry/The Poetry of Economics." *Critical Inquiry*, vol. 14, no. 1, 1987, pp. 142–172.

Smith, Roger, *Inhibition: History and Meaning in the Sciences of Mind and Brain*. Berkeley, CA: University of California Press, 1992.

Stein, Gertrude. *Useful Knowledge*. London: John Lane. The Bodley Head, 1928.

Stein, Gertrude. *The Geographical History of America Or the Relation of Human Nature to the Human Mind*. New York: Random House, 1936.

Stein, Gertrude. *How Writing is Written*. Los Angeles, CA: Black Sparrow Press, 1974.

Stiles, Ann, *Neurology and Literature, 1860–1920*. New York: Palgrave, 2007.

Szalay, Michael. *New Deal Modernism: American Literature and the Invention of the Welfare State*. Durham, NC: Duke University Press, 2000.

Tratner, Michael. *Modernism and Mass Politics: Eliot, Yeats, Joyce, Woolf*. Redwood City, CA: Stanford University Press, 1995.

Tratner, Michael. *Deficits and Desires: Economics and Sexuality in Twentieth-Century Literature*. Redwood City, CA: Stanford University Press, 2001.

Wicke, Jennifer. "Mrs. Dalloway" Goes to Market: Woolf, Keynes, and Modern Markets". *Novel: A Forum on Fiction*, vol. 28, no. 1, 1994, pp. 5–23.

Williams, William Carlos. *Selected Essays of William Carlos Williams*. New York: Random House, 1954.

Williams, William Carlos. *Paterson*. New York: New Directions, 1963.

Williams, William Carlos. *The Collected Poems of William Carlos Williams, Volume I: 1909–1939*. New York: New Directions, 1986. Winslow, E.G. "Keynes and Freud: Psychoanalysis and Keynes's Account of the 'Animal Spirits' of Capitalism." *Social Research*, 53, no. 4, 1986, pp. 549–578.

Woolf, Virginia. *To the Lighthouse*. New York: Harcourt Brace Jovanovich, 1955.

Woolf, Virginia. *A Room of One's Own*. New York: Harcourt Brace Jovanovich, 1957.

Woolf, Virginia. *The Waves*. New York: Harcourt Brace Jovanovich, 1959.

Woolf, Virginia. *The Years*. New York: Harcourt, 1965.

Woolf, Virginia. *Three Guineas*. New York: Harcourt Brace Jovanovich, 1966.

Zukofsky, Louis. *"A"*. New York: New Directions, 2011.

4

LEAVING THE BODY TO BECOME INFORMATION

Humans are becoming cyborgs, or so it seems in recent economic theory. Philip Mirowski titles his detailed history of the last fifty years of economics, *Machine Dreams: Economics Becomes a Cyborg Science*. He introduces the history by saying, "So what is economics really about these days? The New Modern Answer: The economic agent as a processor of information" (7). John B. Davis similarly summarizes the essence of five recent Nobel laureates in economics—Kenneth Arrow, Paul Samuelson, Milton Friedman, Herbert Simon, and Robert Lucas—by concluding that "Mental processes of individuals are treated as computer processes" (90). The deepest force driving human economic actions is no longer understood to be the body and its unconscious instincts but rather something like an electronic number cruncher.

The dream of humans operating as computers carries with it a new vision of what is most valuable and hence most desirable, namely information. The desire for information is not confined to economics; it permeates the world of romance and sexuality as well. People become attracted to images and texts rather than the physical presence of another person (thus Facebook and Tinder and Match.com). And literary works explore the possibility of people actually turning themselves into information—creating virtual copies of themselves. But there is a strange result that accompanies that process: as people become electronic copies of themselves, their bodies become no longer really part of them. The most popular movie of all time, *Avatar*, is in part a story of a love facilitated by the use of electronics to transfer a person into a non-human form, discarding his human body. When the lovers have their most intense embrace, they are surrounded by cables carrying electronic signals, so sexuality seems to have more to do with plugging into electronic circuits than bodily encounters. In other fictional works, as people in effect leave their bodies, sexual encounters end up being described in quite unusual terms—as mechanical or non-human acts.

The dream of humans becoming information-processors involves denying that anything in human behavior is generated by the body. Much of recent economic theorizing has moved in that direction. As Jack Amariglio and David Ruccio put it,

> economic discourse (especially, but not only, neoclassical economics) in the second half of the twentieth century can be seen ... as a series of attempts to reduce, ignore or eliminate any and all references to the body, in favor of what are considered to be the noncorporeal dimensions of economic agency.
> *(Amariglio and Ruccio,* Postmodern Moments*: 96)*

"Noncorporeal agency" is a fascinating notion, and it is the core of what literary works seem to borrow from economics: people turn into "information-processing units" to alter the way things seem and thereby change what actually happens in the world without having to use their bodies to physically change anything. Economists have turned to this new form of abstract economics in part to correct what they feel is wrong with the previous dominant economic theory, the Keynesian macroeconomics of the early 20th century. As I discussed in Chapter 3, John Maynard Keynes felt that irrational desires, which he called "animal spirits," had a crucial role in keeping the economy going. But economists at the end of the 20th century reject the notion that people are irrational. As John B. Egger puts it, "the actors of Keynes's capitalism are caricatures of real people, partially lobotomized to retain only the properties that would support his cause. The accurate evaluation of the economics of capitalism requires real, choosing and acting, individuals" (463).

The rejection of Keynes's notion of irrational "animal spirits" has been so effective that even those who defend Keynesian policies have felt compelled to completely redefine that term. Two Nobel-winning economists, Ackerlof and Shiller, titled a 2008 book aiming to restore Keynesian notions, *Animal Spirits: How Human Psychology Drives the Economy, and Why it Matters for Global Capitalism.* The title appears to strongly support the Keynesian belief in human irrationality and the animal side of human behavior rather than the "information processing" vision of the new cyborg economists. But Ackerlof and Shiller's account of "animal spirits" does not refer to anything "animal" about humans. They trace the phrase back to the Latin, *spiritus animalis,* and state that "the word *animal* means 'of the mind' or 'animating'" (3–4). Drawing on that Latin source, Akerlof and Shiller define "animal spirits" as forms of information processing, ways people think, with essentially no relation to the body or anything animalistic. They elaborate "animal spirits" into five categories: confidence, fairness, corruption and bad faith (one category), money illusion, and stories. That last category ends up being a kind of catchall because what their explanations show is that all the others are basically various kinds of story. "Confidence," for example, shapes behavior when people circulate stories of good events about to happen, and "corruption and bad faith" takes over when stories circulate of corrupt people running the economy. In an article, Shiller goes so far as to propose a new category of economic analysis that he calls "Narrative Economics," arguing, for example, that "We have to consider the possibility that the dominant reason why a recession is severe is related to the prevalence and vividness of certain stories, not the purely economic feedback or multipliers economists love to model" (967).

Akerlof and Shiller even turn to a contemporary psychological theory of love to support their view that human irrationality is due to our following stories rather than to any bodily functions. They cite a treatise called *Love is a Story: A New Theory of Relationships* by Robert Sternberg. Akerlof and Shiller summarize what they see in this book in terms that make it sound as if love affairs operate exactly the way, in their theory, economic systems operate. They say that Sternberg argues that married "couples create a shared story" so that "ultimately the success of the marriage depends on the partners' confidence in each other and on how that confidence is symbolically reinforced by repeating the stories" (52).

"Confidence" is also central to Keynes's original theory, but confidence is a result of animal spirits, the irrational embodied desires of people. So one might say that a 1930s Keynesian theory of love would say that good marriages and good relationships depend on the bodies of the partners being satisfied, not just on their minds being filled with the right stories.

Ackerlof and Schiller are responding to the economic crisis of 2008, when both the Bush and Obama stimulus packages inspired numerous claims that John Maynard Keynes was back from the dead. But Akerlof and Shiller argue that while they want to bring back some of Keynes's ideas, their conclusion is that his overall theory just doesn't apply any more:

> This recession is different. It is not just due to low demand ... The overwhelming threat to the current economy is the credit crunch ... It is fairly easy now to project the fiscal and monetary stimulus necessary for aggregate demand to be at full employment–if financial markets are freely flowing.
>
> *(86–9)*

Note that they distinguish two different kinds of government intervention: first, the stimulus needed to increase "aggregate demand" to produce full employment—that is, the kind of stimulus Keynes focused upon. They say this is relatively easy to provide; but they see a second kind of intervention, a second kind of stimulus, as necessary to solve the problem of the "credit crunch" and the lack of "freely flowing financial markets." The focus on what needs to be cured has shifted: it is not a bodily state, low demand, low propensity to consume, that is causing the crisis; it is the credit crunch. In other words, this crisis is not about demand, but about financial systems, the systems that we might say produce and manipulate the stories and symbols that shape people's behavior.

That even economists defending Keynes would leave the body out might reflect a broader move away from anything physical as a source of value, in particular a change in the nature of money itself. Until 1971, in the U.S. and many other countries, money was defined by a "species standard," by reference to a physically valuable object, gold. But when Nixon eliminated the gold standard, it carried all sorts of strange implications. Milton Friedman describes what seemed to him as the revolutionary consequences:

> Until 1971, departures from an international specie standard, at least by major countries, took place infrequently and only at times of crisis ... The declining importance of the international specie standard and its final termination in 1971 have changed the situation drastically. "Irredeemable paper money" is no longer an expedient grasped at in times of crisis; it is the normal state of affairs in countries at peace, facing no domestic crises, political or economic, and with governments fully capable of obtaining massive resources through explicit taxes. This is an unprecedented situation. We are in unexplored terrain.
>
> *(Friedman,* The Essence: *379–81)*

Friedman goes on to explain the results of this change to paper money as in effect a move into accepting a fictional version of reality. The gold standard created a vision of money as a copy of something physically real, but Friedman argues that that was always an illusion. Money has always been "a social convention which owes its very existence to the mutual acceptance of what from one point of view is a fiction" (Friedman and Schwartz: 696). Friedman goes on to say that this underlying structure remains hidden because "Money is a veil" (696): what it veils most is its own fictionality. Friedman criticizes previous economic theories for indicating that the fictionality of money made it irrelevant, that one could always substitute the things actually exchanged in any discussion of what money was doing. The move to a general irredeemable paper money has instead made it clear that changes in the sign system itself, in money, are some of the most important determinants of economic events.

This transformation of the core of economics became a central topic not only for mainstream economists such as Milton Friedman but also for cultural theorists from the Marxist tradition. Jean Baudrillard ties his vision of postmodern simulacra to this dematerialization of the economic system, no longer powered by production but rather by finance. In *The Mirror of Production*, Baudrillard concludes that at a certain point in history, production was "elevat[ed] ... to a total abstraction, ... to the power of a code, *which no longer even risks being called into question by an abolished referent*" (129, emphasis in original). Then in a footnote he explains that,

> economically, this process culminates in the virtual international autonomy of finance capital, in the uncontrollable play of floating capital. Once currencies are extracted from all production cautions, and even from all

reference to the gold standard, general equivalence becomes the strategic place of manipulation. Real production is everywhere subordinated to it. This apogee of the system corresponds to the triumph of the code.

(129, note 9)

After the 1970s, the question of what backs up currencies is no longer answered by an image of a huge stockpile of gold, but rather by a reserve system. In the U.S. a dollar is no longer a "silver certificate"; now it is a "federal reserve note." A dollar, then, is evidence that the U.S. government owes the possessor a dollar, and if one tried to get that dollar, all one could get is another promissory note. Money becomes a sign system only referring to other signs.

The notion that signs only refer to other signs is of course a central tenet of the literary theory known as deconstruction, which emerged in the 1970s, founded by Jacques Derrida. And Derrida himself notes the relationship of his theory to the shifts in economics. In *Given time I: Counterfeit* Money, Derrida says it is important to trace the literary consequences of certain events in economic history:

To study, for example, in so-called modern literature, that is, con-temporaneous with capital—city, *polis*, metropolis—of a state and with a state of capital, the transformation of money forms (metallic, fiduciary—the bank note—or scriptural—the bank check), a certain rarification of payments in cash, the recourse to credit cards, the coded signature, and so forth, in short, a certain dematerialization of money, and therefore of all the scenes that depend on it.

(110)

In a sense, this chapter of my book is devoted to doing what Derrida calls for, studying in recent literature the "dematerialization" of money, but I will try to show that this dematerialization goes far beyond just money. The shift in eco-nomics from conceiving of a material base for wealth to conceiving of credit and finance as the base joins with the development in many other realms that fictions, scripts, labels, and discourses are far more important than anything physical. As a result, desires become redefined as fictional structures rather than bodily states. That transformation is part of a broad cultural shift in several fields of discourse and inquiry, each of which informs the other domains. Thus, some biologists are examining the ways that patterns of information could be more important in biological entities than fleshy or chemical structures. Probably the most familiar version of this shift is the role of DNA and the genome in biological theories, which indicate that our fleshy bodies are essentially constructed from DNA pat-terns. Biologists such as Paul Grobstein have recently begun extending this notion to argue that the way animal and human bodies develop—their "morphogen-esis"—is not simply a process of the "unfolding" of chemical and material pro-cesses, but rather is an "information-gathering process ... [in which] each part of a developing organism acquires information about other parts; many, in addition, gather information from the external environment" (9–10). Every organ inside our bodies is now considered a mini-computer connecting to other mini-computers. A similar shift has occurred in many other fields; as Robert Mitchell and Philip Thurtle claim in a recent collection of essays, data has replaced flesh as the basis of everything.

There is a new genre of literature—cyberfiction—that is built on this new valuing of information and computer processing as more important than material objects or human emotions and behaviors; this is the fiction of people leaving bodies behind and becoming cybernetic. Rather intriguing is that Philip Mirowski, in his history of recent economics, uses a cyberfiction work—Steven Milhauser's short story, "The New Automaton Theater"—as the model of the core of recent economic theories. Milhauser's tale describes people in a small town developing a new kind of desire. A theater in that town uses robots to enact human dramas. At first the robots are beautifully operated to imitate human actions, which delights the audience. But then the designer of the show takes a ten-year break and comes back with a new show, in which the robots "can only be described as clumsy" and mechanical in their motions (123). The townspeople are confused because

> In the classic automaton theater we are asked to share the emotions of human beings, whom in reality we know to be miniature automatons. In the new automaton theater we are asked to share the emotions of the automatons themselves ... they do not have the souls of human beings; they have the souls of clockwork creatures, grown conscious of themselves.
>
> *(124)*

People at first dislike the show, but "yearn to mingle with these strange newcomers" and feel "able to shed the merely human, which seems a limitation, and to release ourselves into a larger, darker, more dangerous realm" (125–6). Mirowski concludes that the history of recent economic theory

> is the story of the New Automaton Theatre: the town is the American profession of academic economics, the classic automaton theater is the neoclassical economic theory, and the Neues Zaubertheatre [the redesigned robotic performance] is the introduction of the cyborg sciences into economics.
>
> *(25)*

It is a bit surprising that Mirowski uses this story to represent the new economic vision of how humans act. To turn to the world of information, to become a virtual creature rather than someone in a physical body, would seem to lead to smoother, quicker actions, not to clumsy, mechanical actions. Mirowski clearly chooses this story to highlight the limitations of the new economic theorizing. And Millhauser's story does point to a problem with moving to information processing: while it may seem a smoother, more efficient economic system, it produces problems of its own, glitches due to the technology itself. The crash of 2008 may be seen as partly due to too much reliance on the transformation of physical sources of wealth into purely collections of information. When millions of mortgages were collected together into "derivatives," those derivatives began rising and falling in ways that we could say became utterly disconnected from the physical world of houses and buildings with mortgages, and in a sense these informational systems began acting on their own. As N. Kate Hayles notes in *Unthought: The Power of the Cognitive Nonconscious*, the computer process known as high frequency trading (HFT) took on a life of its own as derivatives expanded:

> HFT has introduced a temporal gap between human and technical cognition that creates a realm of autonomy for technical agency ... The complex temporalities inherent in derivatives interact with the changed temporality of HFT to increase the fragility of financial markets and their vulnerability to feedback loops and self-amplifying dynamics... creating regions of technical autonomy that can and do lead to catastrophic failures.
>
> *(142)*

Realms of "technical autonomy" are regions where the automatons that are computers are acting on their own algorithms, and we could say that sometimes they perform what could be seen as clumsy, mechanical actions, like the automatons in Millhauser's story.

In cyberfiction works, the vision of humans becoming virtual, of escaping the body, repeatedly ends up leading to similar results: actions that are not human, creating what Millhauser calls a "stranger, darker realm." What we see in many works exploring the possibility of humans becoming virtual is that the dream of escaping the body is in part a rejection of the familiar human body, a disdain for or disgust with the human. Bodies do not simply disappear in these works; they remain and certain bodily acts, in particular sexuality, become strangely non-human. Images of disturbing residues of humanness suggest that these books cannot quite fully imagine virtual humanity. They suggest that while we are exploring the desire to become virtual, we have not yet found a way to fully embrace that desire.

Neal Stephenson's *Cryptonomicon* is a good place to start considering literary representations of humans becoming cybernetic. According to Paul Youngquist, the novel is a "convenient introduction to the main obsessions, aims, and effects of cyberfiction," which Youngquist claims is the "preeminent literary genre of postmodern culture" (320). The novel creates a strong sense of a new era emerging by flipping back and forth between World War II and the present. Both eras are focused on the discovery of a "code" that is more important that physical reality. In the WWII section, a group of men break the Enigma code as a crucial step in defeating Nazi Germany; and in the present, another group seeks to create a new form of digital money. The two eras are connected in part because the people in the present are descendants of those in WWII, but also because the new form of money is proposed as a way to stop any recurrence of the horrors of Nazi genocide. Needless to say, this is a strange thing to expect a new form of money to accomplish. Part of the way this is supposed to work is that once the electronic streams which function as money have been set up to pass into every country, one of the organizers, Avi, plans to insert into those streams what he calls a "Holocaust Education and Avoidance Pod" specifically designed to counter any regimes plotting genocide (498). Included in this Pod would be "guerrilla" tactics for an oppressed group to use to resist a coming holocaust.

The Nazi Holocaust is not discussed in much detail in the book; it is just mentioned as the ultimate evil of a government based on the wrong principles, so we might say that what Avi seeks is basically a way to protect citizens from their governments. Hence, a crucial feature of this new form of money is that it will not be created by any government at all but rather by a private company. There is also a kind of logic in thinking that separating money from national governments could help end genocide because such a step might reduce the identification of value with a certain nationality or ethnicity. Also, genocide is often an effort to eliminate bodily difference, so the move into a non-physical economy is tied to the dream of escaping the social effects derived from reacting to bodies.

The book even has a small subplot of someone escaping a kind of genocide by using a form of money. This is the story of how Goto Dengo, a Japanese soldier, survives during World War II. Goto gets separated from other Japanese soldiers and ends up hiding in the bushes in an area occupied by cannibals who initiate their youths by having them kill anyone outside their community. Goto finds a way to convince the cannibals to let him survive when he realizes that they value gold, which he sees is present in a nearby stream. He shows the cannibals that he can pan for gold, and this new technology buys his life because they do not seem to learn the skill very quickly and so value him as a continued source of what is essentially money. Goto's story is a small version of what Avi hopes to accomplish with the Holocaust Education and Avoidance Pod: the cannibals have a policy of killing those not in their culture, a mini-version of the Holocaust, but Goto finds a way to use a "stream" of currency that is also outside their culture, and this external source of value counters the fact that these cannibals devalue anyone external to their culture.

The book proposes that a digital form of money can accomplish something like that for the whole world. But it extends the valuing of the digital beyond economics: individuals, it turns out, are also codes that can transcend the physical and reappear in multiple bodies. One character in particular is presented as existing in multiple bodies, reappearing even in multiple centuries—a mystical figure named Enoch Root. Root ends up proclaiming that the physical doesn't even exist at all.

He proposes that we all live in a version of Plato's cave, seeing only shadows, patterns, never real things. Each culture creates a distinctive pattern of shadows, and would seem thereby to put cultural limits on what people can conceive or know. Root says cultures end up dividing into two different kinds, which he distinguishes as those following Ares and those following Athena. Ares, the God of War, symbolically represents cultures that seek to violently impose their patterns on the rest of the world—which is what was wrong with the Nazi regime. Athena, Goddess of Knowledge, represents cultures that recognize the value of having multiple patterns because that increases the sum total of information in the whole world. Root argues further that those in an "Athenan" culture can discover a way out of their own way of thinking: by discovering certain elements that reappear over and over again in all the different shadow-patterns, across all cultures and throughout history, and realizing that each person has some of those elements. To an Athenan, then, destroying another culture destroys the complexity inside each person. The novel is of course trying to convert the entire world to an Athenan culture.

The book suggests that it requires some pretty amazing persons to bring about this new world order. Root is one such person, a "root" of all cultures, who seems able to exist and recreate himself in multiple cultures and multiple eras. He suggests that he is even in a sense a part of everyone, which is how he explains how another character, Randy Waterhouse, managed to recognize Root in the flesh after exchanging emails. Root says that by reading the emails Randy developed within himself a "Root Rep," a representation of Root, and then upon meeting Enoch, recognized this same Root Rep in the real person (994). The novel goes on to imply that these "roots" can reappear in multiple eras. In this novel, Root dies during World War II but then appears in the tale fifty years later. In the next three Stephenson novels, *The Baroque Cycle* trilogy that is in some ways a "prequel" to *Cryptonomicon*, Enoch Root appears in the 17th and 18th centuries. and Stephenson has confirmed in an interview that this is the same character as the one in *Cryptonomicon*. Root's name is not accidental: he carries the message that patterns or codes are the "roots" of everything, not only of cultures and ideas and the weapons that win wars but also of reality and human bodies.

Root's notion that everything is a shadow, or we might say, a sign without a signifier, is a commonplace of recent postmodern theory, and the book begins in the present with a conference that is all about that theory. The conference focuses surprisingly on World War II, so the participants say the overall topic is "War as Text" (62). The novel seems to mock this topic, but then reverses that tone by switching to a series of scenes of World War II which show that the core battle that decided that war was a battle over control of texts, an effort to break codes and elaborate methods to convince enemies that their codes have not been broken. Some of the most detailed "war scenes" show military personnel blowing up their own ships and weapons while depositing human remains of various sorts to create what appear to be dead spies. The goal of these scenes is to make it seem that spies were physically near the enemy, but then were killed, so that information would seem to have come from those spies rather than from the decoding of intercepted messages. After experiencing many such "war efforts," one of the main wartime figures in the novel, Lawrence Waterhouse, concludes that the war "is every bit as fictional as the war movies being turned out ... in Hollywood" (550).

So in a sense in this book everyone is only a digital code, a "root" that determines the behavior of the body in which it is installed. And those "roots" connect the whole world together. But then there is a very strange result, which has been pointed out by N. Katherine Hayles: the eruption throughout the book of things that refuse to contain hidden coded meanings—purely physical things, which become valueless, or as Hayles puts it, "abject." The characters are trying "to convert the material world into signs, but the abject resists this implicit dematerialization, insisting on its own repugnant physicality" (Hayles, "Performative": 7). As a result, "the abject is everywhere in this text, smelly, slimy, loathsome, and inescapable" (Hayles, "Performative": 7). Possibly the most abject part of the human body—shit—appears endlessly in the text, both as a real substance and as a metaphor. Hayles argues that shit is one of the most dramatic parts of the text:

> Threatening to burst through the sphincters (bodily, social, military, and metaphorical) that seek to contain it, shit refuses to be reduced to only a sign. Expelled in involuntary reaction to intense fear, seeping out in uncontrollable diarrhea, dripping from jungle foliage in brutal marches by the Japanese and Americans in the South Pacific, shit has a material reality that can not be contained solely within the algorithmic and cryptological.
>
> *(Hayles, "Performative": 8)*

While all this "shit" is to be discarded in the creation of the new digital universe, it never quite goes away. It is surrounds everything that is being digitized. To give a simple economic example, the characters face a problem with a private company creating currency: how does that company convince people to use it? How can they create the conditions that will inspire belief in the fictions they produce—belief that their money is worth what they say it is worth? Governments produce belief in complex ways that sometimes intersect with the money they produce, so that ideological decisions can end up distorting the entire economic system. The characters in this novel want to avoid such situations, and the solution proposed is a simple one: instead of relying on trust in a government, they propose convincing people that the new digital money is backed by a huge cache of value or, as one character puts it, "a shitload of gold in the basement" (1008). Following Hayles's argument, I suggest it is as important that the gold is described as a "shitload" as that it is gold: the digital world is always backed up by "shit," by the physical that the digital seeks to escape.

Shit is not the only part of the body that is left out of the move into the digital; as Hayles notes, "Next to shit, perhaps the most conspicuous instance where emotion resists algorithmization is sexuality" (Hayles, "Performative": 8). This is what is crucial to my analysis of the relationship of financial economic theory and some conceptions of love: that sexuality becomes a purely bodily act, rather separated from personalities and thus from the mental processing that makes up economics. Sexuality is never part of the "root" representations that make up people's personalities but something else that nonetheless always accompanies the mental processing that the characters are performing. Lawrence Waterhouse, who is involved in solving the enigma code in WWII, finds his ability to decode is disrupted by his horniness: he needs to ejaculate every few days to stay able to decode, and he uses prostitutes, because a "manual override" doesn't last as long. In other words, bodily drives have a complex relationship of interruption and support for the mental processing that the book seems to be seeking to substitute for the body. Similarly, a long-developing love affair between Amy Shaftoe and Randy Waterhouse in the present era finally turns sexual when she sits on his lap in a taxi and he "pumps something like an imperial pint of sperm" (1080). The sheer physicality and impersonality of that description make it seem almost unrelated to their relationship, and almost unrelated to the goal of the book, creating a pure digital universe of money and "root reps" of personalities. Hayles emphasizes the separation in the book into two halves, the "algorithmized" and the "abject." Those two halves are not easily united: becoming virtual, becoming algorithmic, is accompanied by much of the body becoming abject, so the novel leaves it unclear whether becoming virtual is truly desirable.

But it is not only cyberfiction works that consider the digitalization of human personalities. A work that is generally treated as more a part of mainstream literary culture, Jonathan Franzen's *The Corrections*, also imagines the possibility of an electronic or digital substitute for the human body and, like *Cryptonomicon*, connects this new bodily possibility to recent financial developments. The book tells the stories of several members of one family, all of whom are affected by the emergence of a global financial economy. Immense amounts of money are available for the right investment—Chip, a son becomes an advisor to a country which has decided to become a private corporation and becomes involved in worldwide investments—until that privatized country is ruined by a "Russian currency crisis" (126); the father, Alfred, invents a chemical that is essential for a spectacular new product but sells his patent for very little, and another son Gary, hearing about the chemical, presses Alfred to demand more and become rich, but Alfred refuses to renege on his deal which would make him a fortune, so he is declared decidedly old-fashioned. The title refers most to a "correction," a vast automatic shift in the financial structure of the entire world, which is paralleled to almost everything that the family tries to do to fix their lives.

Unlike *Cryptonomicon*, this novel is not generally thought of as cyberfiction—nobody transcends reality in a virtual world–but repeatedly brought up in conjunction with this global financial structure is the postmodern sense that nothing is actually physically real. Early in the book Chip is teaching Baudrillard and talking about the "detachment of the signifier from the signified" (43–4). He fails as an academic but becomes an important figure in the privatized country, concluding that "here in the realm of pure fabrication, he'd found his métier ... the for-profit nation-state" (436). And Gary, a member of the Federal Reserve Board, starts to think "that the 'real' and the 'authentic' might not be simply doomed but fictive to begin with" (272).

But while everything is becoming presented as an unreal fiction, a financial postmodern universe, moments of sexuality seem quite real, physical, and disruptive. Hayles's description of sexuality in *Cryptonomicon* applies here as well: it is abject. One character states this quite directly: "She had never seen so objectively what an illness sex was, what a collection of bodily symptoms" (411). And that is what we see in multiple sexual scenes—desire and sex so disconnected from personality as to seem merely an illness. It is sex that drives Chip out of his role as postmodern theorist: he has an affair with a student, Melissa, and gets fired. As part of that affair, he uses his expertise to write a paper for her and

> his total mastery of theory ... got him so excited that he began to tease Melissa's hair with his erection. He ran the head of it up and down the keyboard of her computer and applied a gleaming smudge to the liquid-crystal screen.
>
> *(56)*

What starts off as a sense of shared intellectual interest in postmodern theory is suddenly simply two bodies interacting on their own—and then even more striking, the scene ends by paralleling what is inside the body to what is inside the computer that creates the imaginary universe: there is more than a suggestion of a shared identity between the sexual fluids driving Chip to touch the computer and the "liquid-crystal" inside the computer screen. The postmodern fictive world is merely a slight surface, a screen, behind which bodies and fluids and electrons act without consciousness at all.

As another example of sexuality being utterly disconnected from the human personalities of those involved, consider when Gary reconciles with his wife after an argument. He says his disagreement was due to his depression, but "as soon as he surrendered ... as soon as he'd confessed his depression, ... with a locomotive as long and hard and heavy as an O-gauge railroad engine, he tunneled up into wet and gently corrugated recesses" (234). Emotional, personal issues—depression and alienation between husband and wife—turn into thoroughly non-human descriptions of sexual intercourse. Sexuality turns into such a mechanical interaction that it seems that bodily acts do not express personalities but rather replace them.

While people cannot completely escape their bodies, the book does include a vision of a purely digital self that can replace the identity one happens to have within their body. The book envisions an electronic invention, Correktall, that uses electrical circuitry to *"permanently rewire your mental hardware in whatever way you want"* (96). You just put on a wired metal hat and you can change your mind completely. The name of the invention alludes of course to the title of the novel: individuals can undergo corrections just as whole economies can—but as with economic corrections, nobody can really control what happens. One of the ads for the device plays on its relation to economics: "Wherever there's action, though, Correcktall is there to make it stronger! *To help the rich get richer!*" (194). The person who most seems to need Correktall is Alfred, who had invented a chemical essential to Correktall working but was never was paid what his invention was worth. Others who know about this invest in Correktall, get rich, and press Alfred to demand more for his invention. He stands firm, resisting. He is neither postmodern nor financial. Correktall in a sense would add that postmodern personality separated from his body. But it turns out he is too old and his mind too far gone for the product to work, so that by the end of the book he is reduced quite literally to just a body. His mind sort of slips away—but that repairs his relationship with his wife because "His body was what she'd always wanted. It was the rest of him that was the problem" (565). But even then she is not completely happy because while his mind does not seem to work, "the one thing he never forgot was how to refuse. All her correction had been for naught" (566). While she can move his body about without caring for his thoughts, his body can still refuse, can simply be a resistant thing, not a person, and that undoes her "correction," undoes all the ways people think they can escape the resistance and unintelligibility of the physical.

Franzen also undermines the dream of Correktall by noting that the name of this electronic device is also the name of a laxative. As in *Cryptonomicon*, the dream of separating images and money and personalities from the physical body is closely allied to that which is always separated from the body: excrement. There is even a suggestion that Alfred's invention has something to do with urine because in his lab, where he made his invention, there are coffee cans that seem to be full of his urine (8). And Alfred ends up having a scene where shit starts acting and talking on its own. We have to consider the scene his delusion, except that I would suggest it closely mirrors the sexual scenes I highlighted above—the body taking over and acting on its own. Alfred sees a "turd" talking to him. "The turd wheezed with laughter as it slid very slowly down the wall, its viscous pseudopods threatening to drip on the sheets below" (284). The turd calls Alfred an "anal retentive type" (284), which connects this all to economics—anal retentives are in a sense people who are too tightly wound to engage in risky economic adventures. And that is what Alfred is in the eyes of everyone else. Alfred asks the turd what it will take to make it leave, and it says "loosen up the old sphincter, fella. Let it fly." And Alfred responds, "I will never" (285). Alfred resists to the end the acceptance of the imaginary or financial, perhaps because it unleashes shit to act on its own.

Alfred dies at the end of the novel, after the family reunion that seems the tenderest moment of the book. Hence many readers see the book as ultimately rejecting the postmodern financial economics that it explores. For example, Srirupa Chatterjee writes that "*The Corrections* underscores the pernicious effects of consumerism that perverts work ethics, familial values, individual psychology and even sexuality" (para. 2). Chatterjee's summary of the attitudes in the novel seems to say that economics is destroying some non-economic qualities of human beings, such as "individual psychology" and "sexuality." The quote implies that such qualities exist before economics "perverts" them. I suggest that such a view fails to see the way that people are deeply shaped from the beginning of their lives by everything in the social order, including economics. I can agree that "consumerism perverts" some qualities of people, but what that means it that consumerism is changing qualities that were shaped by previous social and economic structures before consumerism became prevalent. Chatterjee does suggest that very idea by putting "work ethic" as the first thing late 20th-century consumerism alters (or perverts); "work ethic" is of course a key quality emphasized by 19th-century capitalism. And one could say that "familial values" are also a core 19th-century economic conception, the family unit being conceived of as the central structure which accumulates wealth. So I would suggest that what Chatterjee is bringing out is that the novel is based on nostalgia for 19th-century economic values. Franzen can also be seen as writing a novel aiming at restoring 19th-century literary forms: he has talked of restoring realism. Chip's embrace of postmodernism is exposed as considerably less valuable than Alfred's reactionary stances. But the tension between the two economic visions in a sense structures the whole novel: Franzen uses postmodern tropes as he delineates postmodern economic structures, to ultimately reject them. So what Chatterjee is accurately noting is the rhetorical stance Jonathan Franzen is taking in presenting oppositions between older and newer economic structures. And so is *Cryptonomicon*, but that novel is presenting the vision of the new "digital" economics, the new information economics, as potentially saving the world from such things as genocide. So the two novels differ in how they evaluate the new economics.

In *The Corrections* and *Cryptonomicon*, the possibility of stepping out of one's everyday body requires a new form of digital existence. I turn now to some works that use other ways to represent the implications for human existence of the new economic structures of the late 20th century. Even before the age of the internet, many social commentators and authors saw a process by which representations were replacing physical selves. Guy Debord, in *The Society of the Spectacle*, wrote in 1967 that "All that once was directly lived has become mere representation" (para. 1). Much of the theory of postmodernism is about this substitution of constructed representations for lived experience. I turn now to two works—*American Psycho*, by Brett Easton Ellis, and *Moulin Rouge*, by Baz

Luhrmann—that trace this new form of existence, in which people become representations of themselves not simply by creating digital copies but by putting on clothing that defines them and performing borrowed personalities. Of course, we could say people have always constructed images of themselves via clothing and behavior, but something different emerges in the late 20th century: credit and digitization have made the sense that clothing and the way people move their bodies seem more than ever before staged performances, directed to an audience not present. In previous centuries these performances seemed to simply supplement the self one is inside the clothing or outside the performance; but now these public displays are viewed more and more generally as substitutes, more the real self than whatever is inside the physical body. Critics often treat this kind of substitution of bought or constructed things for the self as "commodity fetishism," Marx's notion that people see objects as more real than social relations, leaving out the human involvement in producing those objects. But in the postmodern literature I am examining, people are not just substituting commodities for their "real" selves; rather, the socioeconomic order seems able to directly construct the selves people inhabit, though not completely—there remains as we have seen in Franzen and Stephenson some sense of loss or nostalgia for a "real" self.

Some Marxist theorists, notably Michael Hardt and Antonio Negri, have described a new kind of production in the late 20th century that does not rely on commodities as the intermediary that humans use to shape their identities. Rather, aspects of humans themselves are being produced and are becoming valuable entities in the late 20th-century economic system. As Hardt and Negri describe what is developing:

> Images, information, knowledge, affects, codes, and social relationships ... are coming to outweigh material commodities or the material aspects of commodities in the capitalist valorization process ... The forms of labor that produce these immaterial goods ... can be called colloquially the labor of the head and heart, including forms of service work, affective labor, and cognitive labor.
>
> *(132)*

Hardt and Negri call this new source of value "immaterial labor" (139) and "biopolitical production" (307)—the direct creation of the human, the "bios." Furthermore, they say that what these new methods produce are "common forms of wealth" (139). The new forms of wealth are "common" because they gain their value from being shared, and, they argue, these forms of wealth cannot be easily privatized. Thus, Hardt and Negri say that these new forms of production and new sources of value are creating what they call a "common," a worldwide arena of shared products of immaterial labor.

Hardt and Negri connect this new form of labor to finance, arguing that "finance is another vast realm in which we can track down specters of the common" (156–7). In most other Marxist theories, finance is largely seen as the worst form of the separation of wealth from the masses. So much of the language of recent years about the wealth of the top 1% is a criticism of the financial and information sectors. Hardt and Negri recognize this issue, saying, "The wealth produced in common is abstracted, captured and privatized, in part, by real estate speculators and financiers, which ... is a fetter to further production of the common" (157). But note the end of that critique: the privatizing of that common wealth is a "fetter to further production." In other words, privatization is limiting and reducing the growth of this new value.

Hardt and Negri argue that efforts to get around that "fettering" effect—to reduce privatization of the new valuable entities—will emerge, both in acts of resistance and in a kind of unavoidable shifting of the whole system. They claim that "reforms" will arise, "aimed at providing the infrastructure for biopolitical production" (307). Such reforms, they argue, would lead to

> the growing autonomy of the multitude from both private and public control; the metamorphosis of social subjects through education and training in cooperation, communication and organizing social encounters, and thus a progressive accumulation of the common. That is how capital creates its own gravediggers ... it must foster the increasing power and autonomy of the productive multitude.
>
> *(311)*

The notion that the multitude is gaining "autonomy" is problematic in a theory that declares that the images one has of oneself and what one feels are all constructed by social processes. Indeed, one might say that what capitalism constructs in the multitude is the image and feeling of autonomy so that the multitude feels they belong just where they are in the system.

Nonetheless, what Hardt and Negri imagine is a form of possible revolutionary change, ending the oppression of groups because they get defined as "other." *Cryptonomicon* hints at a version of this kind of revolution: the group seeking to create a new, non-national digital money claims that it will help end genocide. In other words, the separations of people into ethnic and national groups that underpin genocide is somehow connected to the physicality of money, or more generally, to the notions of physical production that the novel imagines being replaced by the digital. By including the notion that human bodies have digital roots and so can reappear in different eras, different countries, the novel creates a vision of a mystical "common," a "multitude" including all human beings. The novel does not suggest much about the core issue of Marxist theory, the class distinctions, and certainly the notion of a company creating the international monetary unit as a counter to nationalisms lends itself to a possibility of a more complete capitalist system rather than a revolution. But the novel shares with Hardt and Negri a dream that the new economics constructing selves has potential to liberate people from social oppression.

Both *American Psycho* and *Moulin Rouge* trace developments in the new age of immaterial labor. What we see in these works is people constructing alternatives to their physical bodies, using finance, clothing, and their behavior (which becomes a form of performance) to create their selves. The characters are constructing what they actually are out of just what Hardt and Negri propose: "images," "affects," "knowledges" and "social relationships." The qualities which social commentators often consider separate from the economic system—personal emotions, relationships within families or between friends, and love—are in these works active parts of the economy in which the characters participate: feelings and loves and relations are created by the use of clothing, structured spaces, money, and performances of social relationships. The Duke of Monroth's financing in *Moulin Rouge* and the business of financial transactions in *American Psycho* represent these new forms of economics, which do not consist of payments for physical labor, but rather the pure delivery of non-physical stuff (in other words, information) into the lives of people. What the main characters do is construct selves out of information, out of the socially constructed meanings of objects, and out of money. This does not mean people end up happier or more satisfied with the personalities they construct. But when they are unsatisfied with themselves, it is not the result of finance getting in the way of the more "real" human emotions and relations; rather, it is the result of badly used financial structure, of failing to construct "selves" that work in the social and economic order surrounding them. The constructed elements of the "head and heart" can be unsatisfying, but not because they are unreal—any more than the emotions one inherits from one's childhood family are unreal even if they end up getting in the way of one's finding a satisfying life. Just as one's childhood family provides various emotions and images and words and memories that are used to construct the new self one tries to be, so are all these new products of immaterial labor.

The clothing in particular of these characters—Bateman's suits; Christian's and Satine's costumes on stage—are ways for people to construct themselves: they are not covering up their real bodies; they are truly expressing themselves (though sometimes in ways that don't work very well). And the arts that people use to make their lives more beautiful—Bateman's buying objects for decoration; the songs in *Moulin Rouge*—are not artificial surroundings, but rather real parts of the characters though outside their bodies. But as we will see, bodies remain but no longer hold the newly constructed selves, and as a result bodies are devalued as we saw in *Cryptonomicon* and *The Corrections*.

Moulin Rouge takes quite literally the notion that people wish to merely be representations of themselves: the two central lovers, Christian and Satine, want above all to create performances of characters who are not themselves. These two characters, lovers in Paris at the turn of the 20th century, become on stage a penniless sitar player and an Indian courtesan. Paradoxically, in performing these roles the two are pursuing their dreams of becoming real. Satine wants to be a "real actress" and Christian, the author of the play they perform, wants to become a "real writer." We could say they merely want to become real in the sense of having real jobs that allow them to express themselves by constructing fictions. But the lines they say when they are finally fully in their roles in the staged play are, the movie strongly implies, the truth they need to say to each other and which they haven't been able to say in their usual bodies. In other words, the movie suggests that to tell the truth, to be real in human relationships, somehow requires constructing a complete alternative self one then performs.

The sense that performance constructs the self extends far beyond the staged performance that ends the movie. When people are talking off stage, they keep reciting lyrics of songs well known before the movie was made. Thus, nearly everything is a performance, whether on stage or off. The characters use these performed lyrics mostly to turn their feelings into forms provided by the world around them. Thus, Satine and Christian discover their love for each other by singing lines from dozens of songs in a wildly unrealistic scene ending with the moon singing along. Harold Zidler sings an outrageous version of "Like a Virgin" with the duke to create the feeling that Satine will give a perfect performance of true love in sleeping with the duke to seal a financial transaction to fund the theater. The lyrics allow Zidler to represent to the duke a woman recovering the feeling of being a virgin. The song allows the two men to transcend their bodies and become we might say virtual versions of the bodies implied by the song lyrics. The movie thus carries quite far the postmodern trope that people construct the feelings they share with others (true and false) out of copies of earlier representations of feelings.

To construct the ultimate moment of true love between Christian and Satine, the movie makes them part of an elaborate staged performance, and much of the plot of the film is about acquiring financing for that performance. The financing is needed to construct a theater because it is only in a "real theater" that the "real actress" and the "real writer" can act out the "real love" they have for each other. At its core, then, the movie is about how finance allows people to feel they are "real." And to gain this kind of reality requires an abject form of sexuality: Satine has to sleep with the duke to gain the financing even though she is falling in love with Christian.

However, in the movie the duke never gets to have sex with Satine, so the cost of achieving the image of real love is never paid (except perhaps by those of us who pay to see the movie). Sexuality remains an ambiguous presence in the film, represented as both what is sold to finance performances (Satine has been a courtesan before Christian and the duke enter the scene) and what is the truest expression of love. There are several scenes of Christian and Satine being sexual, but the act always occurs off stage, and the movie quite strikingly distinguishes this sexuality from the very different kind of "real love" that is finally visible in the staged performance at the end of the movie. Most of the movie is shot with very rapid cuts, exciting music, and bright colors that flash through the fast cuts. The scenes of the two lovers in private have few cuts, no songs, and fairly muted colors: they are moments that are in effect cut out of the general performative quality of the rest of the movie. One might say they are the real moments of the movie, but as such they are filmically less interesting, less valuable, than everything staged and performed. Satine and Christian do have some vividly filmed scenes when they sing about their growing love, but those are not the scenes of physical involvement. The movie never unites physical intimacy with idealized, performed expressions of love.

Furthermore, during a number of performances there are sudden interruptions caused by Satine's body failing to be able to continue her actions. She is dying of consumption, and in one scene she passes out and falls from a trapeze, in another the action stops while the camera closes in on blood she has coughed up on a handkerchief. When these moments occur, the rapid cuts stop as they do when Satine and Christian are in their private lovemaking. The movie thus has two kinds of time, the dizzying rapidity of performance and the slow solidity of the body. The actor who plays the sitar player/lover in the play also has a physical disability—narcolepsy—so he too suddenly passes out in certain scenes, stopping the action. The physicality of bodies disrupts repeatedly the magical world of performance.

The ultimate break with the imaginary world of performance occurs at the climactic moment of the show when Satine and Christian both become "real actors"—when they seem to break with the script to declare their love on stage, though they are still using lines that were written before. Their real life situation has merged with the script. This moment is filmed like the off-stage sexuality, in longer takes, with just the two bodies highlighted as they sing, while the rest of the cast is stationary; we could say that the space and time of bodies replaces (or merges with) the space and time of performance at the peak moment of the movie. But immediately after they sing, Satine's abject body finally takes over and she dies. So the perfection of a person becoming the idealized representation of love is accompanied by that person's body becoming a corpse. The movie thus concludes by showing the impossibility of uniting physical bodily states and roles played.

The scene of declaring true love on stage is set up as a counter to an effort by the duke to destroy the entire show by killing Christian. He hatches this plot because he finds out that Satine and Christian have been lovers and he cannot stand anyone "touching my things," which is how he thinks of Satine. This plot of the duke's is what inadvertently leads Christian to join Satine on stage. Satine hears about the duke's plot, and to save Christian's life, convinces Christian that she never loved him, that she was playing a role. In a moment that could be called "real acting," she turns what has appeared an ideal love into an abject melodrama, claiming that she just played up to him to get him to write the great role that would make her career as an actress. Becoming convinced that their love was a sham drives Christian to enter the show and destroy the idealized love in his plot: he takes over the role of the sitar player who is supposed to win the courtesan's love and free her from prostituting herself for the rich maharajah in the play. Christian replaces the narcoleptic actor who played the sitar player, comes onto the stage and seems to twist the plot he wrote: as the sitar player, he throws money at her and says he knows that is all she cares for. So the play threatens to turn into a vision of abjection, with the maharajah, the representation of the duke, winning Satine as his courtesan. The performance would then mirror the reality of finance—that bodies are no longer under the control of individuals, but rather are controlled by the overall financial system. But then a character who plays the sitar—in other words, the embodiment of music—falls from the rafters while saying a key line from the movie's theme song, "the greatest thing you will ever know is to love and be loved in return." That line and that act of falling both represent the transcendence of material reality, and from then on the scripted lines gradually overcome reality: first, Satine and Christian sing lines declaring their love for each other, lines that are apparently the only original song lyrics in the whole movie. In effect, Satine and Christian's "real love" becomes a performance that replaces the previously written script; even the other actors on stage stop moving and smile, becoming an audience.

The duke tries then to reassert the primacy of physical power over images and words by using a gun to destroy the illusion of theater. But the duke is stopped by his theatrical representation—the maharajah—who slugs the duke, knocking the gun out of his hand, and the gun then transcends physical reality to fly out of the theater and hit the Eiffel Tower. At precisely this triumphant moment, Satine dies, which effectively completes the rejection of reality and suggests that to create the fictional world, human bodies have to be left behind. At the end, instead of a lover, Christian is shown in a room with his typewriter. Satine has been completely converted into part of a script, into a representation, which is contained in the typewriter, as it could be in a computer.

That Satine dies of consumption might seem a way to say she is killed by consumerism, and there is something in that—the produced, paid-for version of her replaces the physical. But I would say that she is not so much killed by consumption as that she consumes consumption, transcending bodily needs and desires to become purely scriptural. When the duke is knocked out, in a sense all physicality is removed. The duke is the physical substrate that supports the finance which creates a fictional world. When the duke sees the truth of "real love" performed on stage, he is removed (knocked out) and his financing disappears, which rather ironically ends the movie with the true love affair existing only in the typed document Christian is writing, not in any bodies at all.

To escape bodies and become a part of an imaginary reality is also at the core of the lives of the main characters in *American Psycho*, and finance is once again crucial to that process. The main characters are financiers, and all buy the same expensive products, use the same expensive devices, put on all sorts of chemicals, and exercise excessively so as to turn themselves into such perfect images whose surfaces, smells, and shapes have nothing to do with the "individuals" one would assume they "actually are." To recount Patrick Bateman's morning routine takes three pages consisting almost entirely of descriptions of products used for cleaning and skin care. We could say that people are covering up their "selves" in a form of letting commodities substitute for them, but that is not what seems to be going on. Rather, people are in a very real sense becoming collections of brands and products, becoming signs that do not refer to something "inside them." Their clothes are neither expressive of inner selves nor covers hiding inner selves; rather, the clothes are just part of the image that is the person within the socioeconomic system. The text itself also slips toward becoming information rather than narrative—lists of brands that do not in any way contribute to the motion of any plots. And sometimes the book goes even further, leaving the characters and their clothing completely out of a whole chapter and instead describing some product's development over time, as in a chapter on the albums of Huey Lewis and the News. The chapter reads as a review evaluating the qualities in Huey Lewis's albums—some are New Wave, some are more Punk, some bring out his quintessential bluesiness—and these shifts in musical styles of this band are as much "events" in the novel as anything happening in the lives of the characters. In other words, the book shows that a world of meanings goes on around people with very little relationship to their minds or bodies and even less relationship to their personalities, which in effect don't exist.

Laura Finch provides an acute analysis of the results: "when Bateman is with a group of his colleagues or acquaintances, he experiences the stultifying boredom of a predigested and fully comprehended social field, where individual differences are pared down to a liquid fungibility between characters" (741). Everyone has been extensively shaped by products and social norms, so completely that they constantly make mistakes as they look across crowded rooms at each other:

> "What the fuck is Morrison wearing?" Preston asks himself.
> [...]
> "That's *not* Morrison," Price says.
> "Who is it then?" Preston asks, taking off his glasses again.
> "That's Paul Owen," Price says.
> "That's not Paul Owen," I say. "Paul Owen's on the other side of the bar. Over there."
>
> *(36)*

The novel itself becomes abstract, an endless list of products and expenses that never add up to personalities or plots. Leigh Clare La Berge rather cleverly says that the book has "two narrators: Patrick Bateman, the millionaire financier, and the text's automated teller, which assumes narrative function when the narrator is, in his own words, '"simply not there"'" (286). As we move from chapter to chapter, reading becomes like walking up to an ATM that dispenses the same lists of words (or products) over and over again. La Berge describes this as an "economic and epistemic category of value whose representation foregrounds a series

of tensions between description and abstraction, information and narration"
(275). La Berge concludes that the book is "explicitly linking the financial credit
one receives from an ATM to the basic sense of credible affect required for
interpersonal relations" (288). As Bateman reveals about his relationship to the
ATM, "I stop at an automated teller … Unable to maintain a credible public
persona" (343). Bateman imagines "blood pouring from automated tellers" and
asks himself the very question Millhauser's story raises, "if I were an actual automaton what difference would there really be?" (343). The book thus focuses
intently on that impossible division between blood and the virtual self (i.e. the
automaton) one strives to be. This is perhaps the dream the book is trying to
figure out: how to bring together the new world of clearly defined valuable stuff
(i.e. money) and the very poorly defined innards of the human body, blood that
Bateman repeatedly makes spurt and flow in ways that make no sense. I suggest
Bateman is trapped in the new world of representations, of information, and is
trying to cut a hole in it to release his entrapped body—but of course he only
cuts up the bodies that do not fit in this new world because he cannot actually
step away from the values he shares. The last page of the book has Bateman
"automatically answering … just opening my mouth, words coming out … this is
what being *Patrick* means to me" (399). But even as he recognizes himself automatically spewing what he means to himself, there is a final sign on a door saying,
"THIS IS NOT AN EXIT" (399). There is no end to his self-creation as an
automatic teller who repeats actions endlessly.

Living in such a repetitive and overly designed world, people experience no
satisfying intimacy; bodies are geometric, not biological. And yet the book
repeatedly describes these perfectly shaped persons passing by others who they
regard as imperfect; the homeless, "bums," workers, and persons in marginalized
groups. In reaction to such persons, Bateman recognizes that he is not physically
present though his purchased body is there. Talking to a black Hispanic doorman,
Bateman thinks, "I am a ghost to this man, I'm thinking. I am something unreal,
something not quite tangible" (71). Finch sees in this moment "the heart of the
theory of real abstraction offered by the novel: the unreal feeling of inhabiting a
city invested in finance before sociality" (744). By using the word "unreal," Finch
and Bateman similarly suggest that it is possible to be real, but something has
made them unreal; Finch suggests it is finance. I suggest rather that what Bateman
and Finch are describing is not an unreal existence or an unreal feeling; rather,
the new economic system is leading to a new kind of real feeling that seems
unreal only because we are not fully installed inside the new economic system.

The financiers in this book have developed designs and images to cover and
substitute for their bodies. And as in the other texts I have examined, this substitution of designs and images for bodies leaves bodies themselves abject, disgusting. Bateman has in effect completely suppressed what his body was before
the world of finance took over, substituting a manufactured statue. But that statue
does not feel much when it touches other statues. To feel, Bateman has to engage

with bodies that are not so perfectly turned into products, bodies that are still bodies, which produce a feeling of disgust in all the financiers. But that disgust is thus in a sense what is left of bodily desire in the new world of virtual financial existence. So Bateman is driven to touch precisely that which is so disgusting. And that is why he murders. The language of his murders is the language of pure abject bodies, personality-less, but physically resistant to being shaped into anything perfect. Bateman's first murder in the book follows his saying to a man named Al living on the street, "you reek of *shit*" (130). The full smell of a genuine, abject body produces a desire Bateman cannot resist, and he describes his reaction: "I pull out a knife with a serrated edge and being very careful not to kill him, push maybe half an inch of the blade into his right eye, flicking the handle up, instantly popping the retina" (131). This is true bodily penetration, done with care, but utterly mechanical—like a medical procedure. Bateman then stabs the man multiple times in various parts of his body, and cuts slices in various ways. In the process of slicing and separating body parts, one can imagine that Bateman turns the bum into a Cubist display, no longer simply a body. But of course that leaves the desire that led him to the encounter unsatisfied. He was drawn to Al by a bodily desire that the financial system is transforming into something else. And what Bateman does to Al is turn the presence of a biological body into a constructed set of shapes, which stifles the desire that led him to Al in the first place.

So Bateman tries to put himself into Al's world: after killing Al, he decides

> to go somewhere Al would go, the McDonald's in Union Square. Standing in line, I order a vanilla milkshake … and take it to a table up front where Al would probably sit, my jacket and its sleeves, lightly spattered with flecks of his blood.
>
> *(132)*

Bateman is letting himself be not so perfectly put together, but even the flaws he allows—flecks of blood—are merely "lightly splattered," like impressionist paint strokes.

A part of new materialist theory can help understand what Bateman is seeking: in the terms of Gilles Deleuze, Bateman is trying to escape the "face" that he has so carefully constructed, but which has alienated him from the "head" underneath that face. As Deleuze puts it, in describing the painter Francis Bacon, who creates very distorted and disturbing images of heads,

> the face is a structured, spatial organization that conceals the head, whereas the head is dependent on the body, even if it is the point of the body, its culmination. It is not that the head lacks spirit, but it is a spirit in bodily form, a corporeal and vital breath, an animal spirit. It is the animal spirit of man: a pig-spirit, a buffalo-spirit, a dog-spirit. Bacon thus pursues a very

peculiar project as a portrait painter: *to dismantle the face*, to rediscover the head or make it emerge from beneath the face.

(20–1)

American Psycho shows Bateman trying desperately to dismantle the face and recover what Deleuze and Guattari call the "animal spirit of man," which rather surprisingly parallels the language of Keynesian economics. The new financial economics strives to eliminate "animal spirits" from its theory, but with the cost that we see in these literary works that bodies become abject, incapable of intimacy.

The conjunction of abject bodily matter and financial economics in all the works I have examined is clearly a critique of the new world of finance, and probably most readers would conclude that these works are calling for a return to a recognition of the relationship of the body to the mind. But there is another recent critical development that connects to the visions in these works: ecological—or new materialist—theory, which does not seek to restore the relationship between the body and the mind. Jane Bennett, for example, calls for a new "political ecology" that involves in effect seeking to have non-human "stuff" participate in the governing process. She explores a wide range of stuff which political theory has ignored; in her terms this is the world of "things," which besides the fleshy masses inside humans also includes rocks and electricity and trash. She argues that we need to overcome the "limitations in human-centered theories of action and to investigate some of the practical implications, for social-science inquiry and for public culture, of a theory of action and responsibility that crosses the human-nonhuman divide" (24). Bennett is not denying the value of human consciousness, human minds, but proposing that we need to recognize what she calls "The Force of Things," which could be described as the desires and attitudes of things (1). Bennett is proposing a new form of politics that "crosses the human-nonhuman divide"; we could even see what she is proposing as an information-processing system that involves processing the goals of things (may we call that their consciousnesses?) as well as processing human goals and consciousness.

One recent work creates a vision of just such an information-processing system, one that includes the non-human world in its own agency and totality, and it is the most popular movie of all time, *Avatar*. The movie title comes from the central feature of cybernetic existence—becoming an avatar, an electronic representation of oneself—but which seems far more an ecological vision than a cybernetic one. The movie seems largely a fantasy of leaving the modern industrial Earth for a beautiful, totally "natural" world in another galaxy, where there is no need for any alteration of nature: there is no construction, no human-designed buildings, no automobiles, no guns or bombs (although there are bows and arrows). But the natural beauty is in a sense an illusion because everything physical is only an outer shell that is unimportant. What is important on this planet is that everything has an electronic core that is connected to everything else. The human-seeming creatures in the planet all have an electrical connection, a cord hanging from the back of their heads, that allows them to "plug in" to animals, trees, and each other and thereby be part of an overall mind. That is what the scientist who has specialized in studying Pandora, Dr. Grace Augustine, discovers:

> there's some kind of electrochemical communication between the roots of the trees. Like the synapses between neurons. Each tree has ten to the fourth connections to the trees around it, and there are ten to the twelfth trees on Pandora ... That's more connections than the human brain. You get it? It's a network—a global network. And the Na'vi can access it—they can upload and download data—memories.

And as a result of this vast mental/electronic system, there is no need for construction, for altering the natural world to create wealth. The overall mind directs to everyone and everything all that they need. Pandora is an image of nature as a vast electronic machine.

As Natiri, the Pandoran who teaches Jake, summarizes the way the planet works, "A network of energy connects everything together. All that we have is borrowed and someday must be returned." Pandora is explicitly a world run on borrowing from a central resource: the planet is essentially the ultimate bank. All people do is teach each other how to plug into the central bank, and the better they plug in, the more they will be given by the world around them. Pandorans are essentially computer modules inside disposable bodies, borrowing energy from a giant network.

The movie is a lovely image of an information-processing system replacing the labor force as the driver of the economy. And that information-processing system operates through a central bank that is the source of all wealth, including personalities, which are loaned out to bodies and returned to the system when those bodies die. The movie thus unites the financial and ecological, but it does so by converting nature into that which is the core of the financial model—information—and ignoring the core idea of recent ecological theories, which Jane Bennett says is "to raise the status of the materiality of which we are composed. Each human is a heterogeneous compound of wonderfully vibrant, dangerously vibrant matter." The movie, for all the strangeness of the scenery in Pandora, seeks to eliminate the sense that matter cannot be put fully under the control of minds. While *Avatar* creates a vision of humans and nature accepting and living together in harmony, it does so by turning nature into part of the same mental processing that usually defines humans as unlike nature. Ecological materialism has the opposite goal, to learn to recognize that it is not only nature that is not understandable or controllable but also human bodies. As Jeffrey Cohen describes this ecological vision of humans:

Microbiology, for example, describes the human body not as a self-sealed microcosm, but as a porous environment in which colonies of bacteria symbiotically enable digestion or poisonously invade wounds; in which tiny worm-like creatures contentedly inhabit the follicles of the eyebrows, oblivious to the emotions that traverse the face and animate their home; in which cells are semiautonomous beings that communicate, labor, multiply, die.

(xii)

In other words, the new materialist and ecological theories seek to show that human bodies themselves are as alien as anything else in nature to the usual sense of what is superior about humans—consciousness. *Avatar* reverses that conclusion by showing that the uncontrollable parts of the human body can be brought under control by an electronic process. In his human body, the main character, Jake Sully, has legs that are paralyzed and he is thus not able to perform his duties as a military man. What instigates the plot of the movie is his transformation into a Pandoran: he is placed in a metal container and his mind is electronically transferried to a Na'vi body. He becomes much taller, his facial features are smoothed out, his skin becomes a different color, and his legs work perfectly. He is then able to experience the unity of all the Pandorans, and everything natural in that world, by plugging in. There is no longer any recalcitrant, uncontrollable matter in his body—or in the entire world. The movie itself performs a version of that process of transformation of human bodies into parts of a vast computerized vision: all the important Pandorans are played by actors whose bodies have been transformed by computer generated imagery. The Pandorans are animations, but not drawings: their motions are created by actors, but the computer transforms those motions into those of generated figures. The actors get new bodies that do not quite match their old bodies, but they retain their personalities. Thus, the movie is itself part of the general recent development that is transforming all sorts of things, including actors' bodies, from physical to non-material forms.

The computer transformation of the actors creates a love story at the center of the movie that breaks with the entire previous history of love stories: Jake and Natiri fall in love without her ever seeing his body; she falls in love with his avatar, his electronically projected image. The movie thus presents the ultimate extension of Facebook, Match.com, and other internet sites where people seek love via looking at other people's avatars. In the real world, people who become lovers do eventually see each other's bodies, but not in this movie.

There is an immense economic project that is tied to this new love: Jake transfers his mind into this alien body to help save Earth from total economic destruction. Jake is thrilled to get his new body because his legs have been paralyzed by a military venture. Earth has destroyed the value of the planet by its extensive mining and building, and what humans seek on the alien planet is an insanely expensive ore called unobtainium that it is believed could cure Earth's physical destruction—we might say, restore the planet's legs. But when humans look at unobtainium, all they see is an ugly rock, and the movie suggests that what humans want to do with it will only continue the process of making the planet ugly. Overall, therefore, the movie is a rejection not only of a human body but of the entire human world and all the "accomplishments" of humans: all our buildings and machines and even art works are ugly distortions of a natural possible world that requires no alteration.

Some might object to seeing the movie as rejecting the human since Jake becomes the greatest leader on Pandora, saving the Pandorans from oppressive outsiders—very much like Tarzan. A human becomes the greatest Pandoran, hardly a critique of humanity. But Jake's success is not due to his human intelligence, and certainly not to his human strength, but rather to his fitting into the pattern of Pandora and enacting it. The crucial step in the success of the war against humans occurs when the Pandorans under Jake's leadership are not able to stop the humans; at that point all the animals on the planet attack. It is this pattern that defeats the humans; what Jake provides is something inside him that he was not even aware of when he was in a human body.

Avatar is a fantasy of a completely financial economy as a way of saving the Earth and removing the destruction that is at the core of material production. It may seem strange to suggest such an idea since many observers see the financialization of the rich countries as causing the physical destruction of much of the rest of the world. But the theories of Hardt and Negri suggest a very different possibility: those creating the new forms of "immaterial labor" can become the "gravediggers" of capitalism. Jake Sulley undergoes precisely what Hardt and Negri advocate: on Earth, he was a laborer, following orders, and the result was his paralysis (both literal and metaphoric). Living with the Pandorans unleashes new ideas and new social relations that he had never experienced before, making him part of the global consciousness that is the basis of the immaterial economy of the planet. He becomes the gravedigger of the capitalist exploitative system he was sent to impose.

The movie may be seen as emulating not only the new information economy but also many of the features of the medieval "household economics" which I discussed in Chapter 1: an economics based on the notion that the "initial grant" from a source beyond the entire human world provides everything anyone needs. The critic Si Sheppard argues that the movie even reproduces the early modern rejection of mercantilism that I described as permeating Shakespeare's mercantile plays. Sheppard says that in this movie the invading Earthlings represents a society in which "The Merchant is Become the Sovereign" (141), drawing the phrase from an 18th-century critique of mercantilist English foreign policy. Earth has become a completely mercantilist economy because everything of value on Earth has been used up, so humans are forced to travel away from their "households" in search of other sources of value. But the move to Pandora replaces Earth with a planet that provides everything and more to everyone living there—a "constitutive surplus," as D. Vance Smith labeled a core concept of medieval economics (xvi). But of course this version of a medieval economy is presented as deriving from an amazing cybernetic system, so the movie performs a double move into the future and the past. But the movie does not fully reproduce the medieval answer to mercantilism because there is no royal center that collects and distributes the divine surplus. Pandora directs human actions through "natural" electronic connections, not through the leadership of the non-human people living there. So what the movie more suggests is an ecological source of that constitutive surplus: the planet itself is the royal center.

That the ultimate step in saving the planet is unleashing all the animals via the central electrochemical core epitomizes the way the movie unites an information economy to a world of nonhuman physicality. But the kicker in this is that to unite the nonhuman physical and immaterial information is to reject the physicality of humans, and that rejection ends up taking the form of human bodies becoming strange, inhuman, abject. The end of *Avatar*, the perfect unity of the lovers, requires turning Jake's human body into a corpse, which is left lying on the ground while his consciousness is permanently embedded in the constructed alien body which humans built to allow him to spy on the Pandorans. The new form of value and of love—as virtual or immaterial or purely consciousness—is one with a rejection of the human body.

The sense of seeking some alternative space—digital, fictional, interplanetary—which allows one to become a different person structures all the works I have examined so far in this chapter. The last work I turn to now—*Return to Nevèrÿon*, a four-volume series of stories—goes further than seeking alternative arenas in which to live: it seeks to envision an alternative human history. *Return to Nevèrÿon* is a very strange set of sword and sorcery books that won't allow readers to settle into reading it just as a fantasy because the plot taking place in an ancient society is constantly interrupted by extensive epigraphs and intratextual quotes from late 20th-century critical theory, particularly poststructuralism—Derrida, Foucault, Barthes, Lacan, but also Hannah Arendt and Guy Debord and numerous others. Going back and forth between tales of ancient events and very recent intellectual theories is a jarring experience, but the two halves of the book are subtly woven together, and the very opening of the series suggests the interconnection. Poststructuralism is all about the way that human consciousness is disconnected from reality: we think and act in relation to signs that only refer to other signs, never to anything real. Delany's stories suggest that this substitute of, for instance, written texts and images for real events started long ago with the invention of writing. Writing became a substitute for the physical world and inserted everything that happens into "history." Delany says several times in the stories that he is seeking to alter the history we live within, but clearly he has chosen a strange way to do it, writing a fantasy novel. There is an underlying logic to his actions: he seeks to step outside of history but does not believe he can access anything that is not already "historical" in the current world, which is completely "covered," we might say, by the structure of signs and writing. So what he has chosen to do is to imagine the very beginning of writing and hence of history in order to examine the shift from a physical existence without signs to the world of writing and of history.

The series begins with a preface that describes the overall project. That preface is attributed to by K. Leslie Steiner, a fictional critic invented by Delany. Steiner says the books are a retelling of an ancient document, the Culhar fragment, which scholars think may be the first writing ever, from an ancient regime called Nevèrÿona. The preface declares that "before this ancient nation there is only the unrectored chaos out of which grew (and we watch them grow page on page) the *techne* that makes history recognizable: money, architecture, weaving, writing, capital" (*Tales*, 12). It is striking that Steiner/Delany lists money first in his list of techne that initiate history, and it is equally striking that the last term he includes is "capital," which would hardly seem an element of the most ancient societies. But it is very much the emergence of money and "capital" (or capitalism) that the series of stories traces and equates to the emergence of writing and of history—in other words, to the emergence of a substitute for physical reality.

But while the series traces the arrival of money and writing and thus history in an ancient world, the constant interruption of the tale by quotes from post-rructuralist theorists suggests the book is deeply tied to a much later era, the postmodern world. Steiner/Delany says that "it takes only the smallest critical leap—which we are encouraged toward with the epigraph of each new tale—to realize all we are really learning about is our own age's conception of historical possibility" (*Tales*, 19). A historical possibility in the present, the possibility of creating a different history, a different techne, a different array of money, architecture, writing, weaving, and capital, that is what the stories seek. And at the end of the 20th century, the new form of the techne of money and writing emerging is, I suggest, the financial information economy and poststructuralism.

The preface suggests that the book uses the mixing of recent literary forms to reconsider two stages of economic history:

> sword and sorcery represents what can, most safely, still be imagined about the transition from a barter economy to a money economy … By the same light, science fiction represents what can most safely be imagined about the transition from a money economy to a credit economy.
>
> (Tales, 18)

Delany, known as a science-fiction writer, turns to sword and sorcery in this series to trace the long history from barter all the way to credit. Barter bases wealth on trading physical objects, and in the book that is represented by slavery, wealth defined by the ownership and trading of physical bodies. The book tells a tale of the end of slavery, and what replaces it is economics of money and credit, the creation of wealth by signs.

The character who leads the movement to end slavery, Gorgik the Liberator, speaks in terms that suggest he is seeking to change the way civilization has constructed reality. In the second book in the series, he instructs a young girl who seems to be one of the very few who can write, and his description of the world around him is decidedly poststructuralist. Walking through the "Old Market," he points out some people from "primitive shore tribes ... where civilization has not yet inserted its illusory separation of humans from the world which holds them" (Neveryóna, 59). He says that it is "as if the central process of civilization itself were to take a 'natural' object and possess its every aspect: the thing itself, its material productions, its very image" (Neveryóna, 58). Gorgik's goal across all the stories—to end slavery—involves changing images and their effects on people, and Delany makes slavery itself into a very dense conception that from the beginning challenges what readers would regard as the real history of slavery. For one thing, in this novel, the masters are all dark-skinned and the slaves light-skinned. So the images of slaves that readers in the U.S. bring to the book have to be altered from the beginning. Very little is made of that difference in skin color in the book, but it clearly serves to raise questions of what alternate histories might have occurred.

To treat slavery and its end as an economic transformation tied to the emergence of money, symbolic rather than physical wealth, plays a large role in the book's language. The "history" represented in the book is presented as a transition from physical enslavement to, we might say, textual enslavement. After the era of slavery has ended, Gorgik describes himself as still a "slave to all the forces whose flow and form we have been trying here to mark" (Neveryóna, 61). The forces that once held him via an iron collar now hold him via flow and form, or in other words, via signs that float in and out of everyone's consciousness. Thus, the book is in part also about the ways in which slavery did not end with literal unshackling.

While Gorgik is directly seeking to end slavery, without being able to specify what new structures of thought and force would emerge, there is a character that represents the new emerging economy. That character is named Madame Keyne—after Keynes, of course. And she bears some elements of Keynesian economics. Keynes proposed what we might see as an early form of the information economy, using manipulation of signs (i.e. money) to fuel the economy rather than actual production of valuable things. Keynes sought to create desires by an increase in the money supply so that people would in effect find money around them that hadn't really been earned and would therefore spend more freely. Madame Keyne performs a symbolic version of this by giving a small coin to a slave whom she meets on the street. The young woman she is teaching about the new economics sees that gift as a loss, but Madame Keyne says it is the core of her economics—giving money not as payment for work but merely to alter attitudes. And Madame Keyne says that the coin she gave was made from melted-down iron collars, symbolically transforming direct force applied to bodies into a "fluid" (melted) form of distribution: the iron coins will circulate, and that circulation becomes the new form of control.

But she is not exactly a Keynesian: rather, she is a quintessential poststructural (or we might say, information) economist; as she states quite directly, "I have grown wealthy catering to people's expectations by my manipulations of the real" (*Neveryóna*, 92). Madame Keynes also goes beyond Keynesian economics in describing how she is building what will be called the "New Market," presenting it in terms that seem very much a version of the economy of information. She is financing the construction of boxes and holes where buildings will be built to be this New Market, and she will collect rent from all the industries and businesses that will occupy those buildings. She is not creating an industry but rather constructing another techne that Delany sees as creating history: architecture. She creates the architectural pattern for all industries, and that pattern is the source of value for her, rather than the creation of products. In a sense she anticipates the new industries of distribution and information—Amazon and Google; like them, she provides mechanisms for distribution and sales without actually producing anything—she creates the patterns for sales. It might seem a bit of a leap to equate the formal structure of a marketplace and information, but Delany includes as one of the quotes from a theory text a passage from the mathematician Rene Thom that says, "when we speak of 'information,' we should use the word 'form.' The scalar measure of information (e.g. energy and entropy in thermodynamics) should be geometrically interpreted as the topological complexity of a form" (*Neveryóna*, 154). Geometrical arrangement is identical to information; the arrangement of buildings is a form of information. Jes Battis similarly interprets the markets in these tales as far more sign systems than physical locations:

> The cultural core of Nevèrÿon, and the sign-system that encloses all things within its borders—including Gorgik, Noyeed, the city, the world—is the Market. Everything happens within the Old and New Markets of Kohlhari, and they become the symbolic ground upon which all human interaction—financial and erotic, gay and straight, emerges.
>
> *(481)*

Both finance and erotics are "enclosed" within a sign system.

Madame Keyne suggests that her wealth is in a very real sense inside the formal structures she constructs: when asked where she keeps her money, she says, "It's hidden, carefully throughout the city, where it's protected as much by the accounting acumen of the financially astute as it is by the monetary ignorance of the general populace" (*Neveryóna*, 139–40). She goes on to say that even if she lost her money she would not worry because

> as long as the world in general and the city in particular are organized along the lines they are today I could climb back, simply because I know *where* the ladders' feet are located … But these smiling, sweating, impoverished

creatures below us do *not* know—so that the ladders themselves will always be comparatively free of traffic.

(Neveryóna, *140*)

The source of wealth is knowing the pattern, knowing where the ladders are that allow wealth to accumulate for a person. And the ladders are not just pathways to wealth; rather, they are also pathways to power because power is the core of wealth. And power remains as unknown to the "creatures below" as the ladders to wealth are. As another character, Lavik, says much later in the book, "What real power can buy, of course, is anonymity" (*Neveryóna*, 336). This sense that power is crucially tied to anonymity could be read as a version of Foucault's panopticon, with guards who cannot be seen or identified constantly watching the prisoners. So we could read the "powerful" as the guards of society, but Delany provides a more extensive version of the panopticon, not requiring walls and windows to separate the populace into those being watched and those remaining invisible. This is a vision of an overall socioeconomic system, which distributes power in ways that completely hide and make invisible what and who is actually creating and using the system that produces wealth.

The book thus presents an economic structure of ladders and anonymity as what replaces slavery: slavery is the system where control is entirely visible, written on the body, based on controlling bodies regardless of what desires those bodies actually have. And Madame Keyne's description of the New Market she is creating carries language that speaks of the hope of ending the residues of slavery even in the late 20th century: She says that in her New Market "there will be air, light, room for commercial growth, the encouragement of true diversity among products, marketing methods, competition and profit" (*Neveryóna*, 132). "True diversity" is phrase that resonates in the late 20th century, suggesting the end of all oppressive hierarchies. That she speaks of diversity of products and marketing methods would seem to take away from the dream of diversity of persons, but persons are products in the new information economy: persons are produced, constructed, and marketed and "true diversity" could mean recognizing the equal value in all kinds of persons. But Madame Keyne speaks of keeping the poor poor even as she speaks of "true diversity." And her method of maintaining control focuses on that essential element of Keynesian economics—seeking to modify people's desires by manipulating their relationship to money. She extends that as the new information economy has, by involving not only money but all sorts of signs. She says, "the rich and powerful can exploit desire in the name of labor—the rich who can read and decipher desire's complex signs" (*Neveryóna*, 168). It is not only economic desires that are manipulated by the overall system: all desires are turned into signs—sexual desires in particular. As Jes Battis puts it,

> The sexual relationships that traverse all four *Nevèryon* books are not easily classified, although they can be read as different notes within something vast

and contrapuntal, fragments of a mirror that fit together only to produce a reflection – that is, an *imago* of desire, which is always on the lam, always being pursued even as it pursues something else.

(484)

Desire in this book becomes an image, seen in a mirror: one looks out at this mirror to see one's own desires, rather than looking within the body.

The new economy after slavery merely reshapes the forms of control: the new world of signs shapes desires in ways that "enslave" people. Delany brings out the relation between desires and slavery through Gorgik's story, which traces his sexual encounters as deeply entwined with his rise to Liberator. These encounters involve his putting the collar on men or on himself and enacting slave–master relations as a sexual act. When he was a slave, such sexual acts highlighted the oppression and also made him realize that he was not merely a slave, but a person as well. Thus, as he recounts later,

> There, when I'd been bound round by real oppressions, known and unknown, every gesture had seemed readable: this one luminously sexual, that one solidly political, all showing their true form in the harsh light of power ... Out of that clarity I had constructed my "self."

(Return, 92)

When Gorgik is a free man fighting to end slavery, he continues wearing the iron collar in sexual relations, continuing to act out slave and master, but entirely as a consensual act. Lewis Call writes that Gorgik and his lovers choose "erotic slavery as a liberating alternative to the socio-economic slave system which they fight by day" (290). Call argues that Delany, like Gorgik, is "waging a guerrilla campaign against the institution of slavery while also deploying erotic power relations as a dramatic ethical alternative to the nonconsensual slave system" (289). Delany is thus offering "a way to begin healing the wounds which non-consensual slavery has left upon our culture and its philosophy of ethics" (289). Call is not saying that the erotics of master-slave scenarios is the only way to oppose the residues left in our culture from slavery; rather that we need to recognize that desires, including sexual ones, have been shaped by that history, and if we ignore the erotics of power relations, we ignore much of what is shaping human relations and politics in the present.

Gorgik, finding himself as he said still a slave to the flow and forces of power, turns to erotic use of those forms and flows both to resist and to continue existing within the system of meanings that he cannot escape. The result is the loss of that clear sense of self he had as a slave. Unlike the "clarity" he had when facing "real oppressions"—or we might say the visible oppression of slavery—he finds that when he is free, he no longer has a clear sense of self: "when power was mine and I was as close to being the lord—the perfect, freedom-bearing, benevolent lord, empowering the oppressed—as was possible, I could find nothing clear anywhere about me" (*Return*, 93).

Gorgik provides a very complex explanation of why he lost his clear sense of a "self" when he became free, contrasting his two sexual experiences. In those early experiences as a slave, he says, "I had looked into a mirror, and seized the image within it for my use" (*Return*, 93). But when he is free, he says,

> Now, at a sudden turn of chance, in need of an image to seize, I'd glimpsed that what I'd thought were mirrors and images and an "I" looking into and at them were really displaced, synthetic, formed of intersecting images in still other mirrors ... I couldn't hope to determine ... which, if any, were real and which were merely intersections in others.
>
> (*Return, 93*)

Delany ends up describing his efforts in writing the series in terms similar to what Gorgik ends up feeling after he has ended slavery. Delany considers the series in relation to the sexual politics of his era in a chapter in the third book that alternates accounts of an ancient plague with direct accounts of various aspects of the emergence of AIDS. One might say there was an era earlier when gay-straight relations were as precisely defined as slave-master relations, but after Stonewall there was something of a release from such total repression. However, the result was not so much freedom as a more complex system of signs and symbols such as were circulating around the discourse about AIDS. Delany is engaging with that discourse and those signs and symbols, but like Gorgik he finds himself looking into myriad mirrors and myriad images of what AIDS is. So he defines his goal:

> Perhaps the job is to find a *better* metaphor and elaborate it well enough to help stabilize thoughts images or patterns, that in *the long* run, are useful to those with the disease ... What is most useful in the long run is what destabilizes short-run strategies, the quick glyphs, the clichés, the easy responses history has sedimented.
>
> (*Flight, 187*)

Delany's medieval tale is attempting to destabilize the forms that surround us and are provided for us to "explain" AIDS; the entire four-book series is seeking to "destabilize" the whole system of metaphors and signs—the whole system of biopolitics—which are shaping and controlling desires and economic structures in the late 20th century. The goal of his book is to produce patterns that can change the way society envisions the disease of AIDS and the racial and class oppressions that continue forms of slavery by shaping desires. The book aims to break the power of "the rich who can read and decipher desire's complex signs" (*Tales*, 168). It is not enough to reveal the patterns that are operating or tracing the history that keeps oppressions in place: Delany wants to somehow discover or create alternative patterns, alternative signs, alternative metaphors. Gorgik says, "that what we'd been most denied as slaves here was our history" (*Return*, 73). So he seeks to "construct the start of a personal history," and concludes that "such a personal history, just like impersonal ones, must be founded as richly on desire as on memory" (*Return*, 74). Samuel Delany, as an African-American and a gay man, feels he has been denied the history of people like him, and this series of stories is an effort to construct such a history, centered on a gay man who lived through slavery. But Delany is no clearer about whether his project to construct a new history can succeed than Gorgik is; as Delany asks in appended commentary to one of the books,

> there's a real question where to look for the material? In the past? In the future? On the roaring shore where imagination swells and breaks? In the pale, hot sands of intellection? In the evanescent construct of the here and now— that reality always gone in a blink that is nevertheless forever making history?
> (*Flight, 196*)

In other words, he is not just investigating ancient history or current events but trying to find something that has been left out of history but is almost visible.

The question of what is left after overt slavery is removed haunts the entire series. Gorgik the liberator, who fights slavery and becomes a government executive charged with ending slavery, is asked whether he will continue fighting the inequities and poverty that still exist after slavery. He is asked if there is a slavery after the end of physical slavery, and he simply says he only knows what he experienced—the iron collar—and "cannot tell … what slavery means, for me, beyond slavery" (*Neveryóna*, 189). That question of what the next step is after the liberation from physical oppression persists over the entire series. It is an interrogation of what Hardt and Negri's dream of the grave of Capitalism sup-posedly is creating by promoting immaterial labor: will this new non-physical labor merely create new forms of non-physical oppression? The novel certainly asks the question, and a young girl who joins Gorgik in his fight seems to try to imagine what it would take. She says what would end oppression would be "the absolute freedom of the real" (*Neveryóna*, 189). Such a phrase could mean the end of the turning of the real into signs that obscure the ladders of wealth and the forms of power. But the phrase itself remains quite obscure, and Delany provides a strange metaphor for its promise: what the young girl understood as the free-dom of the real is a "freedom that, in its intensity, had only been intimated by the truth of dragons" (*Neveryóna*, 189). The young girl had ridden a dragon, and felt in that moment outside of everything else, free in a way no one on Earth is free. Is there a dragon that can fly people out of all the geometric structures of oppression? It's only an image, and that is all the book provides.

Every work I have examined in this chapter is at least in part a fantasy. Fantasy seems to be a cousin to the informational model of disembodied identity exemplified in recent economics. To value information is to value what can be separated from physical reality. But every work also presents physical reality resisting or remaining outside the fantasy, outside the world of pure information. And that separation of the physical and the imagined seems to divide desire itself: there is a split between the desires that create images and virtual new selves and the desires that are emerging from bodies quite separate from the images and virtualities. Separating information from bodies splits what is human. All the works negotiate that split in various ways: by suggesting that bodies are the materialization of digital patterns (*Cryptonomomicon*); by trying to totally discipline the body so that it becomes merely an image (*American Psycho*); by using the body in a performance of something other than itself (*Moulin Rouge*); by postulating a future, purely electronic body (*Avatar*); or by dreaming of a new metaphor that can combine the physical and the virtual (*Return to Nevèrÿon*). But all these works mark their merger of body and image as a fantasy, not as a vision of a believable world. It is only in fantasy that the new economics of information can really be considered a place to live, a place where bodies can reside, which suggests that is not completely believable yet. So I end with the caveat that in this last chapter I have been tracing what is not really a distinct new source of value, but rather something on its way to being a new source of value. This is not yet a new era but rather the breaking up of previous eras, the breaking up of sources of value, sources of desires. It is not clear that a new source of desire has emerged in the works I have examined in this chapter. All we can see is the desire for a new desire.

References

Ackerlof, George A. and Robert J. Shiller. *Animal Spirits: How Human Psychology Drives the Economy and Why it Matters for Global Capitalism*. Princeton, NJ: Princeton University Press, 2009.

Amariglio, Jack and David F.Ruccio, "From Unity to Dispersion: The Body in Modern Economic Discourse." *Postmodernism, Economics and Knowledge*. Ed. Stephen Cullenberg, Jack Amariglio, and David F. Ruccio. New York: Routledge, 2001, pp. 143–165.

Amariglio, Jack and David F. Ruccio. "Modern Economics: The Case of the Disappearing Body?" *Cambridge Journal of Economics*, vol. 26, 2002, pp. 81–103.

Amariglio, Jack and David F. Ruccio. *Postmodern Moments in Modern Economics*. Princeton, NJ: Princeton University Press. 2003.

Appleby, Joyce Oldham. *Economic Thought and Ideology in Seventeenth-Century England*. Princeton, NJ: Princeton University Press, 1978.

Battis, Jes. "Delany's Queer Markets: Nevèrÿon and the Texture of Capital." *Science Fiction Studies*, vol. 36, no. 3, 2009, pp. 478–489.

Baudrillard, Jean. *The Mirror of Production*. Tr. Mark Poster. St. Louis: Telos Press, 1975.

Baudrillard, Jean. *Simulacra and Simulation*. Ann Arbor, MI: University of Michigan Press, 1994.

Bennett, Jane. *Vibrant Matter: A Political Ecology of Things*. Durham, NC: Duke University Press, 2010.

Bride, Amy. "Byronic Bateman: The Commodity Vampire, Surplus Value, and the Hyper-Gothic in American Psycho." *Irish Journal of Gothic and Horror Studies*, no. 14, Summer, 2015, pp. 3 18.

Brown, Bill. "The Dark Wood of Postmodernity (Space, Faith, Allegory)." *PMLA*, vol. 120, no. 3, 2005, pp. 734–750.

Burnett, Joshua Yu. "The Collar and the Sword: Queer Resistance in Samuel R. Delany's Tales of Nevèrÿon." *African American Review*, vol. 48, no. 3, 2015, pp. 257–269.

Call, Lewis. "Structures of Desire: Erotic Power in the Speculative Fiction of Octavia Butler and Samuel Delany." *Rethinking History*, 2005, 9, nos. 2–3, pp. 275–296,

Chatterjee, Srirupa. "'Forever Fearful of a Crash': Family vis-à-vis Materialism in Jonathan Franzen's The Corrections." Notes on Contemporary Literature, vol. 39, no. 4, 2007, pp. 6–9.

Cohen, Jeffrey. *Medieval Identity Machines*. Minneapolis, MN: University of Minnesota Press, 2003.

Collins, Marsha S. "Echoing Romance: James Cameron's Avatar as Ecoromance." *Mosaic: A Journal for the Interdisciplinary Study of Literature*, vol. 47, no. 2, 2014, pp. 103–119.

Davis, John B. *The Theory of the Individual in Economics: Identity and Value*. New York: Routledge, 2003.

Debord, Guy, *The Society of the Spectacle*. Tr. Ken Knabb. London: Rebel Press, 2006. First published 1967.

Delany, Samuel. *Flight From Nevèrÿon* (Book 3 in the Nevèrÿon series). New York: Open Road Media Sci-Fi and Fantasy, 2014.

Delany, Samuel. *Neveryóna, Or the Tale of Signs and Cities* (Book 2 in the Nevèrÿon series). New York: Open Road Media Sci-Fi and Fantasy, 2014.

Delany, Samuel. *Return to Nevèrÿon* (Book 4 in the Nevèrÿon series). New York: Open Road Media Sci-Fi and Fantasy, 2014.

Delany, Samuel. *Tales of Nevèrÿon* (Book 1 in the Nevèrÿon series). New York: Open Road Media Sci-Fi and Fantasy, 2014.

Deleuze, Gilles. *Francis Bacon: The Logic of Sensation*. Tr. Daniel W. Smith. London: Continuum Books, 2003.

Derrida, Jacques. *Given Time: I. Counterfeit Money*. Chicago: University of Chicago Press, 1992.

Egger, John B. "Psychologist of the Ills of Capitalism." *Critical Review*, Summer, 1989, pp. 444–466.

Finch, Laura. "The Un-real Deal: Financial Fiction, Fictional Finance, and the Financial Crisis." *Journal of American Studies*, vol. 49, 2015, pp. 731–753.

Franzen, Jonathan. *The Corrections*. New York: Picador, 2001.

Friedman, Milton. *Capitalism and Freedom*. Chicago: Chicago University Press, 1962.

Friedman, Milton. *The Essence of Friedman*. Ed. Kurt R. Leube. Redwood City, CA: Stanford University Press, 1987.

Friedman, Milton and Anna Jacobson Schwartz. *A Monetary History of the United States*. Princeton, NJ: Princeton University Press, 1963.

Godden, Richard. "Fictions of Fictitious Capital: *American Psycho* and the Poetics of Deregulation." *Textual Practice*, vol. 25, no. 5, 2011, pp. 853–866.

Gopal, Sangita and Sujata Moorti. "Bollywood in Drag: Moulin Rouge and the Aesthetics of Global Cinema." *Camera Obscura*, vol. 25, no. 3, 2011, pp. 29–67.

Greenspan, Alan, "Gold and Economic Freedom." *Capitalism: The Unknown Ideal*. Ed. Ayn Rand. New York: Signet, 1967.

Grobstein, Paul. "From the Head to the Heart: Some Thoughts on Similarities Between Brain Function and Morphogenesis, and On Their Significance for Research Methodology and Biological Theory." *Experientia*, vol. 44, 1988. Online at http://serendip.brynmawr.edu/complexity/hth.html.

Hardt, Michael and Antonio Negri. *Commonwealth*. Cambridge, MA: The Belknap Press of Harvard University Press, 2009.

Hayles, N. Katherine. "Text Out of Context: Situating Postmodernism Within an Information Society." *Discourse*, vol. 9, Spring/Summer, 1987, pp. 24–36.

Hayles, N. Katherine. *How We Became Posthuman: Virtual Bodies in Cybernetics, Literature and Informatics*. Chicago: University of Chicago Press, 1999.

Hayles, N. Katherine. "Performative Code and Figurative Language: Neal Stephenson's *Cryptonomicon*." *The Holodeck in the Garden: Science and Technology in Contemporary American Fiction*. Ed. Peter Freese and Charles B. Harris. Champaign, IL: Dalkey Archive Press, 2004.

Hayles, N. Katherine. *Unthought: The Power of the Cognitive Nonconscious*. Chicago: University of Chicago Press, 2017.

Hinshaw, Randall, ed. *Monetary Reform and the Price of Gold: Alternative Approaches*Baltimore, MY: Johns Hopkins University Press, 1967.

Hillis, Ken. "From Capital to Karma: James Cameron's *Avatar*." *Postmodern Culture*, vol. 19, no. 3, 2009, p. 5.

Johnston, Georgia. "Discourses of Autobiographical Desires: Samuel Delany's Nevèrÿon Series. *Biography*, vol. 30, no. 1, 2007, pp. 48–60.

La Berge, Leigh Clare. "The Men Who Make the Killings: American Psycho, Financial Masculinity, and 1980s Financial Print Culture." *Studies in American Fiction*, vol. 37, no. 2, 2010, pp. 273–397.

Martín-Cabrera, Luis. "The Potentiality of the Commons: A Materialist Critique of Cognitive Capitalism from the Cyberbraceros to the Ley Sinde." *Hispanic Review*, vol. 80, no. 4, 2012, pp. 583–605.

Miller, Preston J., ed. *The Rational Expectations Revolution: Readings from the Front Line*. Cambridge, MA: Harvard University Press, 1994.

Millhauser, Steven. "The New Automaton Theater." *The Knife Thrower and Other Stories*. New York: Crown Publishers, 1998.

Mirowski, Philip. *Machine Dreams: Economics Becomes a Cyborg Science*. Cambridge: Cambridge University Press, 2002.

Mitchell, Robert and Philip Thurtle, eds. *Data Made Flesh: Embodying Information*. New York: Routledge, 2003.

Rosenberg, Jordana. "Framing Finance: Rebellion, Dispossession and the Geopolitics of Enclosure in Samuel Delany's Nevèrÿon Series." *Radical History Review*, no. 118, Winter, 2014, pp. 93–112.

Sheppard, Si. "'The Merchant is Become the Sovereign." *Film International*, vol. 13, no. 72, 2015, pp. 41–66.

Shiller, Robert J. "Narrative Economics." *American Economic Review*, vol. 107, no. 4, 2017, pp. 967–1004.

Skidelsky, Robert, ed. *The End of the Keynesian Era: Essays on the Disintegration of the Keynesian Political Economy*. New York: Holmes & Meier, 1977.

Skidelsky, Robert. *Keynes: The Return of the Master*. New York: Public Affairs, 2010.

Smith, D. Vance. *Arts of Possession: The Middle English Household Imaginary*. Minneapolis, MN: University of Minnesota Press, 2003.

Stephenson, Neal. *Cryptonomicon*. New York: Avon Books, 1999.

Stephenson, Neal. "Interview with Therese Littleton." March 18, 2006. At About.Com, http://contemporarylit.about.com/cs/authorinterviews/a/nealstephenson.5.htm.

Sternberg, Robert J. *Love Is a Story: A New Theory of Relationships*. Oxford: Oxford University Press, 1999.

Youngquist, Paul. "Cyberpunk, War, and Money: Neal Stephenson's *Cryptonomicon*." *Contemporary Literature*, vol. 53, no. 2, 2012, pp. 319–348.

INDEX